ÉDITH PIAF: A CULTURAL HISTORY

ÉDITH PIAF

A Cultural History

David Looseley

LIVERPOOL UNIVERSITY PRESS

First published 2015 by
Liverpool University Press
4 Cambridge Street
Liverpool
L69 7ZU

British Library Cataloguing-in-Publication data
A British Library CIP record is available

ISBN 978-1-78138-257-8

Typeset by Carnegie Book Production, Lancaster
Printed in the UK by CPI Group (UK) Ltd, Croydon CR0 4YY.

Contents

For my granddaughter
Elizabeth (Lizzie) Looseley-Burnet,
with love

Acknowledgements

I WOULD LIKE TO EXPRESS my gratitude to the following, who in various ways have helped me with the research for this book: Jacques d'Amboise, Ewan Burnet, Erica Burnham of the University of London in Paris, Di Holmes, Jim House, John and Josette Hughes, the late Tony Judt, Rhiannon Looseley, Bernard Marchois of the Musée Édith Piaf, Sue Miller, Cécile Obligi of the Bibliothèque nationale's Département des arts du spectacle, Cécile Prévost-Thomas, Keith Reader, Philip Tagg, Florence Tamagne and Vera Zolberg.

I am especially indebted to the late David Whale. David was a teacher of French in the UK whom I never met. He was devoted to French chanson and over a period of some fifty years put together a remarkable collection of books, CDs, magazines and press cuttings on the subject. In donating this collection to me, his widow Ann and David himself have contributed immeasurably to this book.

I should also thank Frederick Kennedy (1926–2014), poet, wit and book collector, for encouraging me to write from a very early age. And most of all my wife, Avril, not only for reading and discussing the manuscript but for her wisdom, enthusiasm, optimism and support beyond description.

Chronology

WHAT FOLLOWS is not by any means a detailed charting of Piaf's life but a sketch to help readers situate and make better sense of the moments highlighted in the book. Some of the dates, particularly those relating to her early life, are approximate or uncertain. A much more detailed chronology appears in Marchois, 1993, passim, but even here the dating is sometimes unreliable.

1915   19 December: birth of Édith Giovanna Gassion in Belleville, Paris. Her parents are Louis Alphonse Gassion (born 1881) and Annetta Giovanna Maillard, known professionally as Line Marsa (born 1895). Louis's ancestry was mainly Norman. Line's was French, Moroccan and Italian. Both came from families of street or circus performers.

1918   31 August: Édith's brother or half-brother Herbert Gassion is born to Line in Marseille.

1921   The young Édith's eyesight problem, whatever it was, is cured.

1922   Louis removes his daughter from his mother's brothel in Bernay.

1922–29   Édith goes on the road with her father, either in the circus or when he works alone.

1929   4 June: Édith's parents are divorced, though they have lived separate lives for some years.

1929   Édith leaves her father and begins singing in the street in Pigalle.

1931   Meets Momone (Simone Berteaut), who collects the money when

Édith sings in the street. The two will also perform sometimes in cinemas, cabarets and *bals musettes*.
8 March: birth of her half-sister, Denise Gassion, daughter of Louis Gassion.

1932   Meets and begins living with Louis Dupont, known as le P'tit Louis (little Louis).

1933   7 February: birth of Édith and Louis's daughter Marcelle.
December (to April 1934): sings in a trio including her father's friend Camille Rebon. They perform a number of times in barracks.

1935   7 July: Marcelle dies in hospital of meningitis, aged two. She is buried in a pauper's grave in Thiais (10 July).
October: meets Louis Leplée.
24 or 25 October: begins performing at Le Gerny's as la Môme Piaf.
26 October: first appears on Radio-Cité thanks to Jacques Canetti.
18 December: makes her first recordings, on Canetti's Polydor.

1936   February: release of the film *La Garçonne*, in which Édith has a small singing part.
6 April: murder of Leplée.
April–May: with Le Gerny's closed, Piaf finds work at more downmarket cabarets, notably Chez Odett and L'Ange rouge. First meets Asso around this time. She records her first Asso song in early May: 'Mon amant de la Coloniale'.
May: the Popular Front government begins.
Spring–summer: tours France with a troupe called La Jeune Chanson.

1937   January: starts a relationship with Asso, who also becomes her manager. Records his 'Mon légionnaire', previously recorded by Marie Dubas.
19–25 February: appears at Bobino.
26 March–15 April: her first appearance at the ABC music hall, closing the first half. She is only contracted to sing five numbers but enthusiastic audience demands more.
19 November: second engagement at ABC begins, for two weeks, this time under the name Édith Piaf.

1938   Sings at an anti-Franco rally in aid of the Spanish Republicans.
January: 45-minute programme devoted to her on Radio-Cité.
15 April–4 May: third engagement at the ABC.

October and November: tops the bill for the first time in a music hall: first at L'Européen, then at Bobino.

1939   August: Asso is called up.
Autumn: meets Paul Meurisse. They move in together sometime near the turn of the year and he becomes her first musical protégé.

1940   Begins writing her own songs.
February: meets Jean Cocteau.
April: premiere of Cocteau's play *Le Bel Indifférent*, featuring Piaf and Meurisse.
May–June: France defeated. Pétain signs an armistice and the German Occupation begins. Piaf leaves Paris, heading south.
Summer: begins touring the free zone.
September: returns to occupied Paris. On 28th, she does her first solo concert, at the prestigious Salle Pleyel and with an orchestra.
December: meets Henri Contet.

1941   Performs throughout France, commanding high fees.
November: release of Georges Lacombe's film *Montmartre-sur-Seine*, in which she stars as Lily, a flower girl who becomes a singer.
Highly personal attack on her in the collaborationist *Je suis partout*.

1942   Meets Marcel Blistène in Marseille.
October–November: at the ABC, she finishes each show with 'Où sont-ils tous mes copains' against a tricolour backdrop, which the German censor forces her to remove.
November: moves in to Madame Billy's, 5 rue Villejust, 17th *arrondissement*.

1943   February: sits SACEM exam to become a professional lyricist but fails.
February–April: her booking in a revue at Le Casino de Paris is interrupted for five weeks, either because of a dispute with its director or, in some versions, because she was banned for singing a song by a Jew (Émer's 'L'Accordéoniste').
June–July: at both the ABC and Bobino, she innovates by having her two combined orchestras hidden behind a stage curtain.
Summer: in a press interview, she protests that she is not a realist singer.
August: Line Marsa is sentenced to six months in prison.
14 August: travels by train to Berlin for a seven-week tour of French POWs and STO workers in Germany.

December: resits SACEM exam and passes.

1944   2 February: second concert at Pleyel.
14 February: second tour of Germany begins.
3 March: two days before her return from Germany, her father dies, aged 63.
June: meets Yves Montand; they become lovers.
25 August: the Liberation of Paris begins. Shortly before, probably in July, she moved out of Madame Billy's potentially compromising establishment on the rue Villejust.
September: the Purge begins.
October: she claims in the press to have helped 118 French POWs escape from camps in Germany.

1945   6 February: her mother Lina Marsa dies, aged 49.
9 February–8 March: booking at the Théâtre de l'Étoile, with Montand.
September: back at L'Étoile, she is accompanied for the first time by Robert Chauvigny on the piano. He becomes her conductor and arranger for many years.
October: breaks up with Montand.
November: Marc Bonel joins her as her accordionist. She also meets Louis Barrier, who joins her team as manager and agent.
30 November: her case is examined by a Purge committee; she is exonerated and congratulated.

1946   Leaves Polydor and signs with Pathé Marconi (Columbia).
Meets Marcel Cerdan fleetingly.
April–May: working and performing with Les Compagnons de la chanson.
3 April: release of Blistène's film *Étoile sans lumière*, Piaf's second starring role.
12 April: Piaf has her daughter Marcelle exhumed and re-buried at Père Lachaise, along with her own father.
May: she and the Compagnons appear at the Théâtre de Chaillot. She is accompanied by a 50-piece orchestra.

1947   Sings at a French Communist Party rally; meets the party's leader, Maurice Thorez.
September: triumphant return to L'Étoile, with the Compagnons, whose leader, Jean-Louis Jaubert, is now her lover.
October: sets off for New York on the *Queen Elizabeth*, with the

Compagnons, Aznavour, Barrier and others (9 October). Affair with Cerdan begins.

30 October: opening night at the Playhouse (performs until 6 December inclusive).

9 November: Virgil Thomson's article appears in the *New York Herald Tribune*.

1948 14 January–10 March: engagement at the Versailles club.
March: release of the film *Neuf garçons et un cœur*, directed by Georges Freedland, in which she stars with the Compagnons.
Spring: she is introduced to Princess Elizabeth, future Queen of Great Britain.
May: sings at a Gaullist rally held by the new RPF party.
September: Cerdan beats Tony Zale and becomes middleweight champion of the world.
September: she flies back to New York to start another tour.
22 September: starts a second run at the Versailles, until 14 December.
18 December: flies back to Orly with Cerdan.

1949 14 and 22 January: sell-out shows at Pleyel.
16 June: Cerdan loses his title to Jake LaMotta.
Late spring: Piaf writes 'Hymne à l'amour' with Monnot; first recorded by Yvette Giraud in June.
14 or 15 September: opening night of her third stint at the Versailles.
27 October: Cerdan boards night flight to New York for a return match with LaMotta, after Piaf has pleaded with him to come by plane rather than boat. The plane crashes, killing all on board.
28 October: learning of Cerdan's death, Piaf refuses to cancel her performance that night at the Versailles. Announces at the start that she is singing for Marcel Cerdan. Breaks down while singing 'Hymne à l'amour'.

1950 Danielle Vigneau becomes part of her team; she will marry Marc Bonel in 1951.
March: back from America, Piaf begins touring France. She does her first performances in Paris for almost a year. They include her first French renditions of 'Hymne a l'amour'.
7 September: flies back to New York with her new love, Eddie Constantine. Begins another three-month booking at the Versailles on the 13th.

By the end of the year, she is extensively using prescription drugs. She is also regularly trying to contact Cerdan's spirit. Breaks definitively with Momone, whom she accuses of tricking her into believing that Cerdan was responding.

1951   Back from New York (6 January), she begins rehearsing for Marcel Achard's musical *La P'tite Lili*, written for her.
19 January: appears on Henri Spade's TV show *Le Théâtre XYZ*. Begins appearing more regularly on TV around this time.
10 March: *La P'tite Lili* opens at the ABC, directed by Raymond Rouleau, also starring Eddie Constantine. The show is a success.
21–28 March: in the middle of the run, she is admitted to hospital with intestinal problems.
4 April–10 July: *La P'tite Lili* completes its run.
June: wins Grand Prix du disque de l'Académie Charles Cros for her recording of 'Le Chevalier de Paris'.
Summer: touring France and Europe.
21 July: car accident, with Aznavour at the wheel.
14 August: second car accident, with Aznavour and her lover, the cyclist André Pousse. Piaf is hospitalised for five days and is prescribed morphine, which she will become addicted to. Convalesces until November but makes radio appearances and does some recording.

1952   Now addicted to morphine, cortisone (for rheumatism) and sleeping pills; also suffering from exhaustion.
January: release of the film *Paris chante toujours*, directed by Pierre Montazel, in which she stars; release was delayed by last year's car accident.
June: Édouard Herriot, president of the National Assembly, hands her the Grand Prix de l'Académie du disque français for 'Padam... Padam'.
16 and 20 September: civil and religious marriage to Jacques Pills in New York, with Marlene Dietrich as maid of honour.
Autumn: appears twice on *Ed Sullivan Show*.

1953   (Possibly 1954) Jeered at the Casino de Royat for being drunk on stage.
March: on their return from the USA, she and Pills move into their new apartment, 67 bis Boulevard Lannes.
April: they perform together for a month at the Théâtre Marigny.

The show includes a revival of *Le Bel Indifférent*. Luke-warm reception from audience and critics.

May–June: first cure for drug addiction.

June and July: straight after the cure, she is filming both *Boum sur Paris* (directed by Maurice de Canonge) and Sacha Guitry's *Si Versailles m'était conté*, in which she sings 'Ça ira'.

28 September–26 November: attempting to rest.

1954   Start of the Algerian war of independence.

The Olympia re-opens as a music hall.

January: second cure, for morphine and alcohol addiction.

4 January: receives a gold disc for selling a million records, a rare achievement at the time.

3 April: TV special on Piaf in the series *La Joie de vivre*.

July: after a 90-day tour with a show called *Le Supercircus*, third stay in rehab.

1955   January–February: Piaf's first engagement at the recently re-opened Olympia.

March–May 1956: touring North and South America with her new show, called her 'continental revue'. During this trip, the director of the Riviera Casino in Las Vegas pays her not to perform there.

1956   Piaf plays Carnegie Hall: a triumph.

5 January: death of Mistinguett.

7 May: arrives back in Paris after 14 months away.

24 May–12 June: triumphant engagement at the Olympia.

June: Piaf and Pills divorce.

September (–August 1957): leaves for another major tour of North and South America.

1957   13 January: plays Carnegie Hall for a second time, against medical advice. The show is recorded and the recording will later be released as a double album. Three thousand people have to be turned away and extra seating has to be placed on the stage.

8 August: back to France after almost a year. Takes a long break from performing until 25 October, when she starts another tour of France.

9 December: starts filming Blistène's new film, *Les Amants de demain*.

1958   Publication of *Au bal de la chance*.

February: meets Georges ('Jo') Moustaki.

6 February–29 April: second Olympia engagement, extended, due to its success, to a record-breaking 128 performances, before 240,000 audience members. On Sundays, she does three shows. She is taken ill twice on stage, in March and April. Her lover Félix Marten is part of the show.
April: the French government falls.
28 May: De Gaulle assumes power. That day, Piaf is taken ill on stage in Stockholm and has to be flown home in a specially hired plane for hospital treatment. She rests throughout June.
6 September: bad car accident with her latest lover, Moustaki: Piaf hospitalised until 3 October.
5 October: a second driving accident with Moustaki, at the same spot, though not a serious one.
November–December: gruelling tour of France, Switzerland and Luxembourg, with Moustaki.

1959   6 January: her last ever tour of the USA begins, delayed by last year's car accidents.
February: she meets the painter Douglas Davis.
Taken ill twice on stage at the Waldorf Astoria and has to be hospitalised twice for two operations for a stomach ulcer.
March: breaks up with Moustaki, who returns home.
21 April: finally leaves hospital, emaciated.
20 June: returns from the States with Davis, who has stayed by her bedside.
20 July: car accident with Davis driving: Piaf has broken ribs.
21 July: starts her summer tour, despite her injuries.
21 September: back in hospital for an emergency operation for pancreatitis.
14 October: leaves hospital.
November: after convalescing since October, she goes on the road again for what becomes known in the media as her suicide tour.
3 December: taken ill on stage at Maubeuge.
11 December: TV interview recorded in Dieppe with Pierre Desgraupes (*Cinq colonnes à la une*), broadcast 15 January 1960.
13 December: collapses on stage in Dreux and has to be rushed back to Paris. Has a sleep cure.
30 December (–6 January): in hospital again.

1960   6–27 January: treated for jaundice at the American hospital in Paris. She is in and out of hospitals for the next six months.

June: in a coma with an acute liver problem.

End of August: comes out of hospital. Has to cancel her summer tour and sell her country house to pay her bills.

3 October: after a recurrence of the June illness, she cancels her booking at the Olympia for that month.

24 October: Charles Dumont and Michel Vaucaire bring her 'Non, je ne regrette rien'. Legend has it that the song with its upbeat message sets her on the road to recovery. She decides to do the Olympia engagement after all, which will begin in December.

2 December: second TV interview with Desgraupes is televised.

29 December: premiere at the Olympia. The engagement, which saves the Olympia from bankruptcy, will continue until 6 April, with one interruption.

1961   The Académie Charles Cros awards her its Grand Prix in honorem for her entire recording career.

2 January: the official premiere attracts a host of French and American celebrities.

20–28 March: exhausted by her performances and medication, Piaf is taken ill and her Olympia shows cancelled until 29th.

April: soon after closing at the Olympia, she goes on tour.

23 May–8 June: ill again. Back at the American hospital in Paris for her eighth operation in less than three years.

9 June–2 July: returns to the American hospital for yet another operation. Starts working with Jean Noli on serialising her life story.

12 October: Monnot dies.

18 November: presents her latest protégés on the TV programme *L'École des vedettes*.

1962   January: Claude Figus introduces her to Théo Sarapo.

2–16 March: hospitalised again.

1 June: third TV interview with Desgraupes is broadcast.

3 June: Doug Davis dies in a plane crash.

15 June: starts a comeback tour after more than a year's absence from the stage.

25 September: televised renditions of 'Le Droit d'aimer' and 'Non, je ne regrette rien' from a platform of the Eiffel Tower.

27 September–23 October: at the Olympia with Sarapo. Criticisms

in the media of both her singing and her forthcoming marriage to Sarapo.

9 October: marries Sarapo. They perform together that night at the Olympia.

17 November–17 December: the newlyweds tour Holland and Belgium.

1963   21 February–13 March: she and Theo have an engagement at Bobino. Ecstatic reception, though Piaf looks ill. Her chiropractor Lucien Vaimber has to be in attendance every night.

28 March: her last ever performance in Paris.

30–31 March: performs at the Opera House in Lille, to a small audience because of a transport strike. Her last ever live performance.

7 April: makes her last recording, 'L'Homme de Berlin'.

10 April: rushed to hospital for a blood transfusion. Lapses into a coma.

31 May: travels to Cap Ferrat (La Serena, a seaside villa) with her entourage, to convalesce.

1 August: on her doctor's advice, she moves to La Gatounière (near Mougins).

15 August: falls into another coma after a wrong prescription from a local doctor. Hospitalised for 10 days. Proposed US tour cancelled.

1 September: moves to Plascassier, a village near Grasse, to a villa called L'Enclos de la Rourée.

5 September: suicide of Claude Figus, estranged from Piaf. The news is kept from her.

Thursday, 10 October: Piaf dies around 1pm.

10–11 October: her body is covertly transported back to Boulevard Lannes. It is announced that she died there around 7am.

11 October: Cocteau pronounces a eulogy, then dies himself.

11–13 October: an estimated 100,000 people queue to process before her coffin.

12 October: it is announced that the archbishop of Paris has refused to give her a religious funeral.

14 October: funeral and burial at Père Lachaise.

Mid-October: during the weekend after her death, Blistène writes *Au revoir Édith*, published a week later. Sales of her records start to rocket.

24 October: *France-Dimanche* publishes what is reported to be her last letter, but its authenticity has never been proved.

28 December: death of Robert Chauvigny.

1964   Publication of *Ma vie*.
2 October: just before the first anniversary of her death, Pierre Desgraupes's TV special, *La Mort d'Édith Piaf,* based on Marc Bonel's cine films, proves controversial.

1965   Georgette Lemaire and Mireille Mathieu are hailed as new Piafs.

1966   Chevalier unveils a plaque above 72 rue de Belleville claiming Édith was born on its steps.
Death of Jacques Bourgeat.

1967   Léo Ferré writes 'A une chanteuse morte'.
20 October: *Édith Piaf: quatre ans déjà,* a TV tribute by Blistène.
19 December (Piaf's birthday): the Association of Friends of Édith Piaf is set up.

1968   2 April: the Association organises a gala night for Piaf at the Concert Pacra.
October: death of Raymond Asso.
29 October: a second gala night, marking the fifth anniversary, organised by the Association.

1969   Berteaut's ghosted *Piaf* is published; causes considerable controversy but becomes a bestseller. She is sued unsuccessfully by Denise and Herbert Gassion.
Serge Lama, reacting angrily to Berteaut's book, writes his song 'Édith'.

1970   28 August: Sarapo dies in a car crash.
27 December: broadcast in the UK of BBC1 *Omnibus* about Piaf, entitled 'I Regret Nothing'.

1971   Marcel Blistène becomes president of the Association of Friends.
The cinema-theatre of Bernay is renamed Le Piaf.

1974   Guy Casaril's film *Piaf* is released.

1975   Joni Mitchell's 'Edith and the Kingpin'.
May: death of Simone Berteaut.
October: Swiss TV's *Hommage à Édith Piaf* marks her twelfth anniversary.

1976   Elton John's 'Cage the Songbird'.

1977   Claude Nougaro's 'Comme une Piaf'.
       Musée Édith Piaf opens.
       Columbia Pathé Marconi brings out a double album, *Édith Piaf au
       Carnegie Hall* (the 1957 show).
       Catherine Ribeiro's tribute album *Blues de Piaf.*
       February: Juliette Koka at the Playhouse, New York, with *Piaf: A
       Remembrance.*
       June: Libby Morris's production, *Édith Piaf, je vous aime: A Musical
       Tribute*, opens at the Shaftesbury Theatre, London.

1978   Pam Gems's play *Piaf* opens in an RSC production at Stratford
       upon Avon.
       Grace Jones records 'La Vie en rose'.

1979   A street in Chalon sur Saône is named after Piaf.
       Jack Mels's one-man show *Piaf parmi nous.*

1980   Akihiro Miwa's show in Japan: *Amour et chanson: une vie. Histoire
       d'Édith Piaf.*
       France Normand's show *Hommage à la Piaf* at the Cabaret 1390 in
       Montreal.

1981   Gems's *Piaf* transfers to New York.
       September: mayor of Paris Jacques Chirac inaugurates the Place
       Édith Piaf near Belleville.

1982   *Ladies and Gentlemen, Édith Piaf!* in Texas
       Piaf: La Vie! L'Amour! in Kentucky.
       La Chenille theatre company tours their new production *Piaf ou
       qui j'aurai été*, by René Escudié.
       9 October: after a mass at St Germain de Charonne, Jacques
       Devilliers's small monument to Piaf is unveiled.

1983   Twentieth anniversary of her death.
       1 April–8 May: major exhibition, '20 ans déjà' at Forum des
       Halles, organised by the Association.
       13 April: release of Lelouch's film *Édith et Marcel.*

1986   Allain Leprest records his self-penned song 'Édith'.

1988   Year designated 'l'Année Piaf' by TF1.
       The Académie Charles Cros awards Piaf the Prix patrimoine
       category of its Grand Prix international du disque.
       EMI produces a nine-album box set of 300 songs, with lyrics.

June: a street in Bernay, rue du Cimetière, is renamed rue Édith Piaf.

1991   Céline Dion releases 'Piaf chanterait du rock'.

1992   The album *Ma grand'mère est une rockeuse* is released.
Patsy Gallant's show *Piaf: Love Conquers All* in Montreal.

1993   Thirtieth anniversary of her death.
EMI releases another album, entitled *Il était une voix*, which contains Piaf talking as well as singing.
The Lady and the Sparrow, in Chicago, a play about Piaf and Billie Holiday.
Akihiro Miwa's new show of covers of Piaf songs.

1994   *Tribute to Édith Piaf* album, Amherst Records (USA).

1996   Launch of the musical *Piaf je t'aime* at the Cirque d'Hiver, Paris.

1999   8 July: France Culture series *Lieux de mémoire* features Piaf.

2002   Death of Marc Bonel.

2003   Fortieth anniversary of her death.
Six lost recordings are unearthed at National Library.
Paris council exhibition 'Piaf, la môme de Paris'.
Larger-than-life statue by Lisbeth Delisle of Piaf erected at the place named after her at Bagnolet.
Production of *L'Ombre de la rue* at the Théâtre Essaion, Paris.

2007   Nathalie Lermitte in *Piaf: une vie en rose et noir*, by Jacques Pessis.
14 February: release of Olivier Dahan's film *La Môme* (*La Vie en rose* in English).
8 June: Dahan's film is released in the States.
17 July: revival of the 1996 musical *Piaf je t'aime* opens at the Olympia.

2008   Revival of Gems's *Piaf*, starring Elena Roger in the title role.
In the UK, the Specsavers advertisement using 'Non, je ne regrette rien' receives complaints.

2012   A postage stamp is produced jointly by the US and French postal services honouring Piaf and Miles Davis.
3 April: death of Danielle Bonel.
October: Lady Gaga is reported to have bought Piaf's toenail clippings.

5 November: Patricia Kaas performs at the Albert Hall, London, promoting her new album *Patricia Kaas chante Piaf*, released the same day.

2013   The fiftieth anniversary of Piaf's death is marked by numerous events at home and abroad throughout the year.
23 May: death of Georges Moustaki.
4 June: death of Jean-Louis Jaubert.
21 June: the Fête de la musique commemorates Piaf.
4 September (–January 2014): revival at Théâtre Daunou of Pessis's *Piaf: une vie en rose et noir.*
6 September–9 November: Caroline Nin's *Hymne à Piaf*, Théâtre de l'Essaion.
17–18 September: Stavanger Symphony Orchestra does a Piaf concert with singer Britt Synnøve Johansen, who has been translating and recording Piaf songs since 2001.
19 September: the Francofolies festival moves to New York for *A Tribute to Édith Piaf* at the Beacon Theatre.
October: substantial TV coverage of the anniversary, including news broadcasts and documentaries.
5 October: France 2 broadcasts the Francofolies tribute under the title *Piaf: hymnes à la Môme.*
11 October–9 November: the Ministry of Culture and the Bibliothèque nationale mount an exhibition at the ministry's headquarters, rue Saint-Honoré, entitled 'Petite robe noire et autres souvenirs'.
18–20 October: Charles Dumont concert, *Hommage à Édith Piaf*, at the Espace Cardin, Paris.
24 November: in the UK, Labour Party leader Ed Miliband chooses 'Non, je ne regrette rien' as one of his eight desert island discs.

2015   Centenary of Piaf's birth. A major exhibition at the national library opens in April, running through to August.
May: Piaf is voted France's favourite female singer (*Le Point*, 2015)

Introduction

O N 24 JANUARY 2015, the death of British wartime prime minister Sir Winston Churchill half a century before was commemorated. On 22 November 2013, the world had remembered the assassination in 1963 of John F. Kennedy, president of the United States, aged only 46. A few weeks before, on 10 October 2013, France and other countries had marked the fiftieth anniversary of Édith Piaf's equally premature passing, at 47.

Equating two epoch-making world leaders with a popular vocalist sounds incongruous to say the least; but, as fiftieth anniversaries go, it's hard to find more appropriate comparisons. For Édith Piaf was never just a singer. From the very beginning of her career in 1935, when she was not yet 20, she was recognised as culturally singular. And by the centenary of her birth in 2015, she'd become not only France's favourite female singer of all time,[1] but also an instantly recognisable global icon in her simple black dress, like Kennedy with his American smile and Churchill with his V-for-Victory sign. Like them, Piaf lives outside time. She is, of course, an emblem of French chanson,[2] but also of French identity, human resilience in the face of suffering, and that impalpable totem, 'the people'. It was no surprise that during the historic march in Paris on 11 January 2015, when over a million people proclaimed France's unity in the face of terrorism after three days of deadly attacks in the city, Piaf songs were reportedly blasted from apartments along the route from the Place de la République to the Place de la Nation.[3]

In this book, I want to examine how the cultural phenomenon known as Édith Piaf came into being and what it has come to mean, what purposes it has served. My overarching argument is that this phenomenon was deliberately invented. Embedded in the innumerable representations and recollections of her, including her own, there is in fact a paradox. Although she's frequently depicted as all too real, earthy, natural, authentic, she's also said to be keenly self-aware and calculatedly staged in both her performances and her life—or, to put this more contentiously, to be fabricated. This paradox is seldom acknowledged, other than in the conventional showbiz rhetoric which insists that a celebrity is an 'intensely private' person hiding behind a public persona. But I would suggest there's a lot more to it than that.

To describe her as 'fabricated' would have been anathema in her lifetime and probably still is. At Piaf's death in October 1963, Jean Monteaux contrasted her beginnings 30 years before with those of Françoise Hardy, whose career as a young pop star was just starting.[4] Monteaux's argument is that 'the psychological fabrication of the star'[5] scarcely existed in 1935, simply because, with radio and the record still relatively new, the sociological and technological conditions for manufacturing stars in the way Hardy and others were being manufactured weren't yet present. He is therefore unequivocal: 'There can be no question of a trace of fabrication in Piaf's case. [...] She belongs solely to herself'.[6] And her biographer Emmanuel Bonini, citing Monteaux, enthusiastically agrees.[7] For both, her greatness is her uniqueness, universality and authenticity.

This kind of charismatic reading is founded on a hagiographic essentialism and is actually integral to the fabrication process. Unlike Monteaux and Bonini, I don't view fabrication in moral terms, as synonymous with inauthenticity. To see Piaf as an invention doesn't require a diabolical Svengali figure or the manipulative fakery of reality talent shows. Nor should it corrupt the listening pleasure she provides. It's simply a way of understanding how that pleasure was and is generated. Piaf's authenticity is a social construction in the same way as the authenticity of American country music is for the late sociologist Richard Peterson,[8] who speaks of its fabrication without negative connotations. And my concern is with the meanings and uses the constructed Piaf has acquired over time, as she has steadily become a rhetorical figure.

But I need first to address an obvious question. Even if 'Piaf' is an invention, surely there must have been a real Édith somewhere?

Monteaux, Bonini and many who knew her passionately insist there was one, and her biographers regularly set off in search of it. Bonini even calls his book *Piaf: The Truth*. Her faithful accordionist and factotum Marc Bonel believed he had glimpsed the true Piaf during her first trip to America, when she phoned him in the night in a state of extreme distress: 'The night she called me, I realised there was another woman within her. A woman disoriented by success and money; a woman who'd made it because of her talent but also a poor unfortunate, a poor little bird, a child deprived of tenderness.'[9] But the problem with any account of her life that claims to reveal this real Piaf is that the full circumstances of her childhood and youth and even aspects of her adult life remain a mystery for want of reliable sources, even though some useful biographical detective work has been done. As a result, the biographer can easily fall into the trap of 'printing the legend': developing an essentially hagiographic account in which the greatness of her singing together with her exotic public-facing self are substitutes for fact. But the legend is problematic by its very nature, because it's the product of decades of accreted narratives which are as questionable as they are hard to shift. Foremost among them are Piaf's own.

'Nobody can tell Piaf's story', claimed her friend Pierre Hiégel, who had known her since she was singing in the street at the age of 13, 'because she was different for each of us. You couldn't work her out and she enjoyed maintaining that ambiguity, because she was the one searching for herself and finding herself'.[10] And Danielle Bonel, Piaf's long-term secretary, shrewder than her husband Marc, is conscious of the same problem:

> How can anyone know who the real Piaf was? She played so many roles! She was a chameleon. She would adopt the ambiance of the man she was with at the time. She couldn't remain herself the whole time. I knew her in all sorts of guises. The real Édith was the one who had to face up to herself, when she no longer had to play a part and would ask herself 'Who am I?'[11]

Piaf too was aware of this: 'By the time I die, so much will have been said about me that no one will know any longer what kind of person I was.'[12] A poignant remark but disingenuous, given how much of her life she wilfully obscured: 'As for my private life, the real one, nobody knows that', she warned shortly before her death. 'People only know what I choose to reveal'.[13]

Little wonder that French writing about her life has become locked into standard reflexes which from one book to the next make up an intertextual loop largely shaped by her own strategic statements. We're told repeatedly of the painful episodes of her childhood that she has carefully selected for us, of her belief that love conquers all, of her restless search for a lover who might live up to her expectations. And it is she who informs us that only the boxer Marcel Cerdan, who died in a plane crash in 1949, did live up to them. Some biographers struggle to maintain our and even their interest in the years after Cerdan, as her career seemingly resolves into frenetic touring, unsatisfying affairs and frequent spells in hospital. Olivier Dahan's acclaimed biopic *La Môme* (2007), released as *La Vie en rose* in English-speaking countries, gets caught in the same loop in the sense that for all its acrobatics with cinematic time, it contents itself with the already known. What it doesn't do, as *Le Monde*'s Véronique Mortaigne points out, is illuminate the central Piaf mystery: 'What did Édith Piaf represent, given that she generated so much popular support, abroad as well as in France?'[14]

Some French biographies—Bonini (2008), Brierre (2003), Duclos and Martin (1993) and Lange (1979)—stand out from others by the depth of their research or their sensitivity to the subject. So too does the memoir by Danielle and Marc Bonel, her close associates during her last 18 years, who insist that much of the Piaf legend is false and are determined to correct it.[15] But, valuable though their account is, their loyalty and resolve to exonerate her from the unflattering myths that surround her suggest they are merely replacing one legend with another.

A handful of English-language biographies have also appeared. David Bret's *The Piaf Legend* is as uncritically celebratory as one might expect from his title and his opening confession that the book 'is an attempt to thank her for the immense, heart-warming pleasure which she has given me'.[16] Margaret Crosland's portrait (1985) is more solid, though much has been revealed about the singer since then.[17] The best biography in English is by Carolyn Burke (2011). It's better researched than many that preceded it, in French or English, and is an effective introduction to what Burke calls the 'texture' of Piaf's life and 'her complex humanity'.

But there's still a touch of sentimentality here. Burke conceived the book while standing at Piaf's grave, as a 'homage to the little star who taught me her language and, in the process, gave me a more generous view of her life, and of my own.'[18] And she concludes it in a similar mode by describing Piaf as 'a soul who gave of herself until there was nothing left but her voice and the echo of her laughter.'[19]

The best-researched biography to date in either language is undoubtedly by journalist and biographer Robert Belleret (2013). He undertook considerable archival research, unearthing police reports about the young Piaf and even the proceedings of the committee that looked into accusations of collaboration straight after the German occupation of France (1940–44). This material is important, as we'll see. Belleret too undertakes to discover the real Piaf beneath the myths, but he doesn't start from a position of unquestioning admiration and his book has exploded some cherished illusions. Yet even he is obliged at times to fall back on reasoned assumption rather than evidence, stumbling once again on the 'true' Piaf's unknowability.

Before 2012, there were no published academic monographs on Piaf in English or French, though a handful of perceptive shorter studies by Anglophones had appeared.[20] That these were in English is significant. For some time, Anglo-American scholars, influenced by cultural studies, had been much more receptive than their French counterparts to the study of popular culture. Furthermore, it has conceivably been more difficult for French writers to cast a dispassionate eye on so sacred a national monument. But in 2012, an interesting exception to, and illustration of, this difficulty was provided by the first book-length scholarly study of Piaf, by Joëlle-Andrée Deniot.

Wisely avoiding biography for once, Deniot's imaginative book asks what the different uses of the Piaf figure are. But in practice, extending Catherine Dutheil Pessin's anthropological study of the evolution of the *chanson réaliste* from popular sentimentality to tragic myth,[21] Deniot is more interested in the close textual analysis of the singer's stage perfor-mances, with a view to establishing 'frameworks for a more generally applicable analysis of vocal gesture on stage'.[22] This makes for a complex skein of theorised argument which I will refer to as the book progresses. But her monograph also stands out from traditional French scholarship by resorting to 'an intrusive "I"', which expresses Deniot's 'personal connection to chanson' but also constitutes an experiment with 'radical subjectivity as a privileged pathway into intersubjectivity'.[23] A related singularity is that the book includes not just photos of Piaf on stage but some 40 sketches by graphic artist Mireille Petit-Choubrac. These, Deniot insists, serve not to illustrate her argument but as a second sensibility, separate from Deniot's own, contributing to the intersubjectivity she aspires to. Significantly, too, the book is published by a fine-art publisher. In addition, then, to the rich insights afforded by its elaborate analysis, the book's conception, appearance and admiration for Piaf as a fully fledged artist are meaningful in themselves. They invest her with a national aesthetic importance.

These tendencies in past writing on Piaf underline the need for a different starting point. My aim is not to write another 'definitive' biography, or to undertake further analysis of the aesthetics of performance. Instead, I want to explore a Piaf of words, representations and judgments, an imagined Piaf. To assert that she was fabricated doesn't simply mean that she was a different person on stage and off. Nor are we talking about the kind of ludic self-invention of a David Bowie or a Madonna, where fabrication is acknowledged with the audience's complicity. Performers like these are admired because they play with multiple identities which they creatively control. Piaf is admired for supposedly having just one identity: truth to self. This is her particular business plan and it's what her followers have long invested in; it's how they have insisted on imagining her. With her, the natural is a signifying artefact, though with evolving meanings or uses. I want to look closely at the diversity of these meanings or uses, which are often different from or more complex than the commonplace media representations built into the Piaf 'legend'. In his pioneering study of film stars, Richard Dyer is concerned with 'stars in terms of their signification, not with them as real people'.[24] My focus is not dissimilar, but I want to explore what one particular star has signified culturally over time. This is what I mean by a cultural history of Piaf.

A relatively new discipline in France, cultural history is usually defined as the social history of representations, tracing the ways in which societies imagine the world around them.[25] Adapting this definition to include representations of a single individual, I want to trace historically how Piaf came to mean what she means at the centenary of her birth. As

Simon Frith has argued, cultural history has often come up with more satisfactory, more nuanced analyses of popular culture than cultural studies, which, with a particular liking for French theory, has at times seemed to have a 'cavalierly postmodern attitude to the past'.[26] But Frith is also aware that popular-musical history, in Britain at least, has itself become a commodity, with endless biographies, coffee-table histories and TV documentaries. Amid this 'cacophony', history is 'constructed and sold with little respect for the niceties of academic methodology'.[27]

This assertion echoes my own concerns about biographies that promise to lay bare the truth. In a sense, I am more interested in the legend than the 'truth', though this doesn't mean simply printing the legend. A cultural-historical approach means critically analysing the legend: its origins, evolution, contradictions and cultural significance. Piaf's raw talent as a singer, the qualities of her voice, her stage performances, have always been read through a succession of mediations. As Frith contends, music always comes to us mediated; Dyer's stance is much the same. To make sense of Piaf, we have to accept that her meanings over time have been the result not of direct, uncomplicated communion with her audiences but of various interpositions through which she's been heard. These range from the genre or form of the songs themselves and the manner and medium of their performance (cabaret, music hall, record, radio and television) to the prevailing social, cultural and political conditions and collective representations— among them, evolving notions of chanson, popular culture, gender and national identity. And, crucially in Piaf's case, the meanings of the songs are mediated through narratives of the person and vice versa. Dutheil Pessin is right to point out that 'no woman singer more than Piaf has so combined life and song that it becomes impossible to distinguish one from the other'.[28] But if we're to advance existing understanding of Piaf, we need to approach this inseparability more cautiously and interrogatively.

Another cultural-historical concern of the book is cultural memory. I want to examine Piaf as a 'site of memory', a 'lieu de mémoire'. This concept, developed by the French historian Pierre Nora and a team of researchers in the 1990s, endeavours to explain the modern 'commemorative consciousness', illustrated in those anniversaries of Churchill, Kennedy and Piaf herself, as well as in the incremental rise of genealogy and museums of everything.[29] I shall come back to it at the end of the book, since one of my key questions is why a France as obsessed with the future and the modern as Nora contends resolutely commemorates a singer who was born a hundred years ago and who has been dead for more than half a century. Why does remembering Piaf still matter?

A cultural history of Piaf also needs to take account of her internationality. It's sometimes said that French cultural historians have been too exclusively concerned with France as a nation state and need to make a transnational turn by examining cultural circulations between national and regional spaces, 'movements of agents, ideas and knowledges' ('déplacements d'acteurs, d'idées et de savoirs')[30] that in fact transcend or blur conventional national boundaries. The French music historian Ludovic Tournès argues that colonial history and postcolonial theory, among other approaches, have shown that 'national cultures are constructed without as much as within frontiers' and that 'the notion of national identity is fundamentally plural, shifting and dependent to a large extent on phenomena taking place beyond the borders of the nation-state'.[31] In this perspective, French cultural history has begun identifying '"passeurs" from one civilisation to another' ('"passeurs" d'une civilisation à une autre'):[32] mediators who transgress frontiers and are responsible for such circulations. In the process, there's an increasing engagement among French cultural historians with cultural studies, or more precisely, as Érik Neveu puts it, with the argument that popular practices can be as rich in meaning and as subtle as those of elites.[33]

There's a good case for seeing the imagined Piaf as one such *passeur*, crossing national and cultural boundaries. She became an international star not only in Europe but in North and South America and in the UK. This particular direction of transatlantic travel has largely been ignored by cultural historians, who, Tournès maintains, have tended to essentialise international cultural transfers as a one-way process labelled 'Americanisation'. But 'circulation' is a more apt metaphor. Piaf in fact circulated cultural meanings and in the process acquired new ones which themselves began to circulate. There are different Piafs orbiting in transnational space, taking constantly mutating interpretations of chanson, Frenchness and French culture back and forth between the Francophone and Anglophone worlds. The imagined Piaf—the rhetorical figure—is at once exclusively French and stateless.

For some, this global relativism might be problematic. Touching on the linguistic specificity of chanson, Deniot underscores the problem of untranslatability in chanson. Gesture, voice and words are so tightly imbricated that, contrary to received opinion, she insists, a chanson's meanings can't be grasped without linguistic understanding. The 'music of the words' argument cuts no ice with her. Listening to a chanson without native or 'similarly mastered' linguistic competence will lead only to superficial understanding or misunderstanding.[34] This indirectly poses the question of my own analytical standpoint, as a native English speaker with French as an acquired language and with some awareness of the sameness and otherness of French culture.

I'll return to this question as my argument develops, but for the moment I want to point out that while Deniot is no doubt right when it comes to the semantic meanings of a chanson's lyric, its shifting cultural meanings are another matter. Even if I meet Deniot's criterion for understanding chanson by having adequate familiarity with the French language, I still remain at least a partial outsider culturally, and my approach will inevitably differ from that of a native-French scholar by virtue of an ethnographic distance.[35] I don't, however, see this distance as something I need to compensate for or try to eliminate by becoming as 'French' as possible. Rather, I believe that what native French speakers sometimes see as the cultural 'misunderstandings' of non-French observers who don't quite 'get it' can have an epistemological value—provided, of course, that they aren't simply based on ignorance— as agents of defamiliarisation. As I've argued elsewhere,[36] the dimensions of language and location introduce different complexities to the study of popular music from those perceived by scholars studying the musics of their home cultures. They provide an intercultural optic which is possibly unique to those working in the liminal territory between linguistically distinct cultures. If Piaf may herself be described as a 'passeur', so too might the non-French scholar working in French cultural studies. But such scholars aren't just neutral interpreters who allow Francophone and Anglophone cultures to have a two-way conversation. As professional interculturalists, they are in the conversation; in a sense, they *are* the conversation, decoding and re-encoding with their every utterance. An intercultural perspective of this kind can shed light on Piaf's national and transnational meanings.

All translations from the French are mine unless otherwise indicated; I supply the original French in the endnotes. The book consists of three parts. Part I examines the imagined Piaf's early years, from 1935 to 1945. Part II deals with the high point of her career, from the Liberation to the mid-1950s, followed by her gradual decline. Part III is concerned with her death and afterlives, from 1963 until the 2015 centenary. But we have to start with a brief look at who she was before she became that imagined Piaf, even though we must fall back on her own accounts and those problematic biographies.

PART I

NARRATING PIAF

CHAPTER I

Inventing la Môme

'How monstrously she wanted to become something else'
(Henri Contet)[1]

É DITH GASSION was born on 19 December 1915, daughter of
Annetta Giovanna Maillard, herself a street singer using the alias
Line Marsa, and of Louis Gassion, a circus performer and itinerant
acrobat and contortionist.[2] Both parents came from circus or fairground
backgrounds. They married in September 1914, the month after Louis
was called up, separated probably in 1919 and finally divorced in 1929.
Left alone, Annetta appears to have consigned her baby daughter to her
half-Moroccan mother Aïcha until Louis, returning from the front to
find the little girl dirty and unhealthy, removed her to his own mother's
brothel in Bernay, where she found a degree of security and love. Around
the age of seven, she moved again, joining the Caroli circus with her
father and living in a caravan. When he later went solo and began
performing acrobatics in the street, Édith passed the hat and, so the
story goes, did a little singing to soften the hearts of the crowd. She
recounts that the first ever song she sang publicly was the only one she
knew at the time, the national anthem, the 'Marseillaise', though in an
interview in 1936, at the time of the left-wing Popular Front government,
she claimed it was the 'Internationale'.[3] Aged about 15, Édith struck
out on her own, first taking several short-term jobs, then turning to
street singing.

The French popular music economy of the 1920s and 1930s centred on Paris and involved three types of venue, though in practice the boundaries between them were unstable. One was the commercial music hall, where the dazzling revues for which Paris was famous had taken hold in the 1910s at the Folies-Bergère, the Olympia and the Casino de Paris, with their sequinned, feathered and bare-breasted dancing girls, glittering staircases and up-to-the-minute electrical effects.[4] In the aftermath of war, the halls emulated the mass spectacles of Broadway in a wave of Americanisation, popularising jazz and associated dance styles like the charleston, the shimmy and the black bottom.[5] Within the revue formula, established stars—among them Maurice Chevalier (1888–1972), Yvette Guilbert (1867–1944) and Mistinguett (1873–1956)—would deliver cheery, comic or salacious numbers. The hit songs of the time usually came from these revues, as did the latest singing stars, like Josephine Baker (1906–75) and the Corsican crooner Tino Rossi (1907–83).[6] Nevertheless, with the rising popularity of spectacle, rhythm and big-band music, singing for its own sake was sidelined in the halls for a time.[7]

The second type of location was the cabaret, where Piaf would have her breakthrough. More intimate and convivial than the music hall, cabarets were in reality diverse, ranging from the sophisticated or literary to the squalid and licentious. Customers were seated at tables rather than in rows and would listen to singers while smoking, talking, drinking or dining. This said, in the post-1918 era, many cabarets, especially in Montmartre, imitated the music-hall revue in an effort to attract tourists, drawn to Paris for precisely that kind of entertainment.[8] The third location was the street. Buskers traditionally made their money performing on street corners or in the courtyards of residential blocks, where those listening at the window might throw a few coins wrapped in paper. Before records became widespread, street singers also sold rudimentary copies of sheet music known as *petits formats*, enabling those who stood listening or singing along to take the song home.

The rise of cinema from the 1910s caused a great many music halls to close or become film theatres. So it was in the cabaret and the street particularly that songs and the styles in which they were performed gradually formed into the self-contained, increasingly self-conscious subculture that is understood and designated in English by the French word 'chanson' and that, to an extent, underlies the French phrase *la chanson française*.[9] The street and the cabaret were sites where the vocal and the verbal took precedence over rhythm and spectacle, and songs were primarily meant to be listened to.[10] By the mid-1930s, new technologies were also creating new resources for the popular singer: radio, the microphone for live performances, cinema and, to a lesser extent, recording. So the young Piaf arrived at a propitious time for singers. Traditionally, a song would be identified by its lyricist and composer, whose names were announced by the performer, a nineteenth-century practice audible in the first recordings of Aristide Bruant (1851–1925) and Yvette Guilbert and which Piaf herself retained. But with the singer and actor Damia (1892–1978), who achieved stardom in the 1910s and 1920s with a varied repertoire and a theatrical delivery, a song became publicly identified with its performer.[11] This would be decisive in the development of both the imagined Piaf and the distinctive notion of *la chanson française*, as we'll see.

Street singing provided Édith, along with her friend and assistant Simone Berteaut, known as 'Momone', with a living, though a meagre and unreliable one. As a child living in Paris's 20th *arrondissement* (district), the singer Odette Laure recalls hearing Piaf's 'cathedral-like voice',[12] which she loved so much that she would collect 25-centime pieces ready to throw down whenever the singer appeared, once or twice a month. Momone would pick up the money, since Édith was lost in the music. When in February 1933, at the age of 17, Édith had an illegitimate child, Marcelle, she would carry her with her when she went busking. Laure remembers once following them to the Pelleport metro station, where Piaf met a young man pushing a pram, presumably the baby's father, Louis Dupont, known as le P'tit Louis (Little Louis). Because he disapproved of Marcelle being hauled round the streets, Louis eventually took her to live with his mother, where she died of meningitis in July 1935 aged only two. She was buried in a pauper's grave. This was the first of the misfortunes that would befall the adult Piaf, and it would haunt her all her life.

For the more motivated street singers of the early 1930s, there were also opportunities to perform in barracks, cafés, dance halls and the more downmarket cabarets. Édith was already taking such opportunities as they arose. In 1933–34, she joined a small troupe performing in barracks, led by Camille Rebon, a friend of her father. For cabarets like Le Juan-les-Pins (better known as Chez Lulu) or Chez Marius,[13] she would sometimes adopt exotic stage names like Tanya, Denise Jay, Huguette Hélia or even 'Miss Édith', an echo of the famous 'Miss', Mistinguett.[14] But an upturn in her fortunes, and a new stage name, came with a chance meeting in October 1935, while she was still mourning her daughter. The details of this encounter are contested but immovably embedded in Piaf's grand narrative. As she and Momone sometimes did on weekdays, they were working in the upmarket Étoile district. Here (or possibly elsewhere), Louis Leplée, a well-known nightclub impresario and one-time drag artist, offered her an audition at his elegant cabaret restaurant, Le Gerny's. Signing her up to appear a few days later, possibly on 25 October,[15] he also gave her a new name: la Môme Piaf, literally 'Kid Sparrow'. She was an instant hit and ended up with a regular booking there until Leplée's mysterious murder in April 1936 caused the club to close.

An overnight success at Le Gerny's, she was immediately invited by the soon-to-be-famous talent-spotter for Polydor, Jacques Canetti, to appear the following Sunday on the popular Radio-Cité station, where Canetti was in charge of programming. The station was owned by the advertising magnate Marcel Bleustein-Blanchet, who like Canetti had seen her first performance at the club, on Leplée's recommendation.[16] Listeners to the 15-minute radio slot fronted by Félix Paquet, who introduced a new hopeful every Sunday morning at 11.30, immediately jammed the switchboard wanting to know who she was. Canetti promptly booked her for another 13 weekly slots, for which Bleustein-Blanchet found a commercial sponsor. Radio was the making of her as a national celebrity. Canetti's Polydor connection also allowed her to make four studio recordings, on wax, in December of that year, the first of 120 tracks she would record for the company.[17] Then came her first music-hall appearance, in March 1937, at the prestigious ABC, owned by Mitty Goldin. By the end of the year, she had even sung in a film, released the following February, an adaptation of the controversial 1922 novel by Victor Margueritte, *La Garçonne*, published in English as *The Bachelor Girl*.

The young woman who experienced this breathtaking ascent only months after the death of her daughter was inexperienced professionally yet street-wise and self-aware, with a quick intelligence cultivated by her harsh childhood. She was marked by her mother's abandonment of her, and although she is said to have loved her father,[18] his treatment could be brutal, and his lifestyle was unstable, with a succession of lovers who were uninterested in being her surrogate mother. Constantly on the move after Bernay, she'd had little schooling. Leplée was warned that he was adopting a wild child: binge-drinking, semi-literate, dirty by some accounts,[19] and promiscuous. The men she frequented in Pigalle were pimps, petty crooks and organised criminals. She only avoided prostitution, the story goes, by paying for 'protection' out of her takings and pointing out to her 'protector' any women in clubs wearing jewellery expensive enough to steal.[20]

This background was inscribed in her very being on stage. In his memoirs, Bleustein-Blanchet describes seeing her at Le Gerny's for the first time: small, visibly undernourished and unattractive.[21] The writer Carlo Rim, on a visit to the cabaret on 9 November 1935, saw 'a pathetic little woman in a cheap dress, with the hunted look of someone who's just had a good hiding'.[22] A journalist with *Les Nouvelles littéraires* in 1950 recalled first seeing Édith there 15 years before, while she was rehearsing. He'd been taken aback by 'this little scrap of a woman, wearing a pleated skirt like a Les Halles streetwalker and a white sweater' and bringing to mind 'all her sisters of the Paris streets. With a good line in repartee, she was humming street songs'.[23] In company, she was by all accounts upbeat and fun-loving, but for those who knew her better she was fragile and insecure, desperate to be loved unconditionally, afraid of solitude and the dark. For Tino Rossi, she was a lonely woman surrounded by people, 'unpredictable and hard to understand, with bizarre mood swings, suddenly changing from manic jollity to inconsolable despair', and, for Aznavour, 'a child dictator [...], whose reactions could be totally infantile'.[24]

Her physical appearance and psychological vulnerability call to mind characters from nineteenth-century fiction: Cosette in Hugo's *Les Misérables*, Cissy Jupe in Dickens's *Hard Times* and, in her impractical romanticism, Emma Bovary. Literary analogies of this kind have been drawn repeatedly over the decades, with Zola a particular point of reference. Etched into collective representations of Piaf from the outset, they have served a vital function as intertextual components in the machinery of invention. That machinery was initially designed and set in motion by three identifiable individuals. First among them was Piaf herself.[25]

She invented herself not simply by skilfully exploiting the physical properties of her voice but by narrating herself from the very beginning with what Crosland calls 'a novelist's imagination'.[26] Chanson was the ideal vehicle for this. Simon Frith argues that all songs are implicitly narratives: 'to sing a song is to tell a story'. He admits, though, that *la chanson française*—exemplified by Piaf in his argument—is a case apart because it is explicitly narrative, verbal as much as musical.[27] Yet with Piaf, I believe, we need to go further. Collective representations of her have grown out of the stories she told in her songs, but these stories have from the first been read both through and into her own creative recounting of her life. In Piaf's work, there's in fact a double narrative: within the explicit narrative of the song, there's the watermark of a second narrative—Piaf the woman.

Berteaut, for example, recounts how, even before she was famous, Piaf would identify spontaneously with certain songs, seeing them as in some ineffable way about her. Some time after having a brief affair with a legionnaire, she heard 'Mon légionnaire' (My legionnaire), a lyric by Raymond Asso set to music by Marguerite Monnot and recorded by Marie Dubas (1894–1972) in May 1936. Piaf was angry about this: 'The Foreign Legion belongs to me and no one else [...]. It was "my" song, "my" story.'[28] Years later, when she was short of money, she agreed to have her autobiography ghosted by Jean Noli, a journalist on the populist weekly *France-Dimanche*. Noli later recalled with admiration the canny awareness she brought to the task: 'Her life as she served it up was a subtle, skilful mix of Zola, lonely hearts serials, Aristide Bruant and romantic fiction'.[29]

This impulse to live through fiction is complex. Belleret is more negative about it than Noli, accusing her of self-pity, exaggeration and a more or less conscious attempt to construct or encourage a myth that the truth would have destroyed.[30] Certainly, her self-narration is a form of image-building. Responding to a journalist in 1941 who asked whether the story in 'Mon légionnaire' really happened, she replied: 'Some of it's true, some of it's false. It all depends how you tell stories.'[31] Her being born with the help of two policemen on the steps of 72 rue de Belleville is probably a tall tale (her birth certificate indicates the nearby Tenon hospital). So too no doubt was her professed childhood blindness. And Noli is perfectly candid about one episode in the autobiography, in which she supposedly sold herself to pay for her child's funeral. The part where her understanding punter, moved by her tears, gave her the money without demanding her services was concocted by the two of them.[32]

Yet there is more to her fictions than cynical manipulation. Rather, she seems to have experienced herself more completely through narrative and role-play. Piaf 'acted out her life as she did her songs' ('jouait sa vie comme ses chansons'), writes Danielle Bonel.[33] More than once, she likened herself to the heroine of Jean Anouilh's play *La Sauvage*, citing the protagonist's admission that there will always be 'some stray dog somewhere to stop me being happy'.[34] Self-constructions of this kind, drawing explicitly or implicitly on literary antecedents, have the effect of making her culturally identifiable, while also allowing her to see herself through the eyes of others, as a character in a true-life drama. Danielle Bonel, her principal apologist, admits that the poverty of Édith's childhood has been overstated.[35] Bonini too concedes that though her early life certainly wasn't easy, 'it wasn't Zola either'.[36] But journalist and future minister Françoise Giroud understands this complex psychological need differently, arguing that telling and re-telling her story made Piaf grasp just how wretched her early years had been.[37]

Identifying this intervention of the other's gaze in Piaf's self-consciousness is essential to an understanding of how her myth was elaborated. We can make sense of Piaf as a social chameleon, wilfully plural, always aspiring to be something other than she was. This connects with another aspect of her self-invention, which is her will to better herself. With scarcely any formal education, the young Édith, once she went professional, developed an ethic of self-improvement which turned her into an autodidact. 'All the things she did in order to raise herself up socially and culturally [...] left us all quite flabbergasted!' reveals Henri Contet, one of her lyricists and lovers.[38] In particular, she would ask better-educated acquaintances like her lifelong friend Jacques Bourgeat, bibliophile and occasional poet, to recommend books of literary or intellectual merit, which she would devour.

Self-reinvention was equally critical to her singing. As her brother (or possibly half-brother), Herbert Gassion, observed, in life she was a joker, but on stage everything changed: 'When she sang, she took on a second personality, as tragic as the first one could be comic.'[39] This capacity for switching moods also makes sense of the ease with which she took to acting: on stage beginning with Cocteau's *Le Bel Indifférent* in 1940 and on screen with the 1941 film *Montmartre-sur-Seine*. But above all it sheds light on the methodical construction work she undertook for her singing performances, which relativises the common perception of her being a spontaneous, intuitive performer. Here again, though, we mustn't assume that the crafting of a stage persona, common to all popular singers, is in some way at odds with sincerity. It's rather that sincerity—'authenticity', as Peterson might have it—is itself a performance, on stage and in life.

She soon learnt to prepare her stage performances to the last detail, as we'll see later. But her first efforts in this regard were to rethink her existing repertoire. When she started at Le Gerny's, her act was a rag-bag of evergreens like the street favourite 'Nuits de chine' (China nights, 1922), 'Comme un moineau' (Like a sparrow, 1925), other numbers borrowed from Damia, Fréhel, Josephine Baker ('J'ai deux amours'/I have two loves, 1931) and Tino Rossi, and even a few opera standards.[40] But Leplée wanted her to be more selective so as to foreground the down-at-heel exoticism that was captivating his middle-class clientele, so she took to trawling the offices of music publishers for suitable new material. At that time, newcomers could only 'create'[41] a new song if it was unwanted by established singers, who were generally granted first refusal because the publisher was taking less of a gamble. Or, if the newcomer was lucky, they might be allowed to cover a song already adopted by someone else. Piaf's illicit appropriation of the excellent 'L'Étranger' (Malleron-Juel-Monnot, 1934)[42] is an illustration of the kind of problem these arrangements could cause. She purloined the song from the established singer Annette Lajon during one of her regular visits to publishers by praising Lajon's version of it and asking her to repeat it several times, though according to Lajon Piaf actually stole the sheet music. In Piaf's account, her rival, turning up at Le Gerny's and hearing her song performed without permission, graciously forgave her, but eye-witnesses have Lajon slapping her face. Either way, Piaf was forced to withdraw the song.[43]

As with 'Mon légionnaire', this determination to have the number testifies to her awareness that she needed a style. Both songs belonged to the tradition of the 'realist song' (*la chanson réaliste*), a feature of the popular music scene in interwar France. With the social changes brought by the Great War and the rise of Americanised dance music and revue, it had already become a nostalgic form by the 1930s, harking back to cabaret and the *café-concert*[44] and to the social realism of Bruant and Montéhus (1872–1952) in the late nineteenth century. Bruant's version used street slang to stylise a marginal world of crime, prostitution and cruel destiny. It was subsequently appropriated and adapted in the *café-concert* in the late nineteenth and early twentieth centuries by women singers, notably Eugénie Buffet (1866–1934), Berthe Sylva (1885–1941), to an extent Marie Dubas, and the two main exponents, Damia and Fréhel (1891–1951). The style eventually trickled down to street singers like Piaf's mother, Line Marsa.[45]

Although the realist song was a fluid category by the mid-1930s,[46] it did have some well-established conventions. Performed by women, it was clearly gendered. Far removed from music-hall spectacle, realist staging was minimal and austere, with the singer alone in the spotlight and made up to look pale with strong red lipstick, to intensify emotion and focus attention on voice and body.[47] The first *chanteuses réalistes* typically began their careers with songs by Bruant or Montéhus. But this masculine rhetoric of social populism was soon replaced by melodramas about female dependency, unrequited love and the heartbreak of motherhood among the urban poor. The realist song also had a familiar cast of characters from melodrama: fallen but naively romantic women, small-time crooks, sailors on shore leave. One of the characters, usually a woman, would invariably fall victim to a cruel destiny. Realism expressed nostalgia for the old, pre-war Paris too,[48] drawing inspiration from Zola, popular fiction (Dabit, Carco, Mac Orlan), 1930s cinema (Carné, Duvivier, Renoir) and the photography of Brassaï.[49] The city it depicted wasn't the dazzling capital imagined by tourists seeking saucy delights. Nor did it have the contemporary effervescence of jazz, Cocteau, Stravinsky or the surrealists. It was the Paris of Bruant and the *fortifs*, the former fortifications that marked the boundary between the city and its down-at-heel suburbs, the *faubourgs*. This Paris had become a stereotype by the 1930s as a result of urbanisation, a reality melancholically acknowledged in the songs themselves.[50]

Yet realism acquired a new if imprecise topicality with the post-1918 moral crisis (unreturning sons, fathers, husbands, lovers), subterranean shifts in social structures, and economic depression. In this context, its chief appeal for women[51] was its constructed identity between singer and song. In Piaf's own version of it, this identity was signed visually by her waif-like appearance. The singer Rina Ketty first saw her perform as Édith Gassion in 1932 at Le Lapin agile, a legendary cabaret of La Butte-Montmartre where Ketty herself had a booking. Piaf sang only briefly with the house band before passing the hat: 'She delivered realist songs with such force, such intensity, that she was already tearing our hearts out. [...] She put into her songs all the misery of her youth.'[52] In fact, Piaf had arrived at a significant time in the history of chanson, when the singing voice was no longer just to be heard but also, under the influence of cinema, to be seen.[53] The 'sung voice' as Deniot calls it became 'the seen voice', part of a total-theatrical performance. So in moving from street to stage, la Môme had to adapt to a new dramaturgy. She had difficulty replicating the gestural semiology of others[54] so was forced to make up her own, drawing unconsciously on an existing rhetoric harking back to the great tragic actresses of the past like Réjane and Sarah Bernhardt.[55] In this way, Piaf re-invented the *chanson réaliste* visually and scenically.[56]

But Piaf also arrived at a time when what we now call 'authenticity', prefigured in earlier *chanteuses réalistes*, was becoming an expectation.[57] This was another result of the microphone, the cinematic close-up, the record and radio, which all made possible a new kind of intimacy. As Cocteau once wrote: 'the airwaves carry the poignant voice of our singer into the most intimate of rooms and that voice becomes part of the lives of a mass of people'.[58] Whereas older entertainers like Chevalier or Mistinguett switched in and out of character, the new taste for intimacy required younger female singers to be seen as singing about themselves. And the *chanson réaliste* was ideally suited to this expectation. But Piaf's interpretations of it brought a stronger visual dimension to this intimacy, not only because of her child-like height and appearance of vulnerability but also by an economy of gesture and scenic space (there was in fact no stage at Le Gerny's), facilitated by her prompt conversion to the static microphone.[59] In her case, then, the identity between singer and song became instantly visible. Possibly the first ever article about her, in *Le Petit Parisien* of November 1935, is entitled 'A singer who lives her songs' ('Une chanteuse qui vit sa chanson'), and its anonymous author associates this identity once again with a literary trope: 'This girl from the street gives the songs of the street the same poignant, penetrating and discreetly toxic poetry as Carco does to his stories of the street.'[60]

The perception that she was authentic, that she'd experienced the suffering her songs depicted, would become the chief component of the imagined Piaf, and the longest-lasting. And at a time when truth to life and intimate self-revelation were becoming an obligation, it was arguably a perfectly conscious strategy of her self-invention process. She chose the well-worn realist formula precisely because it identified singing with being, though she would mould it and later try to relinquish it altogether. But she would never escape it—unsurprisingly, because she would persistently narrate her life through the lens of the *chanson réaliste*, deploying its codes and grammar as a common language and, where necessary, adjusting her self-narration to it in order to get a better fit between singer and song.

Her lifelong fatalism, for example, was entirely consistent with the *chanson réaliste*. This is well illustrated in the song 'Elle fréquentait la rue Pigalle' (She hung around the rue Pigalle, Asso-Maitrier, 1939),[61] written at her request.[62] A sex worker, smelling of 'cheap vice' and 'black with sin', is removed from her milieu and moment by a man who tells her she's beautiful. She asks him to take her away from dingy Pigalle, encrusted with sordid memories, to the brighter Montparnasse. But, once she moves outside her 'natural' environment, where she somehow made sense, into a space where she doesn't belong, he sees her as she really is: fallen, ugly. Sin is indelibly inscribed in her features. He promptly sends her back to Pigalle, to a fate she had never really had a hope of escaping. Piaf's narratives of her own life often echo this kind of populist determinism, as with her whirlwind affair with the legionnaire. In the song supposedly based on it, the handsome legionnaire, after a night of passion with the protagonist, goes off to fight and dies. In *Ma vie* (*My Life*), the autobiography ghosted by Noli, she describes the corresponding 'real' encounter with epic self-regard: 'Oh, how I loved him, "My Legionnaire"! [...] For a long time I couldn't sing it without a shudder. Maybe that's why I sang it so well?'[63] She lost him, she laments, because she wasn't destined for happiness, though for good measure she also mobilises the realist trope of sacrificial motherhood. Forced to choose, she left the legionnaire 'for my daughter's sake'. Naturally, the spurned lover did what any self-respecting legionnaire would: he requested a posting to Africa and dutifully lost his life.[64]

Piaf, however, wasn't the only one working at that better fit between singer and song. One of the persistent leitmotifs in writing about her is Pygmalion. Leplée was her first Pygmalion, though his efforts didn't go all that far and weren't especially inspired. As she would reveal in 1936 during the investigation of his murder, he treated her as a child, trying to regulate her carousing and stop her mixing with undesirables—one of several possible explanations of the killing. In the process, he made her work on her act. In 1934 and 1935, the most popular tunes were still largely from the revues. They were light-hearted numbers like Chevalier's 'Prosper (Yop la boum!)' and 'Quand un vicomte', both from the 1935 Casino de Paris revue *Parade du monde*. Or they were romances like Rossi's Corsican-themed 'Vieni vieni', from the 1934 revue *Parade de France*. Similar styles also featured in films and light operas.[65] The problem for Piaf was that these styles didn't suit her. There was also her look: small, thin and pale rather than voluptuous or sophisticated like the standard female singer. Rather than attempt a makeover, Leplée opted to retain her street appearance and encouraged her to shape her repertoire accordingly.[66] At his behest, she introduced more socially marked numbers: 'La Valse brune' and Bruant's 'Nini peau de chien', both street standards, the more recent 'Les Mômes de la cloche', composed by Vincent Scotto (Street girls, lyrics by André Decaye, 1936),[67] and more borrowings from Damia and Fréhel. These choices steered her further towards the *chanson réaliste*. And he chose her a stage name to match. Aliases weren't unusual at the time; nor was his choice especially original, as young women were often called 'mômes' and 'la Môme Piaf' was only a slang variant of the name of an existing performer, la Môme Moineau (Lucienne Dhotelle), who had also begun as a street singer.[68] It was Leplée who, introducing her at Le Gerny's, first told the story, true or false, of their encounter on a street corner. In doing so, he produced a narrative which embellished the truth for the sake of launching a new act with a particular style, turning her street origins into a consumable product for his audience of bankers, lawyers, wealthy foreigners and the occasional government minister.[69] He knew they might be taken aback by the rough and ready nature of her delivery, but he was shrewd enough not to dilute their agreeable sense of roughing it.

The knowingness with which Leplée fashioned Piaf anticipated the repackaging of artists that would become prevalent in the mass-cultural industries of the 1950s and 1960s. But its real significance is that, hand in hand with Piaf's own self-invention, Leplée helped imagine a persona that would eventually evolve into a myth. After his death, a much more significant step in this direction was taken by Raymond Asso, whom Piaf met by chance in January 1936 in the publishing house where he worked, though he only became her manager, and lover, a year later, after Leplée's demise had left her rudderless. She would adopt his songs for the next two and a half years, until the summer of 1939. 'I made Édith', he would later boast ('Édith, je l'a façonnée').[70] Aged 35 when he began managing the 20-year-old, he had reputedly been a shepherd, a cavalryman, a legionnaire in North Africa, a smuggler and, since 1933, a lyricist who had tried his hand at fiction[71] while working as Marie Dubas's secretary. With no qualifications other than an intuitive understanding of live performance in the burgeoning French music industry, he became the architect, strategist and publicist of the imagined Piaf, taking her own and Leplée's first achievements a good deal further. He recognised her talent but could see that it remained undisciplined and that she had little stagecraft. He therefore moulded her to the cultural expectations of the time, transforming her from the Kid, gifted but freakish spectacle for the comfortable bourgeois, into the accomplished Édith Piaf. He made her work ceaselessly on stage presence, diction and interpretation. He also introduced the signature plain black dress she wore at her first Bobino appearance.[72] The choice of black was indebted to Damia, but the dress was shorter than the gowns usually worn. Asso even dealt directly with Piaf's dress-maker, Marinette Mousquès, to regulate matters of design, material and repairs.[73]

French singing stars at the time were made in music halls, not cabarets. Only in the halls could they reach a sizeable, sociologically diverse audience. The ABC, a 1200-seater that opened in 1934 on the Boulevard Poissonnière in the 2nd *arrondissement*, rapidly became the most prestigious live venue, boasting of the 'note of aristocracy' it conferred on its performers.[74] It did so by only booking each act for a short run to ensure a rapid turnaround, and by featuring only established performers. Asso nevertheless assailed its owner, Mitty Goldin, until he begrudgingly signed up Piaf for a bottom-of-the-bill slot of five songs, on 26 March 1937. After that first triumphant night, Goldin needed no more persuading. Asso had made her study other singers, most notably Marie Dubas, who was then performing at the ABC. Later, Piaf would cite this experience as the most important event in her career. Still young and inexperienced, Piaf had herself been approached by Goldin about appearing at the ABC but was so convinced of her genius that she had imposed ridiculous conditions and Goldin had withdrawn the offer.[75] Asso insisted she learn from Dubas, and Piaf observed her every day for two weeks. The experienced singer's work allowed her to measure how much rigour and contrivance was required to master her trade: 'in this magnificent performance nothing was left to chance; nothing was improvised. Facial expression, gestures, pose, intonation, all were carefully planned.'[76]

Asso similarly understood that, for a true star, on-stage and off-stage images are interdependent. Like Leplée, he worked on Piaf's social and cultural skills, even her table manners, teaching her how to function in polite society. He made her read and go to the theatre so that she might better understand tragedy.[77] He took her away from the underworld she'd been consorting with and banned her from seeing Momone. In short, he became Professor Higgins to her Eliza Doolittle, though reports that he hit her on occasion suggest a less benign relationship. A sense of possession and power in fact emerges from his recollections of that period: 'Over two years, she would lose her vulgar side, evolve and completely transform herself. Her face took on a purity that was deeply moving'. He also makes out that their love was of a different order from her other relationships: 'It was the birth, the procreation, the delivery of a whole new being'.[78] In 1968, just before he died, Asso returned to his awkward obstetric metaphors: 'Édith was the flesh of my flesh. I made her. I gave birth to her, labour pains included!'[79] He objectified her in other ways too, referring to her as an uncut diamond or a work of art that the war had prevented him completing.[80] And she in turn internalised his view of her, developing a disturbing capacity for self-loathing. Before Asso, she writes in *Ma vie*:

> I was wallowing in stupidity like some disgusting insect in the mud. I basked in it. And in ugliness too. [...] Raymond transformed me. He taught me how to be a human being [...],

to become a woman and a star, not just a phenomenon with a voice people listened to as they might look at some rare animal on show at a fair.[81]

In September 1938, she replied to a letter from him: 'How you must be hurting, to write such horrible things to me, but you're right, I am stupid [...] and I disgust myself, I've lost all confidence in myself; basically I'm nothing according to what you said in the letter.'[82] As we'll see later, such asymmetrical gender relations would recur throughout her life.

Artistically, Asso's achievement was to write an entire repertoire of lyrics, which she sang until the war separated them. The intensity of this process was never matched by her later writers. Like Piaf, he had grown up with the *chanson réaliste*, for which he had a talent, overlaid with a taste for noir fiction, cinema and jazz. But, again like Piaf, he succeeded in refining the form, injecting it with, in her words, a whole new style which would set the agenda for her future lyricists.[83] He produced songs with plots, sometimes based on episodes in Piaf's early life or his own. Telling a complete story in the three minutes available on the 78 rpm record required ingenuity. But Asso made a virtue of constraint through what he called 'verism', a kind of *chanson-vérité*: limiting his narratives to 'real, human matters' ('des choses humaines, vraies'). Accessibility through simplicity.[84]

Asso's songs have the directness, narrative economy and morality of the folktale, urbanised and dramatised into pocket operas. Like his relationship with Piaf, his characters are conventionally gendered. Women are helpless victims of desire and emotion: rejected lovers, seasoned street girls or unworldly maidens drawn to the sins of the flesh. As in 'Elle fréquentait la rue Pigalle', they are also determined by their socio-urban status. Men are much freer, more mobile geographically, socially and emotionally. Often they are dashing adventurers, both driven and empowered by elemental forces like the sea or the desert, though they may reluctantly or unwittingly reveal a degree of vulnerability. There are also elements of crime fiction and noir cinema, evident for example in 'Browning' (Asso-Villard, 1936), a cynical tale of gangsters and guns, 'Le Contrebandier' (The smuggler, Asso-Villard, 1936), and 'Paris-Méditerranée' (The Paris-Mediterranean line, Asso-Cloërec, 1938), where the female protagonist falls for a stranger on a train, who is arrested when they arrive at their destination.[85] Piaf displays remarkable skill in interpreting these songs, setting up a vocal narrative which dramatises or completes Asso's verbal narrative. In her recording of 'Mon amant de la Coloniale' (My lover in the colonial army, Asso-Juel, 1936) and in one recorded version of 'Le Fanion de la Légion' ('The flag of the Legion', Asso-Monnot, 1936),[86] she half-speaks her lines with the stylised, exaggerated drama of an adult telling a story to a child.

The composer too is essential to this musical counter-narrative, and we encounter here a third inventor of la Môme, alongside Asso and Piaf herself. Marguerite Monnot was a gifted, classically trained musician and composer from a musical family. Her input at the very early stage of the invention was intermittent, so less immediate and direct than Asso's. But it was already decisive by the end of 1937, as she had written the music for three key songs: 'L'Étranger', 'Mon légionnaire' and 'Le Fanion de la Légion'. She and Piaf became friends and continued to work successfully together for a quarter of a century, long after Asso had left the scene. Her refined yet popular melodies for over half of Piaf's songs, including many of Asso's lyrics, are therefore just as vital to the characterisation of the imagined Piaf. When Monnot died in 1961, Piaf acknowledged her strategic importance, declaring that her talent had 'helped me be Édith Piaf!'[87]

The prototype designed and realised by Piaf and Asso was unveiled during her second booking at the ABC, in November 1937. 'La Môme is dead', announced the presenter of the show. 'What you're about to hear is Édith Piaf!'[88] Critics got the message: 'Certainly, la Môme was charming and her success justified', explained one. 'But clearly, Édith Piaf and the triumphant reception the general public now gives each of her songs, that's something else. She's an artist, a great artist.'[89] Nevertheless, the original design team didn't last long. Although Monnot would remain for many years, she would eventually be replaced rather abruptly by Charles Dumont, composer of two of Piaf's most famous songs: 'Non, je ne regrette rien' (No, I regret nothing, Vaucaire-Dumont, 1960) and 'Mon Dieu' (Dear God, Vaucaire-Dumont, 1961). But from 1940 Asso's place was taken by two new lyricists: another lover, the journalist Henri Contet, and Michel Émer, both of whom developed the formula that Asso had established.

A number of others played a part, large or small, in the invention of

Édith Piaf, and we will encounter them as the book goes on. But two are worth singling out here. One is Jacques Bourgeat, much older than her and a self-taught scholar, who befriended her in the mid-1930s and stayed true as confidant, tutor and father figure until her death. He also wrote the first song lyric tailor-made for her, "Chand d'habits' (Buyer of second-hand clothes, music by Alfred Roy, 1936).[90] Their correspondence covers three decades. As well as working on her social and personal habits, like Asso, even teaching her how to clean her teeth, and supporting her through the trials of her career and love life, Bourgeat helped shape the Piaf she became by assisting in her programme of self-education, to a large extent drawing it up for her. Despite his own impecuniousness, he would supply her with edifying books and discuss them with her: Sainte-Beuve, Ronsard, Molière, Baudelaire, Plato. When, years later, she thought of becoming a Rosicrucian, it was to him she turned for an explanation of the movement and appropriate reading. Effectively, he taught her to read and write, working particularly on her spelling, and this labour of love steadily produced a different dimension to her public image.

This enculturation was continued by her next lover, after Asso but before Contet: Paul Meurisse. From an educated and wealthy background, Meurisse was trying to make a career as a comic singer when Piaf changed his life, turning him into a successful actor. But his indebtedness didn't alter his sense of being another Higgins to her Eliza:

> Her manners were still those that she'd learnt in her youth, despite the luxury that now surrounded her [...]. I tried to initiate her in the finer things and a healthier lifestyle better suited to my own tastes. [...] When we met, I insisted she buy her clothes from the best couturiers and didn't wear the same kind of make-up off stage as on! You know, she was really pretty and she didn't need to do much to embellish that pretty face. [...] With me, she went up a rung in terms of social class and she knew she needed to do that.[91]

But the male vanity that encouraged both Asso and Meurisse to give themselves the starring role in the fabrication of Piaf shouldn't obscure an important limit to their power. The creative relationship between

Piaf, Monnot and Asso, then Meurisse, became symbiotic and reciprocal, making the line between fabrication by others and self-fabrication impossible to draw. 'People say it was Asso who made her what she was', Serge Hureau concedes. 'That's true but the important thing is that she understood what he said.'[92] Similarly, with Meurisse, the tables were quickly turned when he became the first of a string of performers for whom she herself would become Pygmalion, as we shall see. Her years with the circus and on the street had given her a more advanced sense of the artifice of performance than an outright beginner and prevented her being inert clay to be moulded. Reading also developed her cultural awareness and self-consciousness. And the more her familiarity with her invented self grew, the more autonomous she became. She developed a style, arrived at a sophisticated understanding of it, and continued to bend and shape it to her own designs. After the initial stage of dependency and collective creation, she started managing her own persona. She became her own power source.

What is clear about the invented Piaf is the complexity that persona was already acquiring by the 1940s, a complexity that would continue to develop in the postwar period. She and Asso, with Monnot too perhaps, were also perfectly aware of the fabrication they were engaged in. Yet what they were fabricating wasn't a mask. The private Piaf, paradoxical and volatile though it was, formed the malleable matter of a stable public identity, while also, by its very volatility, remaining distinct from it. There was, however, one further, indispensable inventor at work in this collective creation: the public.

CHAPTER 2

Piaf and her public

WHATEVER THE ORIGINAL HOPES or intentions of Asso, Monnot and the singer herself, the imagined Piaf was only forged in the crucible of public consumption. It's her public meanings from 1935 to 1945 that I'm concerned with here: what were audiences at her early performances hearing and seeing?

For a long time after those first two memorable engagements at the ABC in 1937, Piaf performed in both cabarets and the larger music halls, even featuring in revues occasionally. Never shy of hard work, she would sometimes go from one kind of venue to another in one evening. In spring 1943, for example, she featured in a revue at Montmartre's Casino de Paris, then switched immediately to the nearby cabaret La Vie en rose, in the basement of the Théâtre Pigalle. In the process, she barely altered her act, apart from cutting one or two of the more theatrical numbers for the cabaret.[1] In music hall, she shared the bill with variety performers, but by the early 1940s a new mode of performance was available to her. In September 1940, she did her very first solo concert at the prestigious classical venue the Salle Pleyel. But in all three types of venue—cabaret, music hall and concert hall—her self-presentation was essentially the same. She performed intimacy rather than spectacle, foregrounding the lyrics and the emotions they contained. 'In a song', she later declared, 'the lyrics are what interest me first.'[2]

And yet in the impressions recorded by observers of Piaf's earliest performances, at Le Gerny's, Bobino and the ABC and on her first recordings, it wasn't the lyrics that seized the attention but the voice. What's especially revealing are the verbal acrobatics deemed necessary to communicate these impressions, for the uniqueness of that voice seemed almost to defy description. This is well illustrated by Pierre de Régnier's virtually synaesthetic account of a performance at Le Gerny's in 1935:

> And then that voice, that cold voice, the colour of oysters being opened in wet baskets in front of bistros, that indefinable voice, husky and full, at once ordinary and unique—ordinary but unique, I should say—that moist, nasal, still child-like and yet already despairing voice grabs you in the pit of your stomach, inexorably, just when you'd stopped thinking about it.[3]

It's the physicality, the fleshiness of her voice that Régnier is struggling to articulate, together with its power to transfigure banality: '[that voice which] makes the stupidest of words in the most ridiculous and familiar of songs sound unrivalled among their type and irrevocable'.[4] And over the next decade, critics continued to wrestle with its ambiguities: 'It's the voice of a street singer', attempted one in 1941, 'abrupt, with sudden surges. A harsh, muffled voice which cracks. The voice of a poor wretch dreaming, a child wide-eyed with amazement.'[5] Whether she's working in a large music hall or an intimate cabaret, her voice is heard through her staged body. A critic observing one of her first appearances at the ABC writes:

> This little scrap of a woman sings with her lovely harsh voice 'Le Légionnaire', 'Le Contrebandier' and ten other strong numbers, in a dress of black velvet [...], her face pale, her mauve, feverish eyes miming distress, suffering, misery and love; and she does it so painfully well that you want to comfort and protect this little girl who looks as though so many sad things are happening to her![6]

The phrase 'little scrap of a woman' has echoed down the decades as a shorthand for her stature but also her perceived vulnerability and resilience. Piaf was only 1 metre and 47 centimetres (4′10″) tall, and the paradox of so immense a voice issuing from so tiny a body was to become a standard trope of her reception throughout her career. At the same time, as Roland Barthes would argue years later when speaking of the 'grain' of a voice, body and voice are consubstantial in the projection of her meanings.[7] In 1939, a Spanish journalist described the start of her act at a Paris club:

> She arrives wearing her plain black dress, her big eyes luminous and grave. She weaves her way between the tables and steps onto a small platform [...]. No smile, no bow. [...] she looks at the audience and in her eyes there is something resembling a fear of life, the fear of someone who has experienced every blow that fate metes out. [...] Her voice, laden with a gravity that grows ever deeper, opens the curtains on the most vivid but also the saddest scenes in the world.[8]

Just as memorable was her way of finishing a number: 'At the end of every song, as the room fills up with applause, Édith Piaf remains silent, unsmiling, biting her lip and looking into the distance, part wounded animal, part passionate woman.'[9] Clearly, she makes no attempt here, at the beginning or end, to come out of role and engage the audience with a winning smile. Even four years into her career, she is still being read as an untutored gamine nervously giving her first performance before grown-ups. Another four years on, in Marseille in July 1943, her bearing on stage connotes much the same unrelieved gravity:

> Now she steps forward into the unforgiving light of the projectors. Her hands like a dying child's, transparent and virtually inert, clasp each other on her narrow chest or her large forehead. Her eyes, where all the terror and distress of this sad world is expressed, grow huge, and her voice rises, first plaintive and muffled, as if choked with tears, then getting louder, higher, turning into the heart-rending, harsh, unending cry of a fatally wounded beast.[10]

The performed Piaf, then, is made up of contrasting but inseparable sensory impressions, which the poet Léon-Paul Fargue, writing in 1938 after seeing her several times in different kinds of venue, endeavours to explicate.[11] The power of her voice to move audiences so intensely comes from its being impregnated with the 'realist' experiences she sings about:

'Not everyone can become a tugger of heart-strings overnight. You need a particular kind of past, a particular way of seeing, and considerable familiarity with different environments and forms of suffering'.[12] And, he goes on, you need a corresponding emotive capacity in the voice, which also can't be acquired. But Piaf's real talent lies in not resorting to the conventional resources of the popular singer: she doesn't 'tell' and she doesn't 'coo'. Instead, she lets us *see* emotion by, literally, incarnating it: 'her whole art consists of [...] herself gradually becoming the strongest and surest emotion of the melody'.[13] And, for Fargue, only a woman's voice is capable of doing so.

A number of conclusions can be drawn from these and other responses to the young Piaf. First, her voice's meanings are the result of its being embodied semiotically. Barthes might think of this as hearing 'the body in the voice as it sings'.[14] Deniot sees it more in terms of visualisation: 'la voix vue', the voice seen as well as heard. Second, this seen voice elicits powerful emotion even in poets like Fargue, whom one might expect to be especially demanding, and in male critics inured to the tear-jerking wiles of realist singers: the paternalistic desire to weep, empathise and protect. Third, this desire is an effect of a woman's voice issuing from a child-like body. Clearly, Piaf is no Shirley Temple: her songs are too explicit and knowing. For Barthes, voices that have a grain don't translate emotion, they make it flesh; they are not transparent but erotic, involving a relationship of pleasure between the bodies of performer and listener. And one senses that for some at least of the men who write about her, Édith's attraction is that of a vulnerable yet sexually available juvenile, like the young protagonist of 'Madeleine qui avait du cœur' (Madeleine who had a heart, Asso-d'Yresne, 1936),[15] who is too naive and generous ever to say no. All of these features are creative developments from the realist tradition. Deniot argues that a key innovation of women realists was to re-imagine the social realism of Bruant not as an external gaze on 'the people', as his was, but as an internal, subjective one.[16] From modest backgrounds themselves, women realists are imaginatively identified with the enhanced subjects of their songs. This subjectivity necessarily means that the realist gaze becomes explicitly gendered. As Dutheil Pessin points out, there is in a variety of cultures a deep connection between the female voice and the expression of suffering and mourning.[17] In western culture, it can be traced back to ancient Greek tragedy, which possibly explains

Fargue's perception. Dutheil Pessin follows this connection from ancient Greece through the diva figure of nineteenth-century romantic opera to the interwar *chanson réaliste*.[18]

In Deniot's view, the *chanson réaliste* is not a genre but 'a convertible category of chanson', which adjusts itself to the times. She is no doubt right, but this doesn't mean the realist label is, as she concludes, nothing more than 'an outer skin we could easily manage without'.[19] On the contrary, Piaf the street singer, still very young when she met Leplée but with four or five years' experience of having to appeal to a crowd if she was going to eat, soon recognised a public need for the gendered emotion that her voice and Asso's songs supplied. The uniquely perceptive Cocteau also recognised this when he first worked with her in 1940:

> the others—those listening—become pitiful, for she condenses the sorrows of their souls and expresses them. [...] She inspires respect with her music of the pavement, her melodies which everybody hums and which sound as though they have sprung from the very tarmac. Yes, for the privilege of these simple love songs is that they respond to a secret plea from the masses and that the masses, when they repeat them, feel as though they are making them up themselves.[20]

Realism, then, was the prism through which all Piaf's work was mediated from the start, and throughout her career. It guided the meanings her audiences attributed to her. Her own inventive re-workings of realist conventions, and the public's readings of her through those conventions, create a tension at the core of her entire work which I'll return to. But for now, we need to look more closely at the meanings themselves.

Society and politics

To some extent, the social meanings of her early work flow from the character conventions of the *chanson réaliste*: disadvantaged girls drawn into prostitution, low-ranking soldiers and sailors, delinquents of various sorts, and the occasional worker. As one critic aptly observed in 1937, she needed songs specially written for her voice, informed by 'a realism of the moment, a realism that prowls around La Villette, gritty with the soot of factory chimneys and buzzing with tunes picked up from the radio in the local bar.'[21]

All the same, the substantive social content of her work comes not from lyrics alone but from her entire imagined being. When she started singing at Le Gerny's, those who encountered her off stage were generally taken aback. She had the ripe accent of the fictional Paris street urchin and an effective line in vulgarity which enabled her to give as good as she got from men. Asso describes the 20-year-old he first met as looking like a Spanish beggar, proud, disdainful and fearful.[22] Burke sees her as never quite adjusting to bourgeois ways but living like a traveller, 'turning each of her many dwellings into a Gypsy caravan'.[23] Leplée's murder of course did nothing to alter such perceptions, especially when Piaf was interviewed by the police and the interrogation filmed. With her louche acquaintances and lifestyle becoming public knowledge during the enquiry, and one of those acquaintances briefly a suspect, la Môme came over in the media as naive, sleazy and off the rails.[24] But even when the episode was forgotten and she became famous, she was still socially marked. When the middle-class journalist Henri Contet first met her in late 1940, he observed, with yet another hint of Henry Higgins, how when she ate fine food she guzzled rather than savouring.[25] At smart restaurants, she had to be told which cutlery to use. Classic Eliza Doolittle.

The social meanings of her appearance and demeanour came across on stage, too, though they took on different resonances. What struck those who saw her debut at Le Gerny's was her naturalness, her lack of staginess. 'La Môme Piaf wears only a cheap sweater and a plain and simple dress; she doesn't know how to gesture and the light from the projectors bothers her; she doesn't even know how to take a bow; to be honest, she doesn't know anything.'[26] Class difference was also palpable, or so she insists in her description of her first night at the club, even if she exaggerates, as she so often did. Leplée drew attention to it in his carefully pitched introduction where he described talent-spotting her in the street: 'She doesn't have an evening dress and if she knows how to bow it's only because I showed her yesterday'.[27] And it was there in the icy silence that greeted her as she timidly walked on stage. This wasn't hostility, she later realised, but bewilderment:

[the bewilderment] of well brought up people wondering whether their host had suddenly gone mad. And of people who, having come to the cabaret to forget their troubles, were probably none too pleased to be reminded that there were on this earth, right next door to them, young girls like me who never had enough to eat and were dying of poverty. With my scruffy old clothes and my face like a ghost, I was out of place in this classy setting. And if they noticed it, I was aware of it too.[28]

In this strategic narrative, she, like Leplée, deliberately plays up social difference. But it is confirmed in the accounts of others who witnessed her at the cabaret. We have to remember that her repertoire itself at this stage, at Leplée's insistence, was socially connoted, particularly the well-known number with which she opened her first night, 'Les Mômes de la cloche': the old favourite of cheap cabarets, backstreet *cafés-concerts* and street singers, which Mistinguett had previously made her own. Piaf's version recorded in 1936 uses working-class Parisian pronunciation and a single accordion to evoke the lovelessness and poverty of sex workers who when the money runs out throw themselves in the canal and are buried without ceremony. The song's social meanings at the time can be glimpsed in the trial of a young man accused of parricide, where the defence lawyer, Maître Maurice Garçon, suddenly burst into the chorus from 'Les Mômes de la cloche'. He then soberly addressed the court: 'What else can you expect, gentlemen of the jury, if after hearing such songs which set a bad example, our young people become louts, thieves and even murderers?'[29]

All of these early social connotations bled into her performances. Deniot locates Piaf's social meanings partly in her gestures. Describing one of her most familiar poses on stage—feet firmly on the ground and slightly apart, hands on hips—Deniot reads it as referencing the age-old gestural lexicon of the French artisan, worker or peasant taking a moment's rest after physical labour. Transferred to the stage before a socially mixed audience, it becomes a signifier which instantly authenticates her popular roots.[30]

But her class meanings are above all signified by her voice. Her natural street speech—'the accent, by turns saucy and warm, of the wretched refusing to be defeated'[31]—was sometimes foregrounded with relish ('Les Mômes de la cloche', 'Les Hiboux'[32]) in order to make a point, although under Asso's influence the accent was generally softened. But her voice was also 'classified' by its imperfections. Twenty-five years after her death, a personal recollection from the subversive satirist François Cavanna, one of the founders of *Charlie Hebdo*, provides a useful insight here. When he was a schoolboy in pre-war France, his wealthy classmates looked down on la Môme. They said her voice was like a cow mooing and was marred by '*dégueulandos*'—badly executed glissandos. She had also stolen her stage name from la Môme Moineau and she was a shameless man-eater and one-time 'tart' ('une pute') controlled by pimps and crooks. But when Cavanna himself heard that voice after the war, he saw his classmates' judgments for what they were: 'OK, so she bellowed. But what a bellow it was! All those things in her voice. All the misery of the world came crashing down on you [...]. So that's what the other kids were hearing, that's what made them turn up their noses? Bloody hell! It left me gobsmacked, sobbing my guts out.'[33] It's in fact the very 'impurities' of the popular voice which explain its emotional appeal.[34] In Piaf's case, the harshness or rawness of her voice, its volume and depth, its vibrato, even its *dégueulandos*, evoke the street singer she was and the hard life she'd had.

Not surprisingly, then, for some in the late 1930s, her voice was ultimately political. It is, one critic declared, 'a voice that hurts like the sight of injustice. A voice that smacks of poverty or rioting.'[35] The pacifist journalist Henri Jeanson similarly asked: 'Have you heard la Môme Piaf? She is the voice of revolt, the maker of waves.'[36] Boris Vian was one of several who would see her as a blues singer, though without the twelve-bar/four-beats-in-a-bar structure of African-American delta blues. The French blues, he wrote in a sleeve note for a Piaf EP of 1957, 'is in the form of a waltz and it's an accordion that drives it; but make no mistake, it's the same strange flower growing out of the sorrows of the poor, the same poignant charm, the same cry of love for life, of revolt against destitution'.[37] Most agree that Piaf took no interest at all in the historic events of her lifetime. All the same, the aphorism that having no politics is a politics in itself was well illustrated in the turbulent period in which her career took off.

Her performances at Le Gerny's, Bobino and the ABC took place against the backcloth of a rallying of the anti-fascist left which culminated in spring 1936 in the first left-wing coalition government in France, the short-lived but fondly remembered Popular Front, which impinged on Piaf at least to the extent of diverting attention from Leplée's death. The Spanish Civil War had also begun. Social or political meanings, therefore, were read into her songs whether she liked it or not. One critic described her second show at the ABC in November 1937 in recognisably Frontist terms: 'Mademoiselle Piaf, passionate and undisciplined, looks as though she is up there on a barricade from which she is railing against the unjust forces in society'.[38] Little wonder, then, that Jeanson chose her to perform at an anti-fascist rally in 1938, organised by the pacifist anarchist Louis Lecoin to raise funds for the Spanish republicans.

Still, Piaf's ideological meanings are a good deal more ambiguous than this suggests. They owe a lot to Asso, whose own leanings are also difficult to pin down, though somewhat less so. He described himself as an anarchist, though his anarchism seems to have been more nominal than active, of the kind later professed by Georges Brassens, who would write favourably about Asso after the Liberation in the anarchist weekly *Le Libertaire*.[39] But Asso's lyrics actually suggest a loosely right-wing ideology, which perhaps explains his writing for the collaborationist press during the Occupation.[40] Certainly, what strikes today's listener to Piaf's renditions of his songs is their virile imperialism.[41] His female protagonists' raunchy attraction to adventurers, legionnaires and combatants in the colonial forces is part of a wave of representations of Empire in both the high and the popular arts at this time, in the wake of the hugely popular Colonial Exhibition of 1931.[42] France's young male population had of course been decimated by the Great War. By the 1930s, the country was also faced with a threatening international situation, a surge in French pacifism illustrated in Jean Renoir's 1937 film *La Grande Illusion*, and occasional dissidence in the Empire, supported by the French Communists. Piaf's songs therefore reassured audiences about France's continuing colonial potency; and chanson as she represented it became a proud confirmation of shared though outdated myths.

The world beyond France is seldom present in Piaf's early repertoire, but when it is, it takes the form of a mysterious, good-looking and nameless 'lad', sometimes blond but unquestionably white, with a lilting accent that adds to his devilish appeal, as in 'L'Étranger' or 'Le Contrebandier'. Or it's in the form of a cartoonish foreigner: the North

African 'bastards' of 'Le Fanion de la Légion' who treacherously besiege the outnumbered legionnaires in a desert stronghold resembling a French Alamo, or the caricatural 'skinny negro' in 'Le Grand Voyage du pauvre nègre' (The great voyage of the poor negro, Asso-Cloërec, 1937),[43] whose simple-minded awe at seeing a 'big boat' docked nearby prompts him to sneak on board and doze off; he soon finds himself en route to Borneo, and bewails his fate in pidgin French to 'Mr God, sir' ('Monsieur Bon Dieu'), no doubt to his colonial masters' amusement.[44]

This political ambivalence, where revolt against poverty sits with unquestioned French imperialism, is exemplified with irony in Piaf's reception at Lecoin's anti-fascist rally of 1938. Warned off singing Asso's paeans to colonial authority before an audience of pacifists and anti-militarists, she encountered an ecstatic crowd calling for more. But when she asked what they would like to hear, they called for 'Le Fanion de la Légion'.[45] This and 'Mon légionnaire' were in fact applauded wherever she went.

As this episode bears out, Piaf's social and political meanings were in the end blunted. Certainly, she may be said to signify popular rather than universal suffering. But popular suffering in her work isn't the product of an economic system. In her own lyric 'C'est un monsieur très distingué' (He's a very distinguished gentleman, Piaf-Louiguy, 1941),[46] there's an embittered statement of class difference as well as a frustratingly brief reference to the Monsieur's unquestioning ownership of his wife, his dog and the singer-narrator herself, who is his bit on the side. This is a man who, as the song points out with admirable concision, can pay for the illusion of being loved by all three. Yet there's no political interpretation of the chasm between him and his well-born wife and children on the one hand and his low-born mistress on the other. It's a social given built into the conventions of the *chanson réaliste* and designed only to underscore the protagonist's misfortune, not to interrogate capitalism. Similarly, in Émer's 'De l'autre côté de la rue' (On the other side of the street, 1943), the poverty of the young woman on one side of a thoroughfare, who observes the wealth of a young woman on the other, isn't historically determined, for their respective situations are easily reversed when the poor girl finds love while the rich one doesn't.

Those who thought they detected social or political content in her work during the Popular Front came up against the same obstacle as those who 30 years later believed Bob Dylan's 'Blowin' in the Wind' was an anthem of countercultural protest, only to find that the fuzziness of its target allowed it to be hijacked by less radical meanings. Politically, Piaf's songs in the realist mode were empty vessels. The characters she sings about and whom she performs in her voice and stage persona rarely come from the urban working class, which she had little experience of and no particular empathy with. They are the opposite of Marx's revolutionary proletariat. Instead, they are literary conventions drawing on a nineteenth- and early twentieth-century typology, just as her own fabricated stage persona does: a typology already familiar in French culture, from the *café-concert* to the fiction of Carco and Mac Orlan and the poetic realism of 1930s cinema. Conventions rather than people, they form a loose community of marginals which we might at a pinch call an underclass but which are ultimately incarnations of the defeatist maxim that the poor are always with us. Piaf communicates the *spectacle* of poverty: she doesn't sing about oppression, she performs it. And there's no Brechtian alienation in this performance. As in the West End musical of Hugo's *Les Misérables*, these characters solicit only comfortable pity.

We need to bear in mind that from the moment she abandoned the street, her audience was no longer primarily drawn from the common people but included various levels of the bourgeoisie. And while those of the working class who could access her work could still identify with her, to her middle-class audiences she proposed not the feared proletariat with a dagger in its teeth but a glimpse from the safety of their seats of an eternal, mythical, exotic demos. The collective role of the *chanteuse réaliste* as she interpreted it was to provide them with a gratifying vision of what could have gone wrong in their own lives had they been as reckless as she was. As a piece in the socialist *Le Populaire* commented with pursed lips just after her mentor was murdered: 'Leplée knew what pleased his decadent clients. This working-class kid he was exhibiting, getting her to sing with that sour voice of hers on the red-carpeted floor of Le Gerny's, was the flavouring, the spice, the dash of pepper that made these ataxic party animals feel alive again.'[47] Piaf the voice of revolt has now become an indulgence, an effete commodity.

Even so, there is a politics of sorts in her early work. The Popular Front was concerned to democratise culture, Piaf to democratise feeling. Underlying her voice, her delivery, her staged body and the content and composition of her songs is a barely articulated, no doubt intuitive ideology of affective citizenship. The scruffy, unremarkable denizens of the Paris suburbs, marginalised by the blows of fate, don't only deserve pity but are capable of emotions as high, as dramatic, as heroic in the face of adversity as those of the elite protagonists of great literature, opera and art. Her songs represent the cultural ascent of the commoner, just as her own life does. Deepening the realist formula, her early work adds up to a people's opera. And although the protagonists of this opera may not be located sociologically as proletarian, they are located geographically as Parisian.

Audiences of the 1930s and 1940s seem to have heard in that voice their own Paris and their own urban experience:

> She brings to life for you a world of images, devoid of joy but not without beauty: gloomy street corners where melodies swirl, October evenings in the city with the smell of the first mists and the first chestnuts, Parisian cobbles gleaming in the twilight [...]. Then there are the desolate places, the wastelands, abandoned spaces, quays, ports... All these images circulate in her songs, inscribed in that voice that reaches you in your very core.[48]

And the famous actor Pierre Brasseur, who had first heard her sing at Le Gerny's, wrote affectionately to her years later that her voice reminds him, as it did then, of the bustling street life of his Parisian childhood: the cries of the newspaper vendor and the greengrocer, 'all those voices of the street, those marvellous voices, [...]. Your voice, your voice. The voice of mates who're hurting, of girlfriends getting dumped or chucking someone out [...]. You're all of that and you were straightway when I first saw you'.[49] Her songs are often set in Paris, either explicitly—through references to specific locations, as in 'Entre Saint-Ouen et Clignancourt' (Aubret and Sablon, 1933) or 'Les Mômes de la cloche'—or implicitly via Parisian slang and accent.[50]

There is nonetheless a temporal discrepancy in these representations. It's the Paris of the turn of the century that they call to mind: the era of troublesome youths in butcher-boy caps (*apaches*), fairgrounds, the *faubourgs* and *fortifs*, and dancing the java to the sound of the accordion. There's certainly local colour here and even some topical comment, as in the comic 'Il n'est pas distingué' (He's not refined, Hély-Maye, 1936),[51] where Zidor the chirpy Parisian urchin loudly announces his views on women, film stars and the rise of the Nazis in the ripest Parisian argot. But technological, political and urban change were turning this Paris into a stylised convention, which Piaf exploited to evoke nostalgia. One curiosity in her early repertoire, quite distinct from her usual realism, crystallises this nostalgia. In 'La Petite Boutique' (1936),[52] with lyrics by Roméo Carlès rather than Asso, a narrator visits a dusty old antique shop tucked away in some deserted quarter, with a drowsy cat on the front step. With a lyrical style verging on the folktale and a wistful accompaniment and gentler vocal delivery, Piaf describes the kindly old gentleman proprietor who greets her with a politeness from another age. Negotiating a price for a musty leather-bound volume, she falls into conversation about current affairs and is amazed to discover he knows nothing about the scandals and political double-dealing that characterised 1930s French society. The tale ends here, other than that, whenever the narrator herself tires of that society, she passes an hour or two visiting the little old shop, which symbolises an idealised French past: a culture of the book, of timeless civility and mythical apoliticism. There are few better encapsulations of the wistful conservatism of her early work.

Piaf's nostalgic take on Paris is the beginning of her iconic identification with the city, as powerful today as ever in the eyes of the world. Marlene Dietrich famously said at her friend's death, 'The only word that could stand in for Paris is the word Piaf'.[53] But part of what makes this identification a myth is that her Paris is a confection. What never comes across is the city's ethnic mix. Belleville, her native corner of Paris, had by then seen waves of inward migration: Auvergnats, Russian and Polish Jews, Armenians and Greeks.[54] Yet her early songs, supposedly shaped out of her own life story, reflect none of this diversity, and certainly do not reflect her own North African roots. A kind of ethnic cleansing takes place which produces a mythically pure and singular French people. They do, however, reflect at least one social division: between men and women.

The body, gender and sexuality

It's especially important when dealing with this theme to distinguish between Piaf the person and the imagined Piaf. From what can be gleaned from autobiographies, biographies and memoirs, her own relationships with the body, gender and sexuality were complex and contradictory. She had few close women friends. And in accounts by both men and women, gender solidarity wasn't one of her virtues, though it's impossible to measure the weight of personal animosity in such claims. The singer Irène Hilda, telling Bonini how Piaf, whom she calls a 'slut' (*pouffiasse*) and a 'bitch' (*salope*), had once been 'odious' to her, goes on to say that Édith utterly detested other women.[55] Mireille Lancelot, wife of a member of Les Compagnons de la chanson with whom Piaf toured America, echoes this view: 'She didn't accept me straightaway. I can even say she couldn't stand me. I was blonde, bourgeois, everything she detested'.[56] And although Lancelot was eventually accepted and now speaks warmly of Piaf's capacity for empathy with suffering, she recounts several anecdotes revealing her to be capable of that special kind of cruelty that masquerades as harmless practical joking.

As for Piaf's feelings about men, here too there is complexity and paradox. Clearly, she enjoyed their company and to an extent their sexuality. She is often said to have needed a man in her life and been unembarrassed about making someone she was attracted to aware of the fact. But although her friends and lovers are usually discreet about her sexual proclivities, they sometimes hint that it was the prospect of warmth and closeness that attracted her more than physical desire. Simone Pills, sister of Piaf's first husband, Jacques, maintains that it was post-coital conversation she enjoyed most about sex.[57] Some acquaintances, Berteaut among them, claim that she liked to be beaten by her lover, even goading him into violence. 'She liked to see her man unleash all his masculinity', as the composer Philippe-Gérard euphemistically puts it,[58] though this is firmly denied by Marc Bonel, among others.[59] But masochism, if it existed, doesn't seem to have been the salient feature of her complex relationship with men. More striking, once Asso's training phase had passed, is her determination to reverse the male teacher–female pupil polarity and become a regendered Pygmalion herself. Hence the familiar tales of her manipulating her lovers (Meurisse, Montand, Moustaki,

Sarapo) and other protégés (notably Aznavour) to make them into the men she wanted them to be. The makeover would start with her buying the new lover a gold watch and a suit, and would progress to her coaching him to become a singer. One senses after Asso a resolve never again to play the compliant little woman. And there's little in her intimate relations with men to suggest a shrinking violet: more dominatrix than innocent flower of the street.

But this biographical dimension reflects only one side of the complexity. In the songs themselves, the underclass evoked is composed largely of women. At first glance, they seem modern, sexually liberated and assertive. They are often young and, like Piaf herself, know how to use street talk to their advantage; they aren't shy or retiring with the 'lads' (*les gars*). They are comfortable alone in bars (not that they remain alone for long), are hard-drinking and seem empowered by sex, which they enjoy and expect to have soon after meeting someone. They relish young men's bodies and are especially attracted to courage and bravado, as with the men who march off to war singing and promising to return in Piaf's own wartime lyric 'Où sont-ils tous mes copains' (Where are all my pals, Piaf-Monnot, 1941).[60] Even so, as Vincendeau convincingly argues,[61] the songs actually 'appeal to a generalized notion of womanhood as suffering, dependent and submissive, but at the same time driven by sexual passion.' Deniot too speaks of 'an element of damnation in desire' ('une part maudite du désir').[62] The women usually fall prey to anonymous, predatory men who are only after one thing and are quick to spot an opportunity. Women's hearts are invariably broken in these encounters because, although they are sexual beings, they also secretly dream of a different life involving stable, conventional, domestic relations with a simple, faithful man; like the sex worker of 'L'Accordéoniste' (The accordionist, Émer, 1940),[63] who dreams of opening a little *bal-musette* with the musician, where he would be the boss and she the cashier.

So, unlike another realist, Yvonne George (1896–1930),[64] Piaf's first social meanings were scarcely feminist. The playwright Jean-François Noël said of a Piaf performance he saw shortly before the Liberation: 'She possesses the premature, quasi-intuitive experience of women who, for several generations, have suffered from hunger, cold and loneliness. She knows in advance the ferocity and egotism of the male and submits to it with good grace because her desire is equalled only by her enslavement as a woman to eternally assuaging the demands of the species.'[65] However, these meanings aren't left entirely open to interpretation, for Piaf deploys her body on stage to give a steer to her reception.

Her body is mediated in part by her self-representation: the knee-length black dress, the tense, anxious posture and, above all, the spare but evocative hand gestures. In the 1941 film *Montmartre-sur-Seine*, her character, Lily, goes from fresh, unselfconscious young woman to slinky cabaret diva. Clad in a shimmering dress, Lily-Piaf performs 'J'ai dansé avec l'amour' (I have danced with love, Piaf-Monnot, 1941),[66] with its louche blue notes and sensual lyric where dancing and sex become indistinguishable. She is accompanied by the Jazz de Paris band, led by the well-known saxophonist Alix Combelle. Throughout, she rocks distractedly from side to side, her hands half-raised either side of her head. But in mid-performance, with her eyes closed in ecstasy, her hands drop briefly to her waist, then rise languorously to caress her breasts for an instant.[67] The sensuality of the performance is quite apparent to a pair of young lovers in the cabaret audience, who seek closer physical contact with each other as it progresses. In many other songs, minimal gestures speak volumes.

But Piaf's body is also mediated through others, particularly in photographs on sheet music, on posters and in the press. The overt performance of sexuality as in 'J'ai dansé avec l'amour' is actually quite rare. Josephine Baker's early iconography emphasises the healthy curves of her semi-naked body, one hip thrust out to the side to accentuate its roundness, one hand raised provocatively, palm upwards, as if to ask 'Like what you see?'[68] The depiction of the young Piaf's body is usually the reverse. In those photos designed to stand visually for what the texts, melodies and performance of her songs communicate, her body is thin, vulnerable, child-like, clothed and closed, connoting female pain, longing or misery. The poses bespeak an ideology of love as suffering and of gender as determinism. Courageous, self-abnegating female victimhood is embedded in Piaf's early visual persona just as it is in the *chanson réaliste* generally, although the victimiser isn't always explicitly the man. Often it's fate that takes him away, though it might be argued that fate itself is objectively gendered as male since its primary victims are female.

This invitation to read her as gendered victim was gratefully taken up by her mainly male critics in the 1930s. One of the more conspicuous features of early media texts about her is the bluntness with which reviewers felt authorised to comment on her looks, as if she were an exhibit in a human zoo. The first reviewers were startled by her tiny stature, which one or two took to be the result of stunted growth. Then, steadily, they began to speak with unabashed candour of her 'ugliness'. This is a perplexing leitmotif and one which she, like Serge Gainsbourg, evidently internalised. She and her close friends evoke her lifelong anxiety about being unlovely and unlovable: 'this insistent, almost morbid need in me to be loved, all the more so as I believed I was ugly, contemptible, not made to be loved!' she writes.[69] Many who knew her well, among them several lovers, deny that she was ill-favoured in this way and some, like her manager Louis Barrier, insist she was beautiful.[70]

But her complex about her appearance is scarcely surprising when we note how forensically it was being examined by the early 1940s. 'She's short, she's ugly, she's misshapen', one observer flatly declared.[71] Jean Cocteau, her close friend and most prolix admirer, described her in evocative but not entirely dissimilar terms: 'Look at this little woman whose hands are like those of a lizard in the ruins. Look at her forehead like Bonaparte's, her eyes like a blind person's who has just learnt to see again.'[72] And one especially vicious review in 1944 went so far as to suggest she shouldn't be making audiences look at her at all but should have stuck to radio and records.[73] We have to wonder where the assumed authority to cast such a pitiless eye over her came from. There seems to be something about the Piaf body that affronted the male gaze; the perceived unconventionality of her looks was taken to be somehow subversive, as if she simply wasn't trying hard enough. There's a tacit expectation that the female singer be conventionally desirable, and that if she has the temerity not to live up to that expectation, she's fair game: a subtext of sexual failure.

Yet this is to miss the point of Piaf's whole self-presentation on stage in her early career. As the contrast with Baker suggests, the quite different parameters that came with the territory of realism offer an alternative to the sexualisation of the female body in twentieth- and twenty-first-century popular music, illustrated today by the likes of Rihanna, Beyoncé or Miley Cyrus. Piaf's body is mediated through the wearing of austere black.[74] When she adopted black, around 1936, Chanel was already dressing women in black and the realist Damia had also chosen it. Black could of course be favoured by men too, but it was differently coded for women, connoting in Deniot's words 'a feminine tragic' ('un tragique féminin').[75] Black, Deniot argues, is in fact heavily gendered in both opera and chanson. It signifies at once the woman in mourning, especially significant in the shadow of the First World War, and the femme fatale. It's the colour of conjoined female suffering and desire. One meaning of Piaf's whole physical and gestural appearance on stage is the acceptance of female sexuality combined with awareness of desire as potentially dangerous, painful, cruel.

The gendering of the imagined Piaf is, then, hard to pin down. Even when she is brutally described as ugly, stunted and undernourished, a different rhetorical note is often sounded, insisting that she transcends that ungracious physicality by inducing psychosomatic changes in the audience, reaching them, it's often said, in their guts (*tripes*). At her first ABC appearance in 1937, a critic confessed:

> I have a weakness for la môme Piaf! She works on me like a drug.
> I can't do without her. I feel an irresistible tenderness for her pale face, her slender fingers, the pathetic look in her eyes, her petite silhouette that's the colour of night! You have to listen to her of course, but above all you have to contemplate her.[76]

And eight years later, when she appeared at the prestigious L'Étoile, another wrote, 'She grabs us in our guts, gently imperious. Her voice, at once warm and harsh [...] thrills us to our very fibres.'[77]

Such changes, it would seem, make the audience re-interpret her body, which is transfigured in performance. One reviewer wrote in April 1941, 'This ugly girl, when she is possessed by her song, takes on a strange, an unbelievable beauty'.[78] This is clearly not the homogenised, desirable beauty of the starlet. It's a spiritual beauty shot through with intelligence. The theme of Piaf's intelligence is already a recurrent one by the late 1930s. In 1939, she's described as having the appearance of 'a girl who's been knocked about and a kid who has thought too hard': 'She isn't skilful, just talented and, developing that talent, an alert intelligence'.[79] This potently captures the complexity of her social meanings at this time: battered, victimised, so singing from the heart, but with a shrewd awareness of her situation and her performance: 'her intelligent understanding of the stage and her intelligence full stop.'[80]

This meta-awareness was soon to put her in control of her self-projection on stage. At the Alhambra in Brussels in 1938, a reporter described how she came on stage looking intimidated and wide-eyed. But this was deceptive, 'for in a few seconds this frail young woman had imposed her will on the audience, which she guided with confident authority through the gamut of sensations she wanted it to experience.'[81] Clearly, this is no longer the timid juvenile of Le Gerny's but a burgeoning star who now understands what Dyer calls 'the artifice of social performance',[82] who knows what she wants from audiences and how to get it.

Religion and spirituality

In contrast to this cool calculation, Piaf's early performances are nonetheless depicted in spiritual terms. This aspect of her stage persona again matches constructions of her off-stage self to an extent. Both she and her biographers bring to the fore her lifelong religiosity. This narrative begins with the largely invented soap opera of her going blind in early childhood while living at her grandmother's brothel in Bernay, her blindness miraculously cured after a procession of sex workers turned out to pray for her recovery at the shrine of the local saint, Thérèse of Lisieux. From here on, her own descriptions of her faith match those of people who knew her: it's a faith that draws unquestioningly on the simple iconography of Catholicism. And there are again literary antecedents for it, notably another naive young Norman girl, Félicité in Flaubert's *Trois contes*, whose blind devotion eventually leads her to identify God with a stuffed parrot.[83] In a letter to Asso dated 15 September 1938, during the Munich crisis when she is away from Paris, she tells him of an encounter, presumably in church, with Christ:

> You're eagerly waiting to hear about my long conversation with Jesus. Here goes. To start with, I cried, I cried a lot and then I talked. I said to him 'stop this war' [...] and then I looked at his feet, his hands and his face all so full of suffering. Finally, I thought of everything he had endured without holding it against anyone.[84]

She cried again and, after praying, felt much better. But such child-like belief didn't prevent the young Piaf living the liberated life she did, about which we are equally well informed. The sacred and the profane, the woman liberated yet repressed—both poles present in the colour black—become the twin buttresses of Piaf's invented self.

Religious practice features spasmodically in her early songs too, as it would in her later ones. A good example is Asso's 'Madeleine qui avait du cœur', where the sacred and profane combine in a narrative reflecting Piaf's early life. Madeleine is a goodhearted, fragile but candid young woman who had a sad childhood, unloved by her parents. In her naive, self-deprecating prayers, she would ask for forgiveness simply for being unhappy. As an adult, this goodheartedness naturally leads to her being unable to disappoint a string of lustful men, and she dies, inevitably, of a disease, though of the heart: she has loved too much.

However, the full spiritual dimension of the constructed Piaf springs much more from her performance, particularly that transfigurative voice and stage presence. As the photographer Hugues Vassal, one of her later image-makers, would write many years after her death, her search for transcendence 'was easily visible in her interpretations of songs whose profane nature often gave way to a quasi-religious enthusiasm that was not unlike gospel music.' Piaf, he went on, 'possessed an innate sense of the sacred which gave depth and nobility to the sentiments she translated into music'.[85] Such descriptions of her performances probably owe something to Cocteau. Seeing her on stage for the first time in 1940, he described her eyes as 'unforgettable': 'the eyes of Lourdes, the eyes of a clairvoyant' ('des yeux de Lourdes, des yeux de "voyante"'). And he likens her to a Spanish statue of the Madonna.[86] Yvon Novy, seeing her at the ABC in 1943, described her voice as having the 'intonation of prayer and imprecation' ('cette intonation de prière et d'imprécation').[87]

It's not irrelevant that these first representations of spirituality in her performances come from the early 1940s. For by then, the social meanings we have been looking at were beginning to evolve, taking on different dimensions under the altered circumstances of occupation. At the same time, new meanings were being forged as the imagined Piaf acquired a greater symbolic importance for France itself. It's her wartime meanings that I'll explore in the next chapter.

CHAPTER 3

A singer at war

'The war was a period of plenitude for Piaf', writes a biographer. 'She was probably never funnier, never more confident about her abilities or in better physical shape.'[1] Certainly, the years of German occupation (1940–44) represent a peak in her artistic achievements, as well as in her self-discovery and self-invention. But making sense of that peak isn't straightforward. One problem is again the shortage of reliable evidence amid all the narrative inventions. Second, those years are still, three-quarters of a century later, a sensitive matter, even as they fall out of living memory. The Vichy era isn't the subject of quite as much overt controversy as it was 40 years ago, when the heroic myths of a resistant nation promoted by De Gaulle began to crumble under scrutiny. But the sensitivity remains. Accounts of any public figures who experienced the Occupation feel compelled to reveal which side their subjects were on, and those that don't are noticed, as happened with Dahan's film *La Môme* (2007), which glossed over that period.

Commonly, such accounts portray their subjects as covertly resistant if they weren't actively so. This is certainly the case with Piaf. For Albert Bensoussan, Piaf was 'definitely resistant'.[2] Both Monique Lange and Anne Sizaire see the fact that she had a Jewish lover during the Occupation as a personal form of 'resistance'.[3] Carolyn Burke is a little more nuanced: the singer 'detested the occupiers' and yet 'had to go on singing—to earn her keep and because she could not do otherwise'. And Burke does at least cite Henri Contet's view that, although Piaf hated the Nazis, 'she was hardly bothered by the Occupation'.[4] But she is still scraping the barrel when she claims that Piaf's performance of 'Le Disque

usé' (The worn-out record, Émer, 1945)[5] in occupied Paris was 'risky'
not just because its composer was Jewish but because the protagonist is
a young woman who portrays 'a proud, haughty stance [...] that could
be taken as a kind of resistance.'[6] But it's David Bret who takes matters
to extremes:

> During the war years Edith Piaf became one of the unsung
> heroines of occupied France. [...] Edith's nerve, courage, and
> love for her countrymen knew no bounds. [...] Edith hated the
> Germans and all that they stood for, [...] flinging Hitler in their
> faces whenever she could. [...] Not enough can be said in praise
> of her exploits during the war.[7]

Such imaginative rhetoric, in which Piaf virtually becomes a bare-breasted
Liberty leading the people, hardly squares with the apolitical hedonism
that others identify during her war years or her ambivalent relations
with the occupiers. It is contagious, though, ratcheting up her Resistance
legend as it's told and re-told. Hence the half-Canadian singer Martha
Wainwright, in a series of 2009 concerts promoting her album of
Piaf songs,[8] describing her as a 'great supporter of "la Résistance"'. It's
important, then, to look more dispassionately at the Piaf of the war years,
which I will do briefly, though I lay no claim to exposing the naked
truth.[9] But my concern in most of the chapter will be with the meanings
she acquired during that period.

Piaf's behaviour under the Occupation was politically and morally
ambivalent, though she wasn't alone in that by any means. There's
agreement that she disliked the Germans and made a few modest public
gestures to this effect. A police report dated 17 October 1944 speaks of
her often having altercations with them and even being arrested briefly
for allegedly facilitating the escape to England of some young French
men. Yet the report's findings according to Belleret were based on rumour
more than investigation.[10] And in 1945 she was summoned before a 'Purge
committee' set up to cleanse the entertainment industry of those who
had collaborated, in her case for having toured Germany in 1943 and
1944.[11] She was let off with no penalty; in fact she was congratulated
in recognition of claims made by herself and her then secretary, Andrée
Bigard (who described herself as being in a Resistance network[12]),

that Piaf had only performed to French prisoners of war and had also materially assisted several Jewish colleagues prevented from working. The police report says the same.[13] Those she assisted include the writer of 'L'Accordéoniste', Michel Émer; Marcel Blistène, an aspiring film-maker who would later cast her in *Étoile sans lumière* (Star without light, 1946) and *Les Amants de demain* (Tomorrow's lovers, 1959); and the classical pianist Youra Guller.[14]

But the most significant case concerned her Jewish pianist and lover, Norbert Glanzberg, a Pole classically trained in Germany who had fled to France in the 1930s and would go on to compose two of her most famous songs, 'Padam ... padam' (Deedum ... deedum, Contet-Glanzberg, 1951) and 'Mon manège à moi' (My merry-go-round, Constantin-Glanzberg, 1958).[15] Like many, Glanzberg escaped south when the Nazis occupied Paris. Living in Marseille with false papers under the name of Girard, he was constantly in danger as the authorities were searching out Jews in the city.[16] He was finally arrested in May 1943. After three months' confinement, he was on the point of being deported to a camp when he was secretly released. It was the Comédie Française actor Marie Bell who contrived this, with help from Tino Rossi. Piaf's assistance was primarily financial and somewhat less risky, though important nonetheless.[17] It's also claimed that having several times refused to sing in Germany, she finally gave in either under duress or, in some accounts, to lift the morale of French prisoners of war. Either way, biographers usually insist that she helped free a number of POWs from Germany. Piaf herself said 118.[18] By having herself photographed with them in the course of the Berlin visits, she and Bigard could subsequently provide them with false papers and even pass some of them off as members of her band.

While there's confirmation of her having assisted Glanzberg, Émer and Blistène, Belleret is sceptical about the rest.[19] How many of the 118 escapees could realistically have been passed off as members of her band? And how reliable is that figure anyway? According to Germain Desbœuf, a senior member of the French federation for prisoners of war, it was as high as 170, though Bigard estimates a more modest several dozen.[20] Bensoussan, apparently convinced of the story's veracity, admits we don't know how many.[21] But Belleret maintains that no escapee ever came forward to confirm the story of the false papers, or to thank Piaf for her courage.[22] Bonini, on the other hand, is convinced that Piaf 'did indeed succeed in getting people out of Stalag IIID in Berlin',[23] including Bigard's own husband. But he then adds mysteriously: 'And what does it matter whether we are talking about one or 100 prisoners!' So, one begins to wonder: is there a chance the great escape involved only Monsieur Bigard? At any event, Contet, speaking from memory, doubts there were ever more than a few escapees, if any.[24]

Belleret is equally sceptical about the rigour of the Purge committee's verdict, suggesting that Piaf got off more lightly than many, including some who had been a good deal less visible than her during the Occupation.[25] At the very least, then, those biographers who cite the verdict to exonerate Piaf do so a little hastily. Berteaut claims the Germans were great fans of Piaf and invited her to tour the big German cities at least 20 times, but confirms that she refused.[26] So did she finally visit the camps out of charitable concern for prisoners or because of the threat of a permanent ban? Was she paid, did she refuse payment, or did she donate the fee to prisoners, as Berteaut has it?[27] None of these questions can be reliably answered. One Belgian press source from 1944, cited unnamed by Bonini and Belleret, reported that Piaf, alongside Arletty, Tino Rossi, Sacha Guitry and others, had been condemned to 'exemplary punishment' (Belleret), even death (Bonini), by the provisional government in Algiers.[28] She was certainly blacklisted by the national radio service for a short time after the Liberation, though unlike Arletty, Chevalier, Guitry and Rossi, she was neither arrested nor imprisoned. Nor was she, like Trenet, banned from performing for several months.

Piaf herself rarely talked about the trips to Germany, apart from telling the press about the 118 escapees. To the Purge committee, she maintained that both trips had been forced on her, the second without payment, and she claimed to have been arrested three times by the Gestapo.[29] Furthermore, she only ever referred, with implied self-justification, to singing for prisoners specifically, though Belleret is sure she also sang in factories where French STO workers were contributing to the German war effort.[30] And she always denied appearing in German music halls and cabarets.[31] She was by all accounts entertained by German authorities, protected apparently by a member of Goebbels's propaganda staff, Colonel Waechter, whom she had met earlier in Paris; and she agreed to a meeting with Goebbels himself. Such invitations might well have been hard to refuse, but in any case the Nazi propaganda minister was called away at the last minute. The historian Frederic Spotts, describing what he calls the 'soft collaboration' that went on in the Parisian music world, briefly considers Piaf's relationship with Waechter, concluding that the Germans used her just as she used them. And he too, sceptical of Piaf's Resistance legend, dubs the escape stories a 'myth'.[32]

Whatever the truth, and however much she may have embellished it, the image of an unsung heroine goes much too far. Her behaviour was at best 'naïve', to use Duclos and Martin's term,[33] at worst self-centred and irresponsible. In France, she sang at a number of benefit concerts and similar events despite the propaganda advantages that accrued to the Nazis and Vichy as a result. Glanzberg's biographer records her once being drunk on a train with the pianist and loudly proclaiming to the assembled passengers that he was a Jew, though she was mortified the next morning. Worse was to come. In 1945, Piaf admitted to him that four years before she had destroyed the visa he had obtained that would have taken him to safety in the USA.[34] The actor Robert Dalban, a close friend who accompanied her on her first trip to Germany, describes her brazenly uncooperative behaviour with the Germans, refusing to attend official receptions, and so on.[35] Yet, like Glanzberg, he encountered a different Piaf during another tour. She'd asked him to join her in Belgium and gave him the name of a *passeur* who could get him across the frontier without his having to apply for papers. When he met up with her there and wouldn't comply with some trivial request, she took umbrage and loudly announced that he looked like somebody who had crossed the frontier without papers, briefly attracting the attention of some German officers.[36] Such irresponsibility is usually glossed as her incorrigible love of practical jokes but in such dangerous times it was reprehensible. The same could be said of her moving into a flat at the top of a high-class brothel run by one Madame Billy. The location's attraction was the plentiful heating it enjoyed because it was frequented by black marketeers, German officers and French collaborators, notably those from the nearby Gestapo headquarters on the infamous rue Lauriston, where Resistance workers were being tortured. Wisely, Contet advised her to move out when the Allied landings began.

Generally, while resenting the Germans, she seems to have continued her indulgent pre-war lifestyle, partying lavishly, working relentlessly and remaining largely unconcerned by the Occupation and its privations. Piaf 'didn't exactly steer clear of the opportunities and creature comforts the sharply contrasting conditions in the country brought her', writes Belleret with pointed understatement,[37] which Berteaut confirms. She and Piaf lived through the Occupation as so many non-resistant French did: 'We felt that nothing was permanent, that we were merely living from day to day. So we made hay while the sun shone. We had never drunk so much; we had to get pissed to forget about our miseries. The Occupation stuck in our throats. Laughter was only a cover-up, it left a bitter taste in our mouths.'[38] And perhaps, as Lange suggests, even Piaf's anti-German feeling was little more than reflex nationalism:[39] an inherited dislike of the 'Boche' after 70 years of Franco-German hostility, rather than a focused revulsion for Nazi ideology. Beyond this, biographers generally agree on her total lack of engagement with the affairs of the world. As she memorably remarked watching the Germans march into Paris: 'Bugger this! If that's history, I'd rather read it than make it!'[40]

The same ambivalence characterises her meanings during the war. By 1942, she had become a national celebrity, hailed as the greatest chanteuse of her time. Her shows always sold out and her life and background were of growing interest to the media. Returning to Paris in October that year after touring the South of France, she wrote to Glanzberg: 'The welcome I got was so enthusiastic! The whole of Paris was waiting for me at the station, flowers, press, the lot. I've never seen such a fuss. It was fantastic. I had to give a press conference at lunch. Like I was a princess!'[41] But this wasn't the whole story. Reviewers continued to be obsessed and disturbed by her body. Indeed, the casual cruelty with which her physical appearance was dissected intensified during the Occupation. She was depicted as stunted, runtish: 'her little body, all tiny and scrawny', writes one journalist in 1943.[42] Another, in Nice in 1941, feigns discretion about her 'unappealing looks' but only to suggest that she might at least have concealed them.[43]

Her body was also interpreted in more conspicuously moral and even political terms. There were occasional insinuations that the grim realism which her 'unappealing looks' were deemed to call for was no longer appropriate given Vichy's aspiration to national remoralisation. One critic noted with surprise the power over the audience of 'this sickly little scrap of a woman, with her taut face and pained expression beneath the dual incandescence of her red locks and the voracious footlights. The songs she sings are miserable, haunted by melancholy images smacking of moral destitution and "cheap vice". This speaks neither to the moral climate of the day nor to the slightest human ideal.'[44] Another merely pleaded for some happier songs: 'Twenty songs about deprivation, vice and death ... that's quite a lot in these times of deprivation and death'.[45] But it was the overtly collaborationist press which took the moral interpretation of her body to new depths.

Her 1941 film *Montmartre-sur-Seine* was the bone of contention here, no doubt because it made her physical appearance nationally visible, beyond the music hall or cabaret—but also, one suspects, because of her sexualised performance of 'J'ai dansé avec l'amour'. The neurotically anti-Semitic *Je suis partout* reviewed the film in November that year. The piece, by a male critic, begins unexceptionally but ominously with a comment about her having lost, by the time of the film, the 'naive sincerity of la Môme Piaf'. She is then accused—quite inappropriately but no doubt with the bluesy 'J'ai dansé avec l'amour' in mind—of imitating Sophie Tucker's 'Some of These Days', 'and other corny numbers by New York Jews' ('et autres rengaines judéo-newyorkaises'). But, more than for her repertoire, full-on misogynistic bile is reserved for her 'sickly' body, with its 'hollow eyes and weirdly large head sunk into hunched shoulders. Since it was deemed acceptable to make us look at her, in my view we are at liberty to say that Édith Piaf could probably be put to use in films as a "freak"'.[46]

Worse was to come. In *Révolution nationale*, a female critic, still disturbed by the film several years later, wrote:

> She is a fine embodiment of our decadent age [...]. Her tiny body, her deficient waistline, her voluminous head, her dented forehead, her expression of misery, her eyes full of distress, it's all there [...]. She reminds one of the end of a race. She is an indictment of our society, our laws, our institutions [...]. In normal circumstances, Édith Piaf should have been a working-class singer churning out tired old tunes on street corners and at fairgrounds. By some miracle, she has escaped that fate, thanks to the snobs who have taken her up, applauded her and launched

her [...]. There are even a few cerebral types who think she's beautiful, admirable.[47]

The article does purport to show sympathy for the way pre-war French society and particularly urbanisation let her down in childhood. It also concedes that she is indeed 'admirable' in the 'colossal' and 'magnificent' self-belief that she conceals beneath her modest appearance on stage.

> And yet, made the way she is, she should have contented herself with making records and singing on the radio. But no. She had the nerve to appear in music halls. [...] Once, she even dared appear on screen [...] in the sadly memorable *Montmartre-sur-Seine*. Every time I think of that film, I can't help feeling deeply embarrassed at the thought that it might be shown abroad, and that Swiss people for example might think that this 'star', who looks like something out of a distorting mirror at a funfair, represents the grace and charm of Paris. [...] Ah, decadence of all decadences! [...] As an old farmer from the Bourbon region was saying to me the other day: 'With everything going on today, no wonder there's a war on!'[48]

The collaborationist obsessions of Vichy are clearly visible in this piece: race and the identification of an alien other, republican decadence, urban sickness versus rural health, intellectual elites versus age-old peasant wisdom. Piaf's body is described with the same pathological repugnance that Nazis applied to Jews. She is in fact similarly ethnicised, though unspecifically because her implied ethnicity is her gender, her subversive female body: unhealthy and scrawny, she is the runt of the litter, the sight of which red-blooded French audiences ought to be spared—and for some reason the Swiss. In Piaf, the decadent Third Republic is made woman; she becomes a pitiful Marianne.

Other meanings, however, did begin to collect round the constructed Piaf in response to the historical context. At their centre was nostalgia once again, but now signifying a number of different things. As I argued earlier, the element of temporal distance in her pre-war re-invention of the *chanson réaliste* had already given her a retro patina, with her evocations of a vanishing Paris harking back to Bruant and the *café-concert*. But the defeat of 1940 gave this nostalgia more intense meanings for an occupied nation that had abruptly ceased to be a Republic after 70 years and could no longer recognise itself. She now came to personify a Paris lost definitively, or so it seemed, and for a very different reason: invasion by the historical enemy.

Under the Occupation, then, Piafian nostalgia becomes doubly identitarian. In September 1940, for example, after she returned from the free zone where she had fled the previous June, she began a string of shows, taking in the ABC, the Folies-Belleville, the Salle Pleyel and some cabarets. Of one of these, an emotional critic wrote: 'Is she singing? No, she's living out the touching images, the despairing popular fictions of her verses. She still looks like a kid, [...]. Édith had tears in her voice she could barely hold back, and I had goose pimples from hearing in her the voices which sang on the street corners of my youth.'[49] For another, three years later, 'These refrains smell of the gutter, the pavement, the street corner, [...] the poetry of Baudelaire and the prose of Charles-Louis Philippe.'[50] And *la chanson française* itself, which she was now deemed to represent, was depicted as the natural vector of cultural memory at a time of defeat, estrangement and loss—not to mention the natural justification for her singing in Germany: 'Surely Édith Piaf is indeed one of the most admirable ambassadors of chanson and surely chanson is the most reliable remedy for soothing the nostalgia of hearts devoted to memories? Over there, far from the beautiful land of France that they [French POWs] yearn for, she will remind them of everything they long to come back to and haven't forgotten.'[51]

Piafian nostalgia was in fact capacious enough to assume a variety of broadly defiant meanings. At the opening night of the ABC's winter revue in December 1940, which featured a number of performers, Piaf sang the popular and proudly militaristic 'Le Fanion de la Légion'. As she turned to face the Germans in the audience, the French went wild and, in some reports, started jeering at the intruders. The next day she was ordered to remove the song from her act. Returning to the ABC in autumn 1942, where the audience included many from the German armed forces, she sang 'Où sont-ils tous mes copains', the stirring march she had written in 1941 with Monnot about France's brave lads going merrily off to war, against a projected tricolour backdrop. Again she was ordered to delete the song but this time refused, though she did remove the patriotic lighting. Once more, in February 1943, she sang Émer's 'L'Accordéoniste' at the Casino de Paris, but was upbraided by the Propagandastaffel for singing a song by a Jew. She again refused to remove it and, legend has it, was banned from performing for five weeks,[52] though her absence may simply have resulted from a dispute with the Casino's boss, Henri Varna.[53]

But there were also pro-Vichy uses to which she could just as easily be put. As Belleret notes, her two tours of Germany, whatever purpose they had in her own mind, could be exploited as part of the strategy of naturalising collaboration. Cultural exchanges involving admired celebrities like Piaf, Trenet and Chevalier suggested that Franco-German cultural diplomacy was the future in the new European order. Intended or not, this was the objective meaning of six published photos taken in Berlin where she appears with apparently happy prisoners who, the pictures carefully reveal, are amply stocked with wine, beer, soup and cigarettes.[54] Days before her first departure for Berlin, she declared that she had selected new songs that wouldn't awaken painful memories in the prisoners, so that they would think less of the life left behind and more of what awaited them on their return. A praiseworthy aim but not one likely to trouble Vichy.[55] The same can be said for the benefit galas for prisoners or STO workers and their families. One such, on 13 August 1943 at the Gaumont-Palace, also featuring Trenet, with whom she would set off for Germany the next day, was given a strong propaganda element. A *France Actualités* newsreel on 20 August covered the gala alongside other items showing the victims of Allied bombing of Paris suburbs, the regime's benevolent concern with the physical and professional development of its young people, and the success of the French team in a football match in Bayreuth between foreign workers. *L'Œuvre*, 'an ultra-collaborationist paper', also covered it on 16 August.[56]

All of this coverage created an impression not only of business as usual but of harmonious cultural relations with the conqueror. Belleret attempts to be even-handed about Piaf's part in such activities but aptly points out that, however ignorant she may have been of the true nature of Vichy, it should surely have become apparent to her in the vile collaborationist representations of her, if nowhere else.[57] Perhaps, though, these representations explain her concern to appear compliant with or at least not hostile to the regime. At any event, the talk of her being condemned to 'exemplary punishment' and the summons to appear before the Purge committee show that, for some at least in the Resistance, her Vichyist meanings were plain. The point is that Vichy ideology was as backward-looking as Piaf's own nostalgic appeal, though in Vichy's case the ultimate referent was not the old Paris but a mythical, pre-republican, peacefully rural past in which the Vichy values of 'labour, family, homeland' were supposedly enshrined. In this respect, Piaf's work with the harmony group Les Compagnons de la chanson, especially their joint rendition of the now famous 'Les Trois Cloches' (Villard, 1945)[58]— adapted into English as 'The Three Bells' but also known as 'The Jimmy Brown Song'—takes on a peculiar significance.

As we've seen, the young Piaf was a city girl, earthily urban. The equally young Compagnons de la chanson, whom she began working with in 1946, were the opposite. Their roots lay in the Compagnons de France movement, formed after the defeat in 1940 with the active support of Pétain's government as part of its ambition to restore the moral fibre and physical health of French youth, weakened in its view by the decadence of a Third Republic dominated by socialists and Jews. This rebirth was to be produced by military-style training and involvement in rebuilding France's infrastructure and culture. Hence the 'boy-scout' style, as Piaf put it,[59] of the Compagnons, with their clean, tight harmonies and traditional folk songs. So, after first hearing and meeting them in March 1944, her decision subsequently to sing and record with them, and take them under her wing, was unexpected.[60] 'Les Trois Cloches' was a recent composition in a folk idiom, which she first performed with them at their request in May 1946 at the Club des Cinq and then recorded with them the following July. It became a hit, selling a million copies and making their name.

Unlike the discordant jazz appreciated by the young 'zazous'[61] of the Occupation, whose music and sartorial style were firmly disapproved of by the authorities, the song's folk appeal and sweet harmonies are atemporal, but, so soon after the Occupation, their connotations were in one sense pure Vichy. The song tells the tale of an archetypal human life mediated through Catholic imagery: the soul, the family, fidelity, eternity. Jean-François Nicot is born, marries sweet Élise, lives in complete harmony with her, and dies as peacefully and naturally as the flowers of the fields, all in the same rural village tucked far away from history, in a valley beneath starry skies. Each stage of his life is marked out, and in a sense imposed, by the church bells. That is the extent of the narrative: birth-marriage-death in the shadow of the steeple. This is the simple life that Vichy's national revolution advocated for all in 'eternal France': authentic peasant traditions, health, hard work, heterosexual monogamy, parenthood and complete surrender to political authority.

These connotations are carried by the lyric but also, and equally powerfully, the polyphony. In the solemn version filmed at the Opéra de Paris, Piaf, rather than being alone on stage as she usually is, stands at the centre of the nine Compagnons, all eyes reverently turned to heaven. A plaintive male solo (the tenor Fred Mella) intones the verse as if it were a psalm, accompanied by the others in the group imitating the bells, while Piaf takes the chorus, whose wording changes slightly with each stage of life. The performance is a shared religious experience, a symbolic communion. No longer the 'decadent' street girl walking the pavements of Third Republic Paris, alone or being pursued by a sinister stranger as in 'Un monsieur me suit dans la rue' (A man is following me down the street', 1942),[62] in peril in the fearful dark, Piaf is now in full light, tiny and feminine, cradled and protected by the nine healthy young men surrounding her, each adopting a manly pose in a clean white shirt, lifting her up to a morally higher plane via their eternal harmonies.

But if the song was so impregnated with Vichy ideology, why did it succeed in 1946, when Vichyism was discredited? The answer has to do with Piaf's ideological importance after the Liberation. The traditional values the song enshrines were not of course exclusive to Vichy but were as universally reassuring as Christmas in a Hollywood movie. The ideal of national rebirth through healthy activities like choirs, scouting and group singing was largely shared by the Popular Front, Vichy and the Resistance, albeit with different ideological framing. This is how organisations founded on those values, such as Uriage, Jeune France and indeed the Compagnons de France, could begin by supporting Pétain's national revolution but subsequently change sides. 'Les Trois Cloches', like the other genuine or imitation folk songs she performed with the Compagnons,[63] evokes not just the ephemeral Vichy but the timeless values of 'deep France' (*la France profonde*) that Vichy sought to tap into. With the help of the Compagnons, Piaf became a remedy for healing national divisions, a sentimental arbitrator between feuding brothers. Her meaning at the end of the war can be epitomised as: politics be damned, we're all friends again.

Cocteau touched on this meaning when in 1946 he waxed lyrical about a performance by Piaf and the Compagnons, though it isn't clear whether he was speaking of 'Les Trois Cloches' specifically. He begins by describing how when witnessing the ancient Procession of the Holy Blood in Bruges he had lamented the fact that such a profoundly religious experience could no longer happen in France. On his way back, however, he happened to hear the Compagnons with Piaf. Of this 'strange marriage' of their two 'solitudes' he writes: 'The miracle has happened that these two solitudes join together to create a sound artefact which so expresses France that the tears start to flow.'[64] And, plainly, for Cocteau this communion between them is as spiritual and moving an experience as the Bruges procession:

> Listen to their voices light each other like the bonfires of St John's Day which spread from hilltop to hilltop. Listen to them each falling silent then responding to the other. Listen to them scatter then regroup like mercury. And say to yourself again that it is foolish to pity France when, ceaselessly and unexpectedly, she provides limitless proof of her secrets and her power.[65]

With his trademark lyricism, Cocteau draws attention, and also contributes, to a new social construction of Édith Piaf, now that the Occupation is over, the Purge is behind her, and the country is bent on rebuilding economically, culturally and spiritually. Culture was enlisted in this crusade, from the government's short-lived initiatives to decentralise and popularise theatre to longer-lasting protectionist measures for French cinema. And Piaf in her own idiosyncratic way did her bit for this national convalescence, though almost certainly unintentionally. Conveniently re-imagining her wartime concerts for prisoners as an act of motherly nurture and a heroic tale of attempted liberation of her 'godchildren', she becomes France's Vera Lynn, the Forces' sweetheart and the nation's 'nightingale'.[66] Or, more appropriately, its Florence Nightingale, whose healing hands helped it pull through. Despite those who had thought her wartime songs too gloomy for such apocalyptic times, they would slip smoothly and reassuringly into the collective memory. This once street-wise, vulgar 'kid' was now subtextually invested with a woman's emotional intelligence, had learnt to commune telepathically with the unvoiced feelings of her contemporaries in time of war: pain, separation, loss, revolt, resilience. As one critic put it in 1943, her songs mark 'a significant moment of the contemporary soul' ('un moment significatif de l'âme contemporaine').[67]

And for this power—judging by the love and glory heaped upon her from the Liberation onwards—the nation was deeply grateful and instantly forgiving. Piaf the approachable, no-nonsense, people's Cinderella could henceforth be remembered as not forsaking them in their hour of need, bravely staying on to lift the nation's spirits. Her ambivalent war record was swiftly forgotten because she offered a reassuring continuity with pre-war cultural traditions which had almost been suffocated by Nazism. Piaf, then, signified the paradox of a forward-facing nostalgia, a France once lost, now found and ready to move on.

What especially distinguished her at this time from male counterparts like Trenet or Chevalier was the hypnotic, gendered, cathartic power of her melancholy, her being identified with 'the sad kind of song which is a release for her kind, girls with very simple dreams, with the same old disappointments, who want to hear of their own regrets and sorrows and be told that nothing is their fault because life is just like that'.[68] This power wasn't, however, exerted only on such young women. It was deemed to transform human consciousness itself. As Pierre Heuze wrote as early as 1941: 'Édith Piaf is that rare thing, a singer who takes people out of themselves, or rather, forces them back into themselves in a procedure akin to being put into a trance'.[69] Her singing here induces a two-way psychic transformation: spectators are led both *out* of themselves—out of the world, out of the Occupation—and *into* themselves, being put back in touch with their innermost feelings and thereby into a state of collective communion. Representations of this transformative power of her voice, songs and performances had begun before the war, but were greatly intensified during it, balancing though not revoking those misogynistic descriptions of her body as unhealthy, unwomanly and un-French.

The Occupation, I believe, is the major turning point in her life, her career and her image. The first invented Piaf relied heavily on a sociologically and nationally located 'popular' identity: French, Parisian, demotic; but primarily an identity of exclusion, marginality, the wretched of the earth. This was a mythified though not exactly false identity. Her actual experiences became the malleable matter of a public persona that would remain with her long after the Occupation. But the persona steadily became a palimpsest, as she sought to invent new selves, or at least more complex versions of the old one, and as her national meanings began to evolve with the coming of mass culture and a steady shift in the French understanding of the popular. However, one problem the nation's gratitude, and its identification with her wartime self, would cause her was that it wouldn't let her change. In part II, I'll look at how this problem developed as her musical, social, national and international meanings evolved between the Liberation and her death. This evolution is inseparable from that of the postwar notion of *la chanson française*.

PART II

PIAF AND CHANSON

CHAPTER 4

A new Piaf

B Y THE END of the war, as Piaf turned 30, her life was changing drastically. Her mother died in 1944 and her father a year later, severing her umbilical bond with the past. In 1946, she starred in the film *Étoile sans lumière*, written for her and directed by Marcel Blistène. She recorded one of her biggest hits, 'La Vie en rose', which she purportedly wrote.[1] There was talk in the press of an American tour and even a Hollywood film, though the movie never materialised. That same year, she debuted at the vast Théâtre de Chaillot with a 50-piece orchestra. Her new orchestral ambitions also made her change record labels from Polydor to Columbia (Pathé Marconi), as Canetti's company was unable to accommodate them. It had become customary for presenters to introduce her on stage with the words 'Just one name, and in that name, the whole of chanson: Édith Piaf'.[2] But she now realised she needed no introduction. From the end of the war to the end of her life, she was simply 'la grande dame de la chanson française' (the grand lady of French chanson). She had also made up her mind to move away from the *chanson réaliste* and began assembling round her a new creative team whom she could control and who would help her refine the imagined Piaf. She had acquired a taste for coaching new talents. In 1947, she cracked America and became an international star. While there, she found the love of her life, the boxer Marcel Cerdan, and lost him again in a plane crash in October 1949.

Thanks to Asso, Bourgeat and Cocteau, she had continued reading widely during the war and her social circle had broadened. Members of the Paris literary scene had long taken an interest in the *chanson réaliste*, among them Cocteau, Prévert, the symbolist Léon-Paul Fargue and the surrealists Aragon and Desnos.[3] In his 1938 article about her, Fargue had even evoked the 'divine brushstrokes' of Goya or Delacroix and the poetry of Mallarmé, Baudelaire and Rimbaud to describe her. Listening to her tales of soldiers and criminals, he had often heard 'the call of a loftier, sparer poetry', connecting her to '[the] most elliptical and refined poets.'[4] Two years later, Piaf's encounter with Cocteau had proven particularly formative. Asso and Bourgeat had introduced her to poetry, but Cocteau taught her to understand his own avant-garde aesthetic. She would sometimes learn his poems by heart, and an unlikely kinship developed between them. As her wartime landlady Madame Billy recalled, 'When he was there, she was no longer with us. She was a violin vibrating beneath a magic bow.'[5] But as her intellectual life developed, her health began to deteriorate. By 1950, then, the parameters of her rise and fall were already in place.

To make sense of this arc, we have to start with her new team. Asso was replaced by Henri Contet and Michel Émer, who, as Asso had done, composed a whole repertoire mixing old and new styles. Monnot would remain her main musical collaborator until the late 1950s, though a new pianist, arranger and band leader, Robert Chauvigny, classically trained and gifted, would help create a new Piaf sound by working and re-working the arrangements of her latest songs. Jacques Canetti maintains that Piaf was over-orchestrated as a result and that her authentic sound lay in the less ornamental settings of the 1930s.[6] There's something to be said for this view, but Chauvigny's innovation was nevertheless to look beyond those early settings and create a more ambitious harmonic language for chanson by combining the popular with the classical. Still, one foot was kept immovably planted in popular styling by her new accordionist, Marc Bonel, who joined the team late in 1945, followed in 1950 by his future wife, Danielle, who would become Piaf's secretary. Louis Barrier, known as Loulou, became her manager in November 1945. He was to play an immeasurable role in making her an international star, while also serving as her long-suffering accountant and prop.

This new team professionalised her to an extent but remained an improvised unit by today's standards. Marc, for example, was informally her general dogsbody as well as her accompanist. Danielle was secretary, dresser and confidante as well as 'artistic technician', according to her payslip, in charge of make-up, sound and lighting.[7] Each team member in their own way helped re-invent the postwar Piaf yet was also part of a substitute family, providing companionship, protection and practical or emotional support as Piaf's circumstances and temperament—endless broken love affairs, accidents and tragedies, mood swings and declining health—became steadily more trying.

In addition to these most loyal intimates, her entourage was made up of friends and associates who came and went as the years passed. Among them at different times were Charles Aznavour, Eddie Constantine, Georges Moustaki, the American painter Douglas Davis, the aspiring singers Félix Marten and Claude Figus, the journalist for *France-Dimanche* Jean Noli and its photographer Hugues Vassal. Some would become lovers; others would claim a different kind of closeness. A few would sculpt the public edifice a little before moving on. Eugène Tuscherer, producer of Blistène's *Étoile sans lumière*, spent several months Hollywoodising her appearance—hair, make-up, teeth, deportment—before he was willing to start filming, having initially rejected her for the role when he first met her.[8] A decade later, Vassal would make his name working on her iconography. Douglas Davis too painted several well-known portraits that have appeared as illustrations in various publications.

One intriguing feature of this entourage is how often the destinies of its members appear to reflect Piaf's own, or each other's. Édith was seriously ill in 1961 when Monnot unexpectedly died that October, two years before her. Chauvigny too fell ill and was 'let go' in 1959, passing away just two months after Piaf. Figus committed suicide shortly before her death. Cerdan and Davis both died in plane crashes. Car crashes too are a recurrent trope in the narrative. Piaf herself had five in all, two with Aznavour in 1951, only three weeks apart, two with Moustaki in 1958, also close together, and one with Davis in 1959. Her second husband, Théo Sarapo, died in a car accident a few years after her death. The best-known coincidence, however, was the death of Cocteau only an hour or so after pronouncing a eulogy to her on the radio, though early reports that they had died on the same day and that her death had caused his were false.

As Cocteau's demise demonstrates, such coincidences are in large part narrative constructions presented as evidence of an implacable doom presiding over Piaf's world, from the deaths of Marcelle and

Leplée onwards. Throughout her career, she was shadowed by such narratives, which were shaped in part by public expectation. Discussing her employer's belief in astrology, fortune-telling and fate, Danielle Bonel perceptively identifies the importance of popular myth-making in the fabrication of this doomed Piaf: 'Édith Piaf is guilty by ancestry. [...] Popular wisdom inscribes the Tables of the Law. It pronounces on good and evil. According to popular wisdom, Édith Giovanna Gassion belongs in that category of women who are predicted to end up on the scaffold.'[9] But it's not quite that straightforward. Piaf did seem to experience her actual life through the image of herself the world reflected back at her, but she also creatively narrated that lived experience for public consumption, as we've already glimpsed. And it was first and foremost she who invested the coincidences with eerie significance. Her sense of pre-destination was both imposed and self-generated. Increasingly, the narrator-in-chief of the imagined Piaf was Piaf herself.

This also had musical applications. When the war took Asso away, she started penning her own lyrics and, occasionally, melodies. In 1944, having failed once, she retook the entrance exam of the society for author rights (the SACEM)[10] and passed, which allowed her to receive songwriting royalties. But even when she worked with other lyricists and composers, she retained creative control. A large number of them would work with her over the years in addition to Monnot, Contet and Émer: Michel Rivgauche, Moustaki, René Rouzaud, Michel Vaucaire, Charles Dumont and more. All wrote within the parameters of her public persona and occasionally helped it evolve. But it was always an asymmetrical partnership in which their job was to do her bidding. Marcel Blistène describes how at social gatherings with her team and entourage she would suddenly go over to the piano and say to whichever composer happened to be there that she had an idea for a tune. She would hum it or tap it out on the keys: 'then, abruptly, like a miracle, the song was on its way; even before it was written, before it was composed, she "felt" it'.[11] Hugues Vassal recalls how she would give her lyricists an idea, a word or a framework to develop:

> This close collaboration was designed to produce songs that were fully adapted to her aesthetic and affective universe, as well as to the specific possibilities of her voice. This is what creation meant

for Édith: each lyric, each melody had to perfectly match her personality, her character and her sensibility. In that way, she could invest in it heart and soul.[12]

The genesis of one of her best-known songs, 'Milord' (Moustaki-Monnot, 1958),[13] illustrates this method. She suggested a range of ideas to Moustaki over dinner in a restaurant, until the word 'Milord' somehow emerged, at which point Piaf decreed: 'That's the starting point. Everything has to revolve round that word. That's where the whole song lies.' Moustaki then set to work and was surprised how easily the lyric flowed.[14] The creative inspiration she furnished is confirmed with some poignancy by the highly talented Émer, who believes that his own creativity died with her.[15]

Piaf would also of course intervene creatively once a song was complete by interpreting it for performance. 'What we write for her is babble', Contet once confided: 'she turns it into cries, pleas and prayers.'[16] This too is illustrated by a famous number. Émer brought her 'L'Accordéoniste' in February 1940 and she recorded it the following May. The song is a three-act drama, each act depicting a different moment in the life of the streetwalker who is its protagonist. But it was Piaf who 'directed' the drama. In the first act, the protagonist is beautiful, so trade is good. Her day's work done, she finds a little happiness by joining her accordionist lover at the local dance hall where he plays. She doesn't dance, but as she watches his expert fingers on the keys, she experiences a thrill both aesthetic and sexual, her body taut and breathless. The second act depicts their wartime separation, which she compensates for by dreaming of their future together when she can leave the street and they can run a little establishment of their own. By the final act, the realisation has dawned that he won't be coming back: the street is her destiny. Yet the masochism of suffering irresistibly draws her back to the dance hall so that her loss can be intensified by a new accordionist playing there.

This interpretation of the song is proposed by Émer and Piaf in tandem. On the page, the song is a third-person narrative. On stage, Piaf the narrator subtly becomes the streetwalker. In the first verse, the sexual dimension of her watching her accordionist play is made explicit by Piaf's hands, which mime his expert fingers stroking first the keys then her breasts. Her face fleetingly expresses ecstasy. But in the famous last verse, Piaf, now more streetwalker than narrator, dramatically disrupts the performance. The protagonist starts whirling deliriously as the music accelerates but suddenly cries 'stop', covering her face because the music has become unbearable. It halts for a few agonising seconds before she delivers a last, pathetic plea to stop the music. But she is pleading with herself, for streetwalker and performer are now one.

Such *mises en scène*, we're told, were instinctive. 'Where I have to watch out is when I start becoming conscious of what I'm doing in a song, when I know I'm singing it, when my gestures become calculated, when they have lost the spontaneity which makes them authentic and "worth it".'[17] And Berteaut confirms this: 'the gestures came to her; she did not have to contrive them, she waited for them to be born quite naturally out of the words', though she does point out that the actual production of a song took place on stage and that Piaf would improve it when she was face to face with an audience.[18] Yet Berteaut gives a rather different account of Piaf's working methods during the Occupation:

> Édith would read hundreds of songs. She'd developed a very clear idea of what she was looking for from a lyric! 'A song is a story, but the audience must be able to believe in it. For them, I am love. It's got to tear them apart, scream at them, that's what my character is. It's OK for me to be happy but not for long; it doesn't go with my looks. The words I use have got to be simple. My audience doesn't think, the stuff I shout at them hits them bang in the gut. I need poetry, the kind to make them dream.'[19]

An unexpectedly strategic approach to performance is disclosed here, modelled on what audiences expect of chanson. A singer so often described as untutored, working by instinct or intuition, wearing her heart on her sleeve, is suddenly revealed as having a cool, professional command of what she's doing. Keenly aware that the imagined Piaf is a narrative and that her body has public meanings, she knows the effects she wants and what she needs to do to get them. To two rejected songwriters, she once explained that she couldn't take their song because the female protagonist was too happy: 'And that, you see, just isn't Piaf. The public knows my life too well... I'm not here to sing about *joie de vivre*'.[20] Likewise, she knew how to perform the body that went with the songs, even in Asso's time: 'I want to keep the look of the streets about me; pale with big eyes and a mouth, no more.'[21] She seemed to know in fact that authenticity in chanson—the audience believing in a song and conflating it with the singer—has to be worked at, fabricated. She may say the contrary: 'My music school is the street, my intelligence is my instinct'.[22] But what she calls instinct, others might think of as intelligence: an alert and intimate understanding picked up on the job.

It was no doubt this intelligence that made her want to break with realism just as she had broken with Asso, whose songs she now considered 'totally out of date'.[23] By the early 1940s, she was being typecast[24] and in an interview in summer 1943 she sounded distinctly cross about it: 'I'm not a realist singer! I hate that genre. I create popular songs. [...] I like flowers, simple love affairs, health, *joie de vivre*'. Today, she went on, it's important to sing for everyone: not just for the lower orders ('le petit peuple') but for anyone ready to be moved by a beautiful love song.[25] The extent of the change she made shouldn't be exaggerated, as songs in the realist tradition—some old, others new—would remain in her act until the end. But from this period on, her repertoire did shift significantly towards the universal love song. With notable exceptions like 'Milord', recorded in New York in 1958 and an international hit single, her most widely known postwar numbers—'La Vie en rose' (Piaf-Louiguy, 1945), 'Hymne à l'amour' (Hymn to love, Piaf-Monnot, written 1949), 'Non, je ne regrette rien' ('No Regrets', Vaucaire-Dumont, 1960)[26]—lack the sociological and national locatedness of her realist work.

One motive was clearly commercial, in that like any popular singer she wanted to reach a wider audience and have an international career. But there's more to it than that. On 17 February 1946, she wrote to Bourgeat asking whether she'd made many spelling mistakes in her last letter, for she needed him to teach her everything she didn't know.[27] On tour in St Moritz the previous year, she had explained to him that she was now moving in different social circles, even diplomatic ones: 'that's why I've no longer got the right to be ignorant. I'm taken seriously, so I've got to take myself seriously too, and that's where I'm counting on you'.[28] This terse self-appraisal carries a lot of freight. Clearly, she's striving to redefine herself through social mobility and her change of repertoire is integral to this. Her early realism embodied a nostalgic and particularist conception of the people redolent of the Popular Front, but both musically and politically this conception was beginning to change. Steadily, the 'popular' song would come to be understood as one appreciated by a diverse, mass audience, not a sociologically specific one.

This shift also helps explain why the critical reception of the new Piaf wasn't uniformly enthusiastic. The change of style and content from Asso to Contet proved particularly contentious. Now that she was widely read and sensitised to poetry, she felt Asso's songs were too populist.[29] And although some commentators admired Contet's greater lyrical ambition ('a true poet in the most perilous of genres'[30]), others thought him too clever for the people's Piaf.[31] The venerable critic Gustave Fréjaville, reviewing her at the Folies-Belleville in January and February 1943, stressed that although her act hadn't changed a great deal, two of her new songs, 'De l'autre côté de la rue' by Émer and 'Les Deux Garçons',[32] 'take their place in a repertoire which is moving towards less straightforward shades of sensibility, towards a visionary poetry with suggestions of mystery and perhaps even magic'.[33] Another new song, 'J'ai dansé avec l'amour', with its 'almost maniacal exaltation', might, he felt, 'disconcert simple souls insufficiently versed in the paroxysms of the imagination and the excesses of lyrical intoxication'. Fréjaville's point is that Piaf was disappointing and alienating her audiences in working-class districts like her native Belleville, accustomed to 'emotions less diluted by literary artifice'.[34]

But it was a booking at L'Étoile two years later, in February and March 1945, which really brought home her new aspirations. The negative responses to the show were occasionally as personal as the article in *Révolution nationale* just a year before. In an open letter that condescended to both her and her simple-minded fans, Serge Weber offered some fatherly advice:

> Don't try to raise yourself up, Mademoiselle Piaf, or to sing above your culture. You have a host of people who love you because you're simple, natural, and because your songs have been as simple as you, with words that everyone gets. [...] Don't go disappointing them with songs that are too literary, that will become increasingly nebulous and where your audience won't understand a thing.[35]

Weber evidently regrets the poetic ambition of Contet's lyrics and the social aspiration that goes with it. The realist song is where she belongs musically and socially. This cultural Darwinism implies a natural homology between the realist style and Piaf's body and class, so Weber feels obliged to put her firmly in her place. In one of her songs, there's a line about her 'maybe' not being pretty. Weber is incensed by that 'maybe': 'we know full well you're not pretty: we're even convinced of it and we don't care. You wouldn't be you if you were pretty. The suffering you enshrine for us doesn't have regular features. It's stooped like you are.'[36] His insinuation is that to abandon the *chanson réaliste* would be to make the same mistake as the prostitute of 'Elle fréquentait la rue Pigalle': she would be attempting to deny the gendered destiny her disgraced body condemns her to. For this male critic, only two identities appear acceptable for the female singer of 1945: sophisticated beauty or unsightly martyr.

A fraction more benignly, Piaf's friend and fellow musician Jean Wiener published a comparable critique, also an open letter. In reflecting on why he didn't cry at the Étoile show as he had when he first saw her in the 1930s, Wiener identifies the problem as being her admirable but excessive experimentation with the modern. The new isn't wrong in itself, Wiener allows, but it has to be introduced discreetly. To make matters worse, her form of modernity isn't all that interesting or all that new. Her latest numbers aren't sufficiently 'defined': 'Art, generally speaking, addresses the masses. The art of chanson even more than any other, only addresses the masses. If your version of the art of chanson lacks definition, it really can't touch anyone, neither mass nor elite'.[37] And this is where the real issue lies, to Wiener's mind: 'you're overdoing the intellectual, overdoing the brilliance. Even your poses, which can be so moving, are excessive, so laden with intent that they no longer come across.'[38] In her resolve to be 'modern' by denouncing realism, she is simply trying too hard. The worst instance of this in Wiener's view is 'Monsieur Saint-Pierre' (Contet-Hess, 1943).[39] The song mixes blues and swing with solemn church music, a funereal bell and an angelic choir that underscores Piaf's extraordinary ability to make her voice thicken and soar with spiritual longing. Contet's lyric features the usual street-wise young woman, who, having shamelessly loved too many 'good-looking lads', arrives at the pearly gates pleading to be let in. 'Pretentiousness' and 'bad taste' of this kind just aren't right for the simplicity, warmth and truth of 'my poor little Môme Piaf' ('ma pauvre petite môme Piaf').

These responses are revealing on a number of levels. What they obviously highlight is the dilemma, familiar today, of the popular singer stuck with a particular style which they can neither repeat without self-parody nor abandon without disappointing loyal fans. But in Piaf's particular case, they also allow us to measure the depth of the change she was undertaking and the national-cultural importance the old Piaf had acquired by the end of the Occupation. Nostalgia is once again the key. What the likes of Weber and Wiener are revealing beneath their condescension, and their assumption that they speak for audiences, is that they want the old, classed and gendered Piaf back. But at the age of 30, the little sparrow, in her own mind, was gone for good.

This tension would be an ongoing one, which she herself aggravated. By the late 1940s, public awareness of her biography was fairly well established and still growing. The media myths of birth in the street, childhood blindness, the circus and discovery by Leplée were all in place and could be built into her act as components of her imagined self. She would also embellish this narrative in interviews and her two autobiographies: *Au bal de la chance* (1958) and the more revealing *Ma vie* (1964).[40] The trouble was that this all made her planned self-reinvention difficult, because these autobiographical reconstructions drew their inspiration directly from the *chanson réaliste*. This is particularly so in *Ma vie* (*My Life*), partly serialised in *France-Dimanche* over ten weeks in 1961 before posthumous publication as a book. Here, she recreates a soap-opera past, with tabloid headings like 'My Man ... My Men', 'My Drugs Hell' and 'Death [Was] My Rival' that underscore her 'scandalous' life of moral turpitude. Her confession of a need for love and her emphasis on misfortunes plunder the tropes of popular melodrama: 'This all sounds like a rather facile serialised novel, I know. But my whole life sounds like a serial that's almost unbelievable.'[41] They also echo Asso's realist lyrics based on her life, like 'Elle fréquentait la rue Pigalle'. This creates a contradiction between her self-constructed, self-promoting autobiographical persona and her artistic desire to move on from realism, a contradiction she would never escape in her lifetime.

As she strove to outrun the *chanson réaliste* and began writing her own songs, awareness of chanson generally, as an aesthetic and a value, became more prominent in her career and was sometimes built into her repertoire. This was already the case in a few of the pre-war songs. The conceit of Asso's 'On danse sur ma chanson' (They're dancing to my song, Asso-Poll, 1940)[42] is that a songwriter hasn't been able to endow his latest composition with the great sentiments he had originally intended because, since he started it last spring, the loved one who inspired it has left him. His deeply felt emotions have thus produced a banal ditty that people are merrily dancing to, which only exacerbates his pain. A value system underpins this lyric, distinguishing chanson from inconsequential festive entertainment. The characters' love wasn't deep enough either to last or to merit a chanson. Roméo Carlès's lyric for 'Simple comme bonjour' (Simple as anything, music by Louiguy, 1936)[43] similarly constructs a narrative so conscious of its banality that the narrator believes it's scarcely worth telling. The presence of such meta-narrative implicitly proposes a conception of *la chanson française* which becomes more common in her 1940s work and helps explain the criticism that she is trying to be clever.

Lyrics by Contet, Émer and Piaf are sometimes self-referential in that chanson is accorded the power to alter emotion. Émer's 'L'Accordéoniste' is a good example, where popular song's capacity for intensifying pain makes sense of that desperate call for the music to stop. In her own lyric 'Un refrain courait dans la rue' (A melody in the street, Piaf-Chauvigny, 1947),[44] a merry refrain with appealing words is anthropomorphised: it stops her in the street and invites her in to mend her broken heart. The bluesy 'C'était une histoire d'amour' (It was a love story, Contet-Jal, 1943)[45] is not so much a narrative as a song about narrative, gloomily aware that in chanson a love story will normally end in tears. In Émer's waltz 'Le Disque usé', the clue is in the title. A scratched record on a wind-up gramophone in the corner of a dingy cabaret keeps replaying the chorus of a song that insists that where there's life there's hope. This persuades the mournful waitress to continue waiting for her sailor, who, 20 years before, promised to return from the sea. In the last verse and chorus, Piaf's vocal imitates the scratches and warping on the disc and finally the gramophone itself as it winds down on one futile insistence that where there's life there's hope.

Awareness of chanson as a distinct form is also evident in her determination after Asso to become Pygmalion for others. The change began when she started writing her own songs. As Reiner hints,[46] this was more than just a practical necessity caused by Asso's being called up. His departure also liberated her from the gendered power dynamic that prevailed in their relationship. Writing her own lyrics, at first in tandem with Monnot, as with the five songs they produced for *Montmartre-sur-Seine*, was a first step in the liberation process, as working exclusively with another woman seemed to help her devise her own creative methods. As Reiner puts it, Monnot 'helped her free herself from the music of men'.[47] A second step came with her next lover after Asso, Paul Meurisse. Piaf brought out the comic potential in the incongruity of his lightweight material in combination with his aloof elegance. This would become his trademark when he abandoned singing for acting.[48]

Another of her projects was Yves Montand, again lover as well as protégé. She persuaded him to abandon the ludicrous cowboy persona he had initially adopted against the background of post-Liberation Americanophilia. As well as writing new material for him herself, she asked Contet to do so. She changed his stage appearance and style, included him on the same bill as her and introduced him to film acting, though unlike Meurisse he would pursue a singing career in tandem. Montand subsequently denied she had moulded him in this way, not surprisingly since her account makes him, like Meurisse, seem her hapless poodle. But the true balance of power is less important to us than her narrative.

As the years went by, a string of other aspirants came under her spell, condemned to stardom, as Noli dryly puts it:[49] the Compagnons; Aznavour; the American singer and actor Eddie Constantine, who took Cerdan's place and was rumoured in 1950 to be about to marry her; her first husband, Jacques Pills; Georges Moustaki; Félix Marten; Charles Dumont, whom she helped become a singer as well as a composer; the musician Noël Commaret; and her second husband, Théo Sarapo. To an extent, we might even speak of a 'Piaf school', though not in the literal sense that applies to the singer and songwriter Mireille's Petit Conservatoire de la chanson, where a number of future stars were trained within a formal structure linked first to a radio programme, then to a TV show.[50] But Piaf's coaching was just as practical. At the very end of her life she told her nurse of her plan to give singing lessons if she could no longer perform.[51] A little excessively, the Bonels claim she literally 'created' the talent of at least some of her young protégés.[52]

She saw herself at the centre of the chanson profession, its infallible magician. Indeed, there were those who felt her influence was too great,[53] since it extended well beyond chanson via her vast network of contacts. But, again, more important than the part she actually played in making careers—important though it undoubtedly was in cases like Aznavour, Moustaki and the Compagnons—is her increasingly deluded belief in her ability to do so. All manner of unlikely lovers, acquaintances and even employees were considered for a career in chanson as soon as they came into her purview: Chauvigny's wife Monique, Sarapo the hairdresser and his sister Christie, even one of Piaf's chauffeurs and the nurse who cared for her on her deathbed. It's as if, as she grew frailer, she needed to believe all the more blindly that she possessed a sixth sense for conjuring talent out of nothing. And the myth of infallibility was amply encouraged by those who admired or flattered her. But there was a deeper dimension to it.

At one level, she was inverting the male/female power regime she had lived with under her father, Leplée and Asso. At another, her invention of new singers was her way of resisting cultural change and assuring her place in history based on her faith that she possessed the alchemical secret of *la chanson française* that it was her duty to pass on. As she commented playfully in an interview 18 months before her death: 'I'm the greatest benefactor of the music hall. We're short of stars? OK, I'll make some. So here's the recipe.' She only has to discover a young man who wants to sing, make him her secretary and be photographed with him, and he will instantly be identified in the media as her lover and protégé. So maybe, she teases, the interviewer himself might like to become a singer?[54] Though she is parodying herself as well as the press, she also betrays a fundamental self-belief. Yet her will to train others wasn't solipsistic. Throughout the 1950s, she made a point of observing other singers at work. She kept up with trends like the rise of Brassens and Brel, both of whom she liked. She also counted famous singers like Trenet, Rossi and later Dalida among her friends, in addition to those in her entourage.

Nor was the music hall her confessional. Her ambition was to expose not her inner self but a carefully engineered avatar of it. And in this, she takes further what Deniot persuasively presents as a turning point in the history of French chanson,[55] emerging from the *chanson réaliste*: the identification of a singer with her or his repertoire, a performing style which for Stéphane Hirschi characterises the modern practitioner of what has become known as the 'poetic chanson'.[56] In this way, with her own songs but above all, paradoxically, those written for her, Piaf made French chanson take a significant step towards auteurism. I will explore this influence, and this paradox, in the next chapter.

CHAPTER 5

High art, low culture

Piaf and *la chanson française*

A T A CONFERENCE in Italy on the influence of the French 'poetic chanson', the introductory rubric began:

> In 2013 we will celebrate the centenary of the birth of Charles Trenet, who is unanimously considered to be the precursor of the French singer-songwriters [*auteurs-compositeurs-interprètes*] [...]. In his wake during the 1950s and 1960s, authors such as Brassens, Brel, Ferré, Gainsbourg, Ferrat, Aznavour, Moustaki, Barbara, Bécaud, Vian [...] have disseminated *la chanson française* across the world and have contributed to an extraordinary encounter— indeed, a fusion, of music and literature.[1]

'Alongside' these great 'authors' but separated from them came the most significant performers (*interprètes*) of French chanson: Gréco, Montand and Piaf. These two groups together, the rubric went on, were responsible for a memorable era of profound renewal in chanson.

The document's deceptively value-free distinction between historic singers and historic singer-songwriters raises an especially intriguing question in Piaf's case. She wrote close to 90 songs, many of which she sang herself. And, as we saw, lyrics were what interested her most: 'Creating a song means bringing a character alive. How can this be achieved if the words are mediocre even if the music is good?'[2] So why isn't she classed as an *auteur-compositeur-interprète* (ACI)? The hyphens here are actually more eloquent than they look. They signify a deeper unity in the talents at stake, an 'integrity' in the dual sense of sincerity and wholeness. They discreetly connote an 'auteur', a single, unifying creative vision. In France particularly, where the concept of auteurism began with film criticism, 'author-composer-interpreter' carries a rhetorical gravitas that 'interpreter' alone doesn't. Likewise, 'author' and 'text' are used in French where English more naturally uses 'lyricist' and 'lyrics'. Singer-songwriters like Trenet, Brel, Brassens and Ferré enjoy a special status because they have a double legitimacy within French republican culture: their work is both poetic and popular, aesthetically demanding yet democratic. They thereby represent within the broader category 'chanson' an elite subgenre variously called the text-based song (*chanson à texte*), the author song (*chanson d'auteur*) or the poetic song (*chanson poétique*).

Piaf, on the other hand, despite those 90-odd songs, is generally classed as an 'interpreter', which here causes her to be placed in the company of Montand and Gréco, neither of whom wrote their own material. This could of course be because her own songs just aren't considered 'poetic' enough. But that qualitative judgment is, I believe, read through the gender coding which, as Eric Drott points out, underlies most critiques of mass culture. Drott's example is early 1960s pop known as *yéyé*, which, dominated by young women (Sheila, Sylvie Vartan, Françoise Hardy and others), 'was cast as a lower, feminized form of expression, deficient compared to genres that supposedly resisted commercial pressures'.[3] But his argument might well be applied to chanson generally, with the commercial pop song (the songs of Claude François, for example) discursively represented as frivolous, inauthentic and effeminate, and the auteurist chanson as serious, authentic and masculine.[4] Certainly, the standard social construction of the great French singer-songwriter of the 1950s and 1960s—not necessarily articulated or even conscious, but in-built—was that they were white, confidently heterosexual and male.[5]

We also need to situate the distinction between singer and auteur against the historical relationship between French identity and the written word. The literacy, dexterity and narrative quality of the ACI's lyrics have given *la chanson française* a national, para-literary legitimacy. Romantic conceptions of personal expression and individual authorship also come into play. Piaf's case for being an ACI is therefore weakened not just by gender coding but also by the process of collective fabrication. Her being the product of concerted teamwork could argue for manufacture and against auteurship. Yet Piaf's particular case challenges that crude binary in two ways.

First, through the creative interventions we encountered in the last chapter, she swiftly became the chanson equivalent of the cinematic auteur, directing the multiple inputs that produced her: developing her own repertoire, writing her own songs or tailoring the songwriting of others, and narrating herself in order that her songs narrate her better. Second, a significant change in public perceptions had come about by 1945, which impacted on her place in *la chanson française*. When she began her new season at the ABC in 1942, one critic rejoiced that the very genre of the *chanson réaliste* had returned in the form of 'the woman who created it' and in whose hands it had become truly unique.[6] Another wrote, 'If there is one name that evokes French chanson and the gratitude of the crowd, it has to be this moving star'.[7] A third, Fréjaville again, praises 'the suppleness and solidity of a talent which is guided by intelligence, which no longer owes everything to nature, which now knows exactly what it wants and where it is going'.[8] Françoise Holbane (pen name of Françoise Giroud) speaks of the 'nobility', 'purity' and 'sobriety' of the 'Piaf style', of which she is now in full possession.[9]

These representations of a mature Piaf—emphasising national representativity, authority, intelligence, accomplished artifice—all concern the cultural status of French chanson as well as Piaf's place within it. They add up to what Simon Frith, building on Bourdieu and Becker, calls an art discourse.[10] He identifies three discursive practices or contexts through which popular music is heard and which produce the terms in which value judgments are made: art, folk and commercial (or 'pop'). In art discourse, the ideal is music that is serious, transcendent, pure. In Piaf's case, this kind of discourse had been gestating since 1937, when she moved up the hierarchy that ran from cabaret to the self-important ABC.[11] But it got properly underway from 1940. A critic said of her performance at L'Aiglon that year: 'Once a century an instrument appears that is a perfect expression of popular poetry. Édith Piaf is it. She is also quite simply a great artist'.[12] In 1942, the young journalist Léo Ferré, who had yet to become one of the three great singer-songwriters of the postwar years, presciently called her a tragedian.[13] Cocteau spoke of her 'genius' in terms suggestive of the ineffability of the greatest art: 'she transcends herself, she transcends her songs, she transcends their melodies and their lyrics. She transcends us'.[14]

At the same time, there are traces left over from the start of her career of Frith's folk discourse, wherein music is valued as the supposedly natural, informal and spontaneous production of communities, though in her case the community in question was by now imagined as national.[15] At a time when a sense of national identity needed to be restored after the defeat and the Occupation, the serious and self-aware kind of song she represented—made so by her voice, her performance style and the autobiographical content—was becoming aware of itself as a French folk art, a generic category in its own right, and a vehicle for self-expression and communication, rather than an everyday commercial commodity (Frith's third discursive practice) in which a simple lyric is set to a simple melody designed to produce simple, marketable pleasures.

The Piaf of the 1930s and 1940s thereby served as a blueprint for chanson auteurism: she embodied an ACI aesthetic in the making. After the war, lone performers like Brassens and Brel would combine the functions of Piaf, Asso and Monnot, hitherto separate in the pre-war French landscape except for the pioneering Trenet, and became fully fledged auteurs with their own artistic vision. Trenet and Piaf together paved the way for this development. Trenet did so more conspicuously but Piaf contributed the vital element of intimate self-revelation. Her contribution wasn't the result of visionary foresight, however, as was evident in her work with a young Georges Moustaki. Footage exists of her giving a plainly embarrassed Moustaki—at that time a songwriter, not a performer—an astringent lesson in her own emotional style.[16] But he would only find his feet as a performer when, several years after her death, he followed the singer-songwriter model as it had evolved by 1968, growing his hair (like Brel and Ferré) and a tousled beard and singing his own compositions with the non-aggressive, understated timbre of the hippy. Perhaps, then, Piaf never wore the mantle of singer-songwriter partly because, belonging to a different generation, she didn't knowingly anticipate the phenomenon. But she should at least be considered an honorary ACI in so far as the songs written by or for her established the parameters of auteurist authenticity.

Authenticity—cherished by aficionados of popular music yet so hard to define—implies here that singers are serious about what they sing and reveal themselves, rather than adopting different masks from song to song in order to entertain. 'You have to be determined to be yourself and only yourself', advises Piaf.[17] Of course, this simple conceptualisation of authenticity can be challenged, but as Deniot and others argue,[18] it was characteristic of a new postwar understanding of French chanson. Singing as self-disclosure was deemed to induce emotional release in the audience, unlocking repressed feeling by means of 'direct identification with the joys and sorrows of the singer'.[19] And this began with a reconfiguring of the realist song by women singers, in whose hands realism became affective rather than social: a realism of the passions for which a taste would eventually spread to all levels of society.[20] Problematic though the notion of authenticity is, then, in theoretical terms, it's built into the social meanings of both Piaf and *la chanson française*.

The word 'authenticity' wasn't actually applied to her all that much in her lifetime, but it's an implicit discursive category in representations of her—her own and those of fans, colleagues and the media. It also underlies (paradoxically, given Deniot's argument) her desire to break with realism, which she felt no longer expressed who she was or wanted to be. And it's implied towards the end of her life when she declares that she really does regret nothing. Everything that has happened to her has given her the experience needed to express all kinds of feelings; as a result, Piaf states, 'I know what I'm talking about. And you need to know what you're talking about when you sing so as to get it across to others and so others can understand you'.[21] Equally, authenticity is present as a tacit concern among critics—like Serge Weber,[22] who regrets her attempt to rise above her own 'culture' because the real Piaf lies in her naturalness; or like Jean Wiener, who calls for a return to 'the true little Piaf, warm and simple, from way back when'.[23] What such criticisms fail to consider is that authenticity is a performance.

In the Piaf of the late 1940s, French chanson found itself at a discursive crossroads. In one direction, a more 'authentic', 'poetic' song which would soon become fully developed in the *chanson d'auteur* of Brel, Brassens and Ferré. In the other, the brash populism of the old *café-concert* and music hall, which was turning into the mass commercial entertainment of the 1950s, or *variétés*, from which the *chanson d'auteur* would always strive to distinguish itself.[24] The postwar Piaf was tarred with both brushes. An intelligent review by the playwright and poet

René de Obaldia of Piaf's first performances at the prestigious Palais de Chaillot in 1946 furnishes an insight into her dual status.

Piaf had announced she would be singing songs by classical composers. And Obaldia believed many in the audience had come to protest at this 'profanation' by a popular entertainer. But she won them over by in fact transgressing the intractable boundaries of high and low cultures. A former street singer reached the transcendent heights of art: 'Édith Piaf made us attain the ineffable in just the same way, though in different genres, as a Chaliapin, a Walter Gieseking, a Marian Anderson, a Yehudi Menuhin, a Michèle Morgan or a Jean-Louis Barrault!'[25] These allusions prompt Obaldia to reflect on the cultural status of chanson itself, too often dismissed as a 'minor art'. If a figure from the world of popular song can succeed in a 'higher' genre, perhaps it's because chanson is 'a truer manifestation of feeling' ('une manifestation du sentiment plus réelle') than many traditional arts and has now assumed 'a subtle, select place in our daily lives' ('une place subtile et de choix dans notre vie quotidienne'). How often do we catch ourselves singing popular lyrics to ourselves, which for Obaldia as for Fargue, whom he cites, are capable of being as 'eternal' and 'beautiful' as lines from Socrates or Shakespeare? And Obaldia adds his own experience as a POW. Somebody would start singing 'Mon légionnaire' or 'Je n'en connais pas la fin' (I don't know how it ends, Asso-Monnot, 1939)[26] and a silence would fall that transcended the barbed wire and the class differences between them, bringing them to a state of quasi-religious communion. It's not that Obaldia is undiscriminating: he makes it plain that he's only talking about 'good songs', as distinct from the 'sickening mediocrity' of most of those played on the radio, where the same high standards of performance aren't needed and 'imbecility' is so often applauded. But he concludes that good songs are especially at home in France because they incarnate 'one of the greatest virtues of our people, by which I mean the genius of spontaneity'.[27]

High and low cultures, good and bad songs, the mediocrity of the mass media versus the special status of 'good songs' in France: all of Obaldia's arguments place *la chanson française* at the threshold of a new national legitimation, with its liminality signified by Piaf herself. The Piaf of the late 1940s sits astride these two worlds, and her meanings in France are accordingly ambiguous, enshrining what was becoming a dominant cultural debate in postwar France, between high French art and low, US-influenced mass culture. However, her decision in 1947 to go to New York to launch a new international career added crucial new dimensions to these meanings and this debate.

New York, new meanings

A tour of America made sense on several levels. With the postwar Americanisation of France, economic, social and cultural progress meant engaging with the United States, whether as model or menace.[28] The USA was the obligatory stepping stone for a singing career in the Anglophone world and it wasn't unusual for a successful French act to try their luck after the war. Chevalier spent a good deal of time there and became world-famous as a result. Trenet too in the same period went to New York and thence California.[29] Even before the war, Mistinguett, Yvonne Guilbert and most successfully Lucienne Boyer had all crossed the Atlantic. But for Piaf the project also made sense as a way of breaking free of the *chanson réaliste* and its social baggage. In New York, she could start with a relatively clean slate both musically and socially. Marc Bonel contrasts the reception she got in France when she did a private performance for one of the Rothschilds—appreciative but cold and, for Piaf, humiliating—with the lively party organised by an equally wealthy oil magnate in Hollywood in 1956, attended by film stars in a restaurant decorated for the occasion, where she was handsomely paid for singing five songs.[30]

Piaf and her entourage—Barrier, Marc Bonel and Chauvigny, Émer and Les Compagnons de la chanson, with whom she was due to tour—set off for New York City on the *Queen Elizabeth* on 9 October 1947. Her opening night was on the 30th of that month, at the Playhouse Theatre on West 48th Street, east of Broadway, in a variety show entitled 'Édith Piaf and Her Continental Entertainers'. In the well-oiled narrative of this adventure, the Compagnons were an instant hit but she wasn't. Towards the end of the Playhouse booking, she even contemplated returning to France alone. A 'wall of incomprehension' was how Brierre would later describe it.[31] But when in one last-ditch effort she was signed to the sophisticated midtown dining club the Versailles in December, everything changed. The switch was facilitated, so the legend goes, by the esteemed classical composer and critic Virgil Thomson, who wrote a dithyrambic article about her. Soon, people were bribing the doorman to get in, diners were standing on tables to applaud, and everyone who was anyone was being ushered in to see her (with the shameful exception of the black jazz singer Lena Horne, who wasn't admitted).

Piaf's career would never be the same. America proved the second major turning point in her career after the Occupation, influencing her meanings at home as well as abroad. Nonetheless, some elements of the story need nuancing. She exaggerates her initial failure, the better to represent her eventual success as triumph over adversity, a common device of her self-invention and one soon picked up by others. Occasional documentaries would still have us believe she had a hostile reception, not realising (or pretending not to realise) that the whistles that greeted her singing didn't signal disapproval in the French way but expressed enthusiasm. To be sure, reviews were mixed.[32] But she wasn't booed or even disliked: audiences applauded and some critics wrote her up favourably. One advertisement for the Playhouse show in the *New York Herald Tribune* contains press quotes, albeit carefully selected, with remarks like 'Last night's audience was rhapsodic', or 'Edith Piaf won an ovation last night', or 'A swanky first night audience blistered its hands applauding'.[33] Of one of her records, Howard Taubman for the *New York Times* told his readers to listen to all six tracks: 'you will come away with the conviction that she is an artist in her field.'[34]

It was just that she didn't live up to American expectations of the seductive Parisian beauty set by Lucienne Boyer in her glamorous Lanvin gowns.[35] With her plain black dress, tousled hair and distressed appearance, Piaf proved difficult to compute for Americans. And, ironically, she was still sociologically, nationally and musically branded, too grittily realist. To her first night at the Playhouse, a writer for the *Daily News* reacted with mild bewilderment though no special hostility ('I liked her all right, I guess'). Recognising that the Compagnons had upstaged her through their burlesque comedy, he tried to make sense of her in terms his readers might understand:

> She has a big, brassy voice like Ethel Merman's, a careless hairdo,
> a simple dress, big blue eyes and a big red mouth. She sings
> French songs mostly, but here and there a verse in Eengleesh.

Mlle Piaf, who grew up as a street singer, affects none of the cooing of a Lucienne Boyer or (if you remember her) a Raquel Meller. She stands smack in the middle of a bare stage on two stocky legs and gives forth. She does not beg for love, nor does she sell any violets, but just ups and lets go, with no frills or fuss—a rare and admirable habit.[36]

In similar tone, the reviewer of the *New Yorker* gently ribbed both his compatriots for only appreciating optimism and Piaf for only singing about dying lovers.[37] Brooks Atkinson in the *New York Times* begins his review of her first night at the Playhouse by lamenting her lack of 'showmanship' and downcast appearance as she stood alone on a bare stage, intimating that she might just as well have stayed at home: 'On first acquaintance, there does not seem to be much here worth snatching out of its normal environment and thrusting out on an empty stage in a preoccupied foreign city.' He does soften somewhat: 'She is a genuine artist in a particular tradition, making no concessions to a heedless metropolis abroad.'[38] But he still connects this artistry ultimately to her transcultural impenetrability.

This problem of cultural boundaries needs unpacking. Her ambition, as we know, was to leave behind both social particularism and national locatedness and achieve universality. New York both helped and hindered in this, but it did endow her with a different aesthetic significance. The well-known sociologist of art Vera Zolberg attended one of Piaf's shows at the Versailles as a young French major at high school.[39] Inculcated with the belief in the superiority of French culture by her teachers, Zolberg saw Piaf as an integral part of that culture rather than a mere entertainer. In her account, the singer's personal style and stage presence, the economy of gesture and setting, the sophisticated cabaret venue, the disconcerting absence of American showbiz glamour, and the rough-hewn tragedy in her voice all added up indisputably to an art discourse. Virgil Thomson's review takes this further.

The part played by Thomson in Piaf's success in New York also needs probing, since Piaf herself is responsible for the story being so widely repeated. In *Au bal de la chance*, his article is made to sound like a challenge to his compatriots: 'Didn't he say in his conclusion that if the American public let me go home after a failure I didn't deserve, it would have demonstrated its incompetence and stupidity?'[40] Piaf's rhetorical question here has been reproduced many times, but the simple answer is no. Assuming she is referring to his piece in the *New York Herald Tribune*, the only article by him about Piaf found in the New York Public Library and the only one reproduced in the volume of his selected writings, he made no such statement. All he actually said in conclusion was that Piaf 'may be strong meat, artistically speaking, for American theater audiences, though I hope our public will long go on loving and applauding her'.[41] Even so, the rest of the article is certainly of importance.

Piaf's presence in New York, he begins, 'is a pleasant reminder that the French chanson is an art form as traditional as the concert song. It has a glorious history and a repertory.' Both then and now, 'its interpreters are artists in the purest and highest sense of the term, easily distinguishable in this regard from the stars of commercialised entertainment', chanson itself being 'the musical art of the urban proletariat'. For Thomson, Piaf is the epitome of 'the art of the chansonnier at its most classical', and he locates her classicism in the spare staging of her body: 'She stands in the middle of a bare stage in the classic black dress of medium length [...], her feet planted about six inches apart; and she never moves, except for the arms. Even with these her gestures are sparing and she uses them as much for abstractly rhetorical as for directly expressive purposes.' All of this is for Thomson the result of carefully choreographed artifice, though, once again, we mustn't interpret artifice in today's terms. The Piaf that Thomson saw is the antithesis of the writhing R'n'B singer who mimes emotion or desire to excess. With Piaf, 'there is apparently not a nerve in her body. [...] She is not tense but intense, in no way spontaneous, just thoroughly concentrated and absolutely impersonal'. And because of this restraint, 'her power of dramatic projection is tremendous. She is a great technician because her methods are of the simplest, in every way classical and direct. She is a great artist because she gives you a clear vision of the scene or subject she is depicting with a minimum injection of personality'.[42]

Thomson's analysis is particularly rich. First, he recognises the distinction between chanson as auteurism and song as commercial entertainment and he unequivocally associates Piaf with the former. Second, he's perfectly aware that her auteurism entails self-conscious fabrication, as are the other American critics who reviewed her. This is surely because they approach her with greater emotional distance than do her French audiences, who adore her for her spontaneity. Richard Watts Junior, for example, in the *New York Post*, is impressed by her work yet fully accepts the natural artifice in popular song: 'Like all exceptional performers in the field of song characterization, Mlle Piaf has created a strongly marked stage personality. [...] She manages it wonderfully, and it is certainly a tribute to her triumphant impersonation of wistfulness.'[43] This relaxed approach to artifice is a fundamental cultural difference between French and American assessments. And it's a difference that requires Thomson to recontextualise her for America, whose virgin gaze has stripped away her accreted meanings in France. In order to do this, Thomson in turn has to strip away American expectations of the French female body—left over from the colourful Boyer but confirmed more recently by conquering GIs' experiences of Parisian nightlife—and re-clothe her unconventional physical appearance. As with Zolberg, French art is characterised in his mind by the asceticism of seventeenth-century neo-classical theatre or Jacques Copeau's notion of the bare stage (*le tréteau nu*). By thus providing American audiences with instructions for use, he endeavours to make their responses to Piaf more nuanced. He implicitly recognises her otherness for New Yorkers and feels obliged to act as intermediary, interpreter between two cultures which have failed to understand each other.

This need for mediation opens up an extra dimension of Piaf's reception in America, which Simone de Beauvoir, in a letter in English to the novelist Nelson Algren, who had raised the subject of Piaf with her, analyses illuminatingly.[44] Attempting to explain why the Compagnons, who 'are not half as talented as she is', met with more success than her, Beauvoir quotes a French friend in New York (Jacqueline Breton, though unnamed in the letter) who had seen Piaf there. Americans, Breton said, 'like what *looks* very French. [...] But the real French things do not seem so French, they are just new'. Beauvoir probes this surmise:

So Édith Piaf in her black dress, with her hoarse voice and very ugly face, does not seem so French, and American people do not know what to find in her—they remain cold. We like her here; we think she is rather wonderful but in this strange way when beauty and ugliness meet. And you [Algren] told me yourself American people do not like so much this mixture. Then, when she touches her neck, the scope of her neck, in a strange, sensual and distressed gesture, the public does not like it: this is the place where men feel the hang-over at morning, and the place where frustrated women would like to feel a man's lips and don't, so everybody is uneasy.[45]

Beauvoir's insights are as rich as Thomson's, showing how not only transnational perceptions of difference but also an unspoken sexual unease about Piaf's unfamiliar stage business intervened to make her undecodable. These also point up how 'Frenchness' means different things to different cultures. Behind the need for Thomson's mediation lies a whole history of Franco-American cultural 'misunderstandings', though in theoretical terms this is the wrong word. Deniot points out that Piaf was interpreted by Americans as a cabaret singer even though in France she wasn't particularly associated with cabaret but with the bigger, brasher music hall. But Deniot recognises that this discrepancy doesn't entirely invalidate American readings. Piaf in fact represents a hinge between the notions of the French singer as voice, to be listened to for its own appeal, and as self-exposure.[46] But 'misunderstanding' is the wrong term for a second reason: because both 'Frenchness' and 'popular' music are ultimately rhetorical artefacts, whose meanings change with time, cultural standpoint and transnational movements.[47] If, as I suggested at the beginning of the book, the ethnographic distance of an outsider's gaze can usefully defamiliarise and re-interpret French culture, the same can be said of New Yorkers' decontextualisation of Piaf. US readings thus become part of her global meanings.

America did indeed make its own sense of Piaf. Brooks Atkinson, identifying her foreignness, nonetheless reached a promising conclusion about cross-cultural relations. Both Piaf and the Compagnons, he wrote, 'are bringing into our small world something genuine that makes you feel a little more hopeful about the UN and the peaceful association of nations'.[48] And certainly, as time went by and she returned to the USA regularly and for longer periods, the American public did become acclimatised to her and, in the showbiz cliché, took her to their hearts. In this way, she began a new international career informed by quite different meanings from those acquired in France. These new meanings were in part founded on an art discourse, as we have seen, which culminated in her playing Carnegie Hall on 4 January 1956, supposedly the first popular singer to perform there, and again a year later, to huge acclaim. At the same time, her art meanings were always mediated through American perceptions of Frenchness. In 1955, a San Francisco critic described her as 'France's greatest gift to the theater since Sarah Bernhardt'.[49] Another, for the *Boston Globe*, wrote: 'Piaf is France [...]. She makes one *believe* what Jefferson, we think, once said: "Every man has two countries, his own and France."'[50] And a third, in 1956, stated, 'We're no longer at Carnegie Hall but in a bistrot on a little street on the Left Bank',[51] confirming in the process Deniot's argument about Piaf's cabaret image in New York. This re-gallicisation of Piaf in America is essentially a version of Frith's folk discourse.

In the USA, then, where few could understand her lyrics, all her existing cultural baggage was recontextualised and reappropriated. And the fact that she quickly learnt English as best she could and began performing and recording English versions of her songs did nothing to alter this, for these versions were unquestionably adaptations, not translations, full of the commonplaces of the Broadway musical and the commercial crooner. So here, too, her original national meanings were altered. She also continued to widen her style and repertoire by absorbing international influences, with the result that her best-known standards in the English-speaking world are, with few exceptions, those with the least national specificity.

Just as importantly, Piaf's cultural recontextualisation by America would have a knock-on effect at home, where her compatriots could no longer see her through French eyes alone. She came home not so much Americanised (though this was the case to an extent) as transfigured, gilded and redefined by the great American other and viewed with a new curiosity and awe, as one perceptive French critic intimated after a homecoming show in 1950: 'Every time she comes back to us from America, she surprises us with the same songs and we are happy to let ourselves be caught out again. [...] She was acclaimed as never before'.[52] In one sense, she returned more French, as a result of that folk discourse binding her quasi-genetically to her national community and giving her the symbolic status of ambassador of *la chanson française* abroad. 'In a

few days' time', one French journalist reveals excitedly during her first
US stay, 'she'll be off to Hollywood [...] with the passionate wish to let
them hear our country's songs'.[53]

In a second sense, she came home aestheticised. In January 1949, she
performed at the prestigious Salle Pleyel, where she had first appeared in
reduced circumstances in September 1940. Like Carnegie Hall, Pleyel was
normally reserved for classical music, but her reception there duplicated
her triumph at the Versailles. In a piece in *Le Figaro littéraire* revealingly
entitled '"La môme Piaf" turns into a princess', Piaf on stage is described
in terms comparable to those used by Thomson a year before. Clearly, the
preoccupation with what she used to be survives, as the reviewer, François
de Roux, wonders with a trace of melancholy how many in the audience
have secretly come to see the frail little sparrow rather than the confirmed
international star.[54] But what now strikes him more than anything is the
signifying power of her act.

The orchestra is hidden behind the stage curtains, an innovation she
introduced in 1943 which focuses attention on her solitude. She unostenta-
tiously walks on stage and immediately announces her first number, after
which comes the applause: 'She doesn't move. With her hands behind her
back, her head up but tilted towards her left shoulder, standing squarely
on her short legs, she looks at the audience without smiling and without
bowing.'[55] The powerful coupling of voice and gesture is again noted:
'The sobriety of her art is extreme. Her voice is not the only one of her
gifts. Each of her gestures assumes an intense meaning. They are rare,
slow and measured. Profoundly eloquent, the movements of hands and
face round off her singing pleasingly once the voice has fallen silent.'[56] As
she warms up and the audience thrills to her singing, she does respond a
little to their enthusiasm. But on the whole she remains aloof throughout,
even refusing an encore, despite the audience's insistence. Transfigured
by both audience rapture and reviewer rhetoric, the little match girl has
been turned into a princess. And as she takes the final applause in front
of the orchestra, now visible on stage, 'one has a vision of a Douanier
Rousseau painting. The evening ends as it should.'[57]

This is the apotheosis of the art discourse we've seen building up
round her since her first ABC appearance in 1937. By the end of the 1940s,
the imagined Piaf has become a work of art. Her act—described here
in a high-cultural newspaper reporting from a high-cultural venue—has

the tightly plotted inevitability of fiction. And the aloofness the reviewer remarks on is a sign of the transcendence and restraint of art. Yet it is simultaneously the aloofness of the star, who as the social theorist Edgar Morin argues has to maintain a precise balance between closeness and inaccessibility, humanity and divinity.[58] Cinema, of course, is the classic generator of this dual effect. Hence Émile Tuscherer's insistence that she be bodily transformed before appearing in Blistène's *Étoile sans lumière*, a process Morin would later call 'starification' but which had already been noted at the time: 'Édith Piaf has a new look [...]. Our singer, who has become a redhead, now looks like a Hollywood star.'[59]

In France, then, her embodiment of national cultural identity after the Liberation was intensified by the American triumph but its meaning was altered. If her wartime identification with national nostalgia accounts for her male critics' wanting to retain the Parisian sparrow girl of the 1930s, who had come to mean so much in occupied France, her American triumph made this reductive representation much more difficult to maintain. As Maurice Chevalier had intuited when he saw her during her first engagement at the Versailles, America showed her that her true place as a performer was an international one.[60] Its gaze gave her a new self-awareness, made her interpret herself and her potentialities differently. After America, she recognised herself as both artist and star.

The essential ingredient of stardom as Morin defines it—the interpenetration of the heroic screen role and the actor playing it—was actually latent in Piaf from the first, transposed as the conflation of song and life. But its presence wasn't fully understood as exceptional until America, after which there was a step change in French perceptions of her. An article in 1952 drives this home: 'Édith Piaf is an extraordinary woman. You can't not submit to her strange charm. [...] She is one of the great personalities of the age. In her profession, she's the tops. The one and only. She has climbed so high that all around her is the void.'[61] Mentioning later that she often irritates other women, the writer goes on: 'Édith Piaf must exert a properly magic power on people's intelligence or sensibility to generate such violent passions—since she doesn't have the beauty of Elizabeth Taylor or the sparkle of Marilyn Monroe'.[62] These comparisons are especially eloquent. It's as if France, long obsessed with her body's wilful subversion of the prevailing codes of sexualised beauty, couldn't bring itself to accord her the semi-divine status of the true star—however famous she was—until she came back from America with her subversive meanings valorised—or, more accurately, neutralised by America's valorisation.

Art and stardom would in fact be the two recurring tropes in narratives of her for the rest of her life. But they aren't necessarily compatible. The two faces of the imagined Piaf co-existed but not always peacefully, as we'll see next.

CHAPTER 6

Ideology, tragedy, celebrity

A new middlebrow

THE Fourth Republic in France (1946–58) may have been a time of political immobilism, with constant changes of government and alliances of convenience, but it also heralded deep social change and ideological conflict. Steady economic recovery, the reconstruction of infrastructure with the help of government planning and nationalisations, new migrations, the start of the baby boom and its consequences for the education system, and the emergence of a consumer society all helped bring about intense modernisation. With the collaborationist right initially marginalised, ideological division was soon reconfigured by the Cold War, as the Resistance consensus broke up. The political and intellectual left dominated by the French Communist Party was hostile to the rise of Gaullism as an organised political force, and the centrist or social-democratic parties of government were hamstrung by France's parliamentary system. Decolonisation would be a new focus of division, with French defeat in Indochina in 1954 followed by the Algerian war of independence (1954–62). By 1958, France was close to civil war over the issue, which brought de Gaulle out of retirement to create an entirely new political structure, today's Fifth Republic.

This whole epic passed Piaf by: she was too busy with her energetic love life, regular tours of America and elsewhere, and declining health. Between 1947 and 1948, she sang at both a rally for the French Communist leader Maurice Thorez and one for the fledgling Gaullist party, the RPF (Rassemblement du peuple français). Both were strictly professional engagements.[1] In May 1958, when the Fourth Republic was tearing itself apart, Piaf was falling in love with Moustaki, had just completed 128 performances at the Olympia before some 240,000 people and was back on medicinal drugs and sleeping tablets due to overwork. In both April and May, she collapsed on stage. Her political horizons were limited to keeping up with current affairs so as not to appear stupid in company and sharing the views of whichever man she happened to be with. She probably never voted and no polling card was found after she died.[2] Piaf seems in fact to have shared popular cynicism about political parties.

Still, the situation is not quite so straightforward. Marc Bonel confirms that she didn't get involved in politics but adds that she was immovably royalist and Gaullist, though he means by this only that she admired de Gaulle and liked watching royal weddings.[3] She was a monarchist, Danielle Bonel explains, only because in 1951 the future Queen Elizabeth, accompanied by the handsome Duke of Edinburgh, had asked to meet her.[4] Danielle places Piaf broadly on the right: 'respectful of institutions, she was in awe of strong personalities'. And she surmises that in the 2007 presidential elections Piaf would probably have supported Sarkozy.[5] So it would seem that, though Piaf had no declared political affiliation, an ideology was another matter. Her fatalism, for example, implies a conservative worldview in which nothing can ever change, certainly not the woes of the downtrodden, who are always with us. Her own biography ought to have disproved this in so far as, like reality talent shows, it demonstrates the possibilities that popular culture opens up for the commoner. But for Piaf both narratives carry the same message: that our fate lies in the stars: 'que sera sera'.

As happened during the Occupation, she did at certain times acquire unintended ideological meanings or uses connected with her postwar status as a national icon. Again, the American gaze proved crucial here, as she re-imported Anglocentric interpretations of France and Frenchness. As Kuisel argues, America was postwar France's other in that it 'helped the French to imagine, construct, and refine their collective sense of self';[6] and Piaf's post-1947 meanings illustrate this quite powerfully. In 1959, with the Algerian situation still at a critical point, a showbiz column in *Combat* by Alain Spiraux announced her return to an engagement at the Empire Room of New York's Waldorf Astoria, after she'd been taken ill there twice on stage.[7] Without intending to, Spiraux argues, she has become France's ambassador to the States. But it's clear from what follows that her ambassadorial function is actually polysemic. On the one hand, she represents an essentialised American ideal of France: 'She sings and as soon as you hear her voice, an image of France in all its detail appears, even in the eyes of those who have never crossed the Atlantic. [...] When they listen to Édith Piaf, Americans in the Waldorf Astoria or Carnegie Hall hear France singing.'[8] On the other hand, her own sickly flesh is deemed to signify France's contemporary sickness in the context of regime change and the Algerian war: 'Just like France, especially last year, she was seriously ill. Both seemed condemned', though both are now in recovery. 'And the words used to describe her [Piaf] are the same as those used by the foreign press to speak of France in danger.'[9] Piaf, then, has become the complex outward face of France for its American other. But Spiraux turns that outward face inward again for his French readership to see: he uses Piaf to reveal France to itself.

America completed Piaf's discursive shift from 'voice of revolt' to 'voice of France', albeit a France refracted through an American lens. Neither she nor *la chanson française* could ever mean quite the same thing after America. Her private understanding of Frenchness seems little more than the sentimental remembrance of her Parisian heritage, coupled with an unreflexive patriotism reinforced by the image reflected back from America. But for her public at home, her Frenchness had more demagogic potential. In *Si Versailles m'était conté*, Sacha Guitry's historical film of 1954, the shot of her heroically mounting the gates of Versailles, raising a clenched fist and lustily singing a famous anthem of the Revolution, 'Ça ira' (It'll be fine), was an eloquent if pliable national symbol in itself. In September 1962, she sang 'Non, je ne regrette rien' from the first level of the Eiffel Tower to mark the release of the epic film about D-Day *The Longest Day*. This too underscores the national-historical symbolism she and the song had acquired, though again the precise meaning of that symbolism was unclear other than as a celebration of wartime heroism. By now, however, the song had taken on a much more specific resonance in the context of the Algerian war. Piaf herself had dedicated it to the Foreign Legion, which she had been associated with in the public imaginary since Asso. The Legion's parachutists involved in the anti-independence putsch in Algeria in 1961 made it their own by singing it when they admitted defeat, and it has remained the anthem of the Legion to this day.

Piaf's in-built ideological meanings are, then, a broadly rightist amalgam of patriotism, nationalism, militarism and Frenchness seen through American eyes. But this didn't prevent her being a vehicle for other meanings. An article from 1958 in the satirical *Le Canard enchaîné*, commenting appreciatively on the 100th performance of her Olympia show that year, describes her voice, despite a bad throat, as 'sensational' but 'dangerous'. She has reached a level of celebrity, the piece goes on, where she could sing anything and still be applauded, as with her rendition of the stirring but bizarre Bonapartist march 'Les Grognards' by the lyricist Pierre Delanoë (music by H. Giraud),[10] with stage lighting forming a tricolour cockade. For the anti-militaristic *Le Canard enchaîné*, this was akin to the famed patriotic renditions of 'La Marseillaise' by the opera singer Marthe Chenal some decades before: 'It's worrying!' ('C'est inquiétant!') Although the tone here is light and satirical, the point is serious: 'You'd have to see her [...] to understand the power this creature has, the magic of this sorceress. If she wanted to, she could make the people rise up and build barricades. No Pasionaria could ever trump her. She's a phenomenon.'[11] In the rest of this chapter, I want to examine how this ability to motivate caused her national meanings to be overlaid with a range of other significations.

After her first triumphant return from New York in March 1948, the emotional character of her reception by French audiences grew exponentially until her death. The reason surely lies in the steady maturation of the narrative that she always sang about her own life. And the death of Cerdan was a crucial intensifier here. Legend has it that her health went downhill after it, though she had begun to suffer from fatigue before his demise, probably due to overwork and over-indulgence. Those closest to her also agree that, had Cerdan lived, he would have likely gone the way of all her lovers. After all, the fierce passion for him that she records in her correspondence is reproduced for other lovers both before and after him.[12] Nonetheless, his abrupt disappearance in tragic circumstances, as well as heralding real physical decline, also assumes a profound symbolic importance, as we'll see.

With endless broken love affairs, easily read as evidence that nobody could replace him, coupled with car accidents, exhaustion and substance abuse, the self-referentiality of her work did become more apparent and was taken for granted. Her songs had long mediated public understanding of her life, but after Cerdan the line between the two became harder to draw. Although she herself had fed this identification from the start, by the 1950s it existed in the eye of the beholder quasi-independently, slipping beyond her control. Turning 40 in December 1955, she began to age before the public's eyes: the 'little scrap of a woman' was becoming smaller still, with thinning hair, arthritic fingers and a stoop. The media's fascination with her body now became even more prurient, since everyone saw for themselves the depredations of her failing health. But the emotional reactions of her public actually went beyond prurience, even if they were informed by it. From the time she started performing at the recently re-opened Olympia on 27 January 1955, at the urging of its owner, Bruno Coquatrix, audience response seemed to reach a peak of ecstasy. So many friends, reviewers and audience members have tried to describe and explain it that, even allowing for hyperbole, it has to be taken seriously.

A reviewer of her show at a packed Salle Pleyel in 1950 tries to capture the emotion of the event: 'With anyone else, you have time to think that she's singing well or badly. With Piaf, you undergo her. Her audience suffers physically.'[13] So too does a 1956 review in *Le Canard enchaîné*: 'She brings out the sentimentality lying deep in the most hardened of hearts, and even the most blasé types, who aren't usually taken in, suddenly feel an unaccustomed tingling, a tugging on their heartstrings.'[14] Among 'the most blasé types' who are won over is presumably this very reviewer, since the paper's tone is usually more flippant than this, as the jokey headline 'Say it with flowers' forewarns. But this is precisely the article's point. Piaf wins over *all* members of her audience, 'workers and aesthetes' (as the reviewer puts it), irrespective of cultural capital or class. She is the cement which bonds a divided nation.

Even Piaf's friends and team members, who had seen her sing countless times, underwent the same transformation according to Marc Bonel. 'At the premieres, all the big names in show business would break down in tears in her dressing room. She was a bit of a psychic, hypersensitive, a real psychologist. She would subjugate an audience after just three or four songs, even those who were against her.'[15] The actor Micheline Dax confesses that when she saw Piaf at the Olympia, after one song she'd shrunk into her seat, after the third she'd got out her handkerchief, and by the end she was stifling sobs.[16] Dax also reports on the reactions of others that night: 'She came on, her face was severe. Ovation. Nobody has ever had the ovations she had. It lasted almost ten minutes. Howls of joy. People were saying thanks. Thanks for being there. Thanks for coming back.'[17] The ecstasy was no different on the other side of the Atlantic: 'As soon as she comes on stage, she hypnotises her audience', wrote one astonished reviewer in Montreal in 1955.[18]

We're dealing here with a kind of collective hypnosis. In a perceptive 'psychoanalysis' at the time of her death, Jean Monteaux calls it a 'spell'.[19] As soon as she came on stage, the audience was bound together in a 'psychic equality', which involved no cognition: 'the mind wasn't affected but the sensibility, in all its most natural, primitive and human dimensions. When you listen to Édith Piaf, everything disappears: the intelligence and the critical faculties, intellectual sophistication and snobbery [...]. The spectator's analytical ability is neutralised.'[20] We should be cautious of the idea that intellection is entirely switched off, but Monteaux as participant observer does bear witness to the cathartic nature of a Piaf performance, in which the audience in the darkened auditorium has the opportunity to express and release its emotions unobserved. However, sounding not unlike an Enlightenment *philosophe*, he argues that Piaf didn't so much touch the 'heart' as 'the guts and the stomach' ('le ventre et l'estomac'), for human thoughts and feelings are only accessed physiologically.

What such first-hand accounts also point to is a sensual, even sexual dimension to Piaf's relationship with her audiences. As we glimpsed earlier, Piaf as body responds to and is responded to by the audience as body, both literally and figuratively. Hence the metaphors describing her affecting audiences in their guts. And as Barthes maintains, this mutual 'embodiment' is essentially erotic.[21] No one illustrates this more graphically than Guillaume Biro, businessman and music publisher, who saw her live for the first time at the Olympia in 1956:

The stage lights go out. A white spotlight moves right. One, two, three... A frail, dark shape steps forward. Only her face and her two hands pressed to her sides are visible. [...] Édith's voice soars through the microphone, fills the entire space, even the highest notes which galvanise me, seemingly coming no longer from her mouth but from her womb, as if their power was without limit. I'm fixed to my seat. [...] By the seventh or eighth [song], I feel as though I'm going into a trance. I can see less and less of the stage, as I feel as though the singer is entering me, guided by the nuances of her voice which feel like a delicious rape I'm helpless to resist, to the point of getting a spontaneous erection. [...] I'm like an animal that's totally possessed and as the voice reaches unimaginable heights which set my insides on fire, an unimaginable pleasure burns into my temples and my heart is beating to bursting point. I literally explode in an orgasm like I've never experienced before, which leaves me prostrate in my seat.[22]

In so carnal a response to her singing, social norms of hetero-sexuality and gender are reversed, as Piaf subjugates then violates her willingly passive male victim. Other forms of regendering have also been identified at Piaf performances. After seeing her at the Olympia in spring 1958, Monique Lange reflects on the way she subjugated men: 'men are mad about Piaf and that's understandable. Yet they are the only ones she fools.' She strokes them as one would a horse, argues Lange; but ultimately, although 'the man is a cruel god', he is an entirely 'replaceable' one.[23] In such descriptions, it isn't primarily the characters or themes that live audiences are moved by but Piaf herself as a woman, a gendered, embodied voice. And in a sense, her audiences are gendered and embodied with her, though this needs some untangling.

Biographers agree that her fan base was largely female, though the intensity of Biro's reaction shows she could cross boundaries of gender as well as class. The 1956 review in *Le Canard enchaîné*, discussed earlier, hints at a further complexity in this regard when it distinguishes between two imagined Piafs. Off stage, the anonymous reviewer writes, her smallness and ordinariness make her come across as 'a good [female] friend [*bonne copine*], an ally who knows about life, you would definitely tell her your troubles because she's made of solid stuff and keeps her nerve.' On stage, however, 'the little street-corner flower girl, awesomely magnified, suddenly becomes the voice of all human misery'.[24] A subtle gendering of her fans is just visible in the French phrase 'bonne copine' (a good *female* friend): an implication that the off-stage Piaf is a sisterly companion to other women because she has experienced and understands their troubles. But, as on-stage awesome myth, she turns those troubles into the dark materials of a universal human condition beyond gender. Of the song 'Bravo pour le clown' (Contet-Louiguy, 1953),[25] for example, the same reviewer writes, 'everyone sees themselves as they really are, a bit of a poor clown, alas, and keeps their tears to themselves'.[26] The mythical Piaf teaches us all, men and women, to recognise and assume the pathos we have in common. Yet the reviewer has said earlier that for everyone in the auditorium, 'restraint no longer applies. Workers and aesthetes, all huddled in their seats in the darkened hall, together feel like romantic young girls at heart'.[27] Here, the audience's shared condition is actually *re*gendered: the emotions spectators are feeling, supposedly irrespective of gender and class, are in fact identified as gender-specific: feminine and foolishly romantic. This hints at a Damascene conversion she is perceived to make male spectators—like Biro and those most 'hardened' and 'blasé' of hearts mentioned earlier—undergo when they come to realise she is their 'bonne copine' too.

If we look closely, then, her effect on the public appears plural and complex. She makes audiences feel when they would rather be blasé about feeling. She unites them across social and cultural differences. And for men she brings out their feminine side. Illustrating Morin's argument that the star always elicits identification and projection in the same instant, she makes spectators identify with her as one of them but also helps them project their own pain and anxiety onto her magnified self,[28] understand themselves better and transcend self-pity. For all this to be achieved, a lot of emotional electricity must be passing between stage and hall. Audiences are responding to her visible frailty as they always have, but now as an augury of her mortality. The imbrication of life and song in the imagined Piaf has become so close by now that the two are indistinguishable, her human frame possessed by her successive public selves.

Yet for all that, this intense emotional response, in all its complexity, is still the result of concerted self-performance. Jean Noli witnessed her interminable rehearsals at home towards the end of her life. As she worked on even the tiniest movement—of neck, hands, eyes, feet—and on every lighting effect, she knew precisely the effect she was looking for: 'If they don't all blub at that bit, they've got hearts of stone.'[29] In the audience at the 1958 Olympia show, Lange writes: 'She knows her job like nobody else. Her act gets better and better because she is always progressing. You can tell she is working.'[30] We may take for granted that this is performance, that she is coolly manipulating our emotions by performing herself. But we never tire of it because she's constantly refreshing it. Ever the show-woman even when she was dying, she would exaggerate her frailty by shuffling theatrically on stage. Was this cynical, exploitative? Not entirely. As we know, she has learnt to live up to the images the world reflects back at her, but these images aren't false: they are reflections of her life as she has lived it and then edited it. The imagined Piaf operates by perpetual motion. Her apparently dishonest stage business is authenticated by the fact that she really is ill and by her public's knowledge that she is. Self-performance thus becomes not trickery but memoir. It's this no doubt that the audience responds to in diverse ways: identification-projection, weeping or orgasm.

Emotional responses like these are so immediate and intense because Piaf's performances, though concerted, contain no irony. The performance reaches out for instant identification, not Brechtian distance or any other form of second-order complexity. Despite, or alongside, the art discourse we encountered earlier, this is, in one sense at least, full-on 'lowbrow' emotion, though not 'lowbrow' in the sense of artless, shallow and simplistic—the kind of dominated culture Bourdieu sees as locking the lower classes in the particularisms society imposes on them. Deniot criticises those who elide emotion from the realm of art, who reduce art to either the exploration of form or (Bourdieu again) the mastery of a code.[31] With Piaf, on the other hand, we confront popular sentiment at its most intense, participative and universal, yet artfully contrived by a mature live performer in full possession of her art. Once again, the intensity has a lot to do with the economy of that performance: the voice, of course, her precise diction, which makes every word count, the spare deployment of gesture, her being alone on stage with band and backing singers hidden behind the stage curtain. And the simple black dress: adorned only with a crucifix to symbolise demure innocence, but black to speak of sex, sin and mourning.[32] With little else on stage to distract them, spectators have to use their imaginations to project themselves into the performed song, as if they were reading a novel.

In the later Piaf's hands, then, *la chanson française*, much like French New Wave cinema in roughly the same period, is proving socially mobile: it's on the way to achieving not exactly high-cultural but 'high-popular' status. Chanson performance as she practises it is becoming a new middlebrow art, alongside the poetic self-expression of the singer-songwriter.[33] There is still, though, an essential difference between the two. By the early 1960s, the work of Brel, Brassens, Ferré and a little later Barbara was achieving middlebrow legitimacy as poetry; Piaf was achieving it as tragedy.

By 1950, Piaf was being labelled the 'tragedian of chanson', as Damia had previously been. Once again, this was to do with her narrated life as much as with her songs, for the key ingredients of the label were the death of Cerdan and the song she had written shortly before it, which took on new emotional resonances after it. In the last verse of 'Hymn to Love', there's a prophecy that if death should steal her lover away, she would die too and they would live together in the eternity of their blue heaven.[34] Trite though the lyric is (triter still in the adaptation into American English), Cerdan's death draped Piaf in a mantle of national tragedy which she would wear for the rest of her life. Burke is right in noting that Cerdan's passing shaped Piaf's creative imagination.[35] But, just as importantly, it shaped her relations with the French public. As celebrity lovers,[36] the singing star and the world boxing champion made the ideal media couple, embodying French greatness in sport and chanson but with a titillating frisson of dangerous liaison. Their archetypal heterosexuality was cinematic, with shades of *Tarzan* or *King Kong*: the gentle giant and the tiny doll helpless in his mighty arms, yet as powerful as him in her own way.

His death united Piaf and the French public in national mourning, though in the longer term it also intensified her odour of sin. As in all tragedy, divine retribution was brought down upon her: for desecration of the sacred laws of marriage and codes of feminine decorum and beauty; and also for hubris, since she had summoned him back to New York earlier than he was due, forcing him to fly rather than travel by sea. His demise and her decline thus turned her into a tragic heroine, the people's Phèdre. More than anyone, Deniot maintains, Piaf points up the ancient anthropological origins of the stage: her audience participates as witness to an immolation.[37] Still, the tragedy she embodies is necessarily popular tragedy, because its flawed protagonists, real or imagined, are of the people, not the aristocracy. The more she suffered, the more the media drew analogies with popular icons, from Mary Magdalene to Joan of Arc.

Indeed, there's a Christian subtext in her suffering, an implication that, like Christ, she had to endure the human condition in all its pain in order to bring her public the balm of identification and projection. She suffers in our stead, dying that we might live. Of a concert at the Salle Pleyel in February 1944, one critic wrote, 'when her voice falls silent, with her head on one side and motionless she looks like a crucified Christ'.[38] Faith and spirituality were present in the Piaf narrative from the first, as we saw with her account of childhood blindness cured by the prayers of prostitutes at the shrine of Saint Thérèse of Lisieux.[39] She also had an affection for Bernadette of Lourdes and made pilgrimages to both places. She prayed regularly. Later in life, with Bourgeat's guidance, she became a Rosicrucian and developed an interest in Teilhard de Chardin. Her later stage costume included that iconic crucifix. Sometimes, her simple faith became confused with astrology and superstition. She was quick to detect signs and omens in everyday coincidences. After Cerdan died, she spent several years trying to communicate with him in the spirit world. In *Ma vie*, she is at pains to confirm the existence of an afterlife and even offers us proof, though this turns out to be that Marcel told her through a medium to meet his wife, which she subsequently did.[40]

True to form, her lyricists and composers picked up on these spiritual associations, just as she herself worked the seam in autobiographies and interviews. From 'Madeleine qui avait du cœur' (1936) and 'Les Trois Cloches' (1945) to Vaucaire and Dumont's 'Mon Dieu' (1961),[41] Christianity was a constant in her repertoire, matched by a sonic paraphernalia of church bells, angelic choirs and the occasional burst of an organ. Religiosity is also present in her voice, with its notes of gravity and supplication, 'that voice which seems to come from the beyond' ('cette voix qui semble venir de l'au-delà').[42] Jean-François Nicot's life in 'Les Trois Cloches' is so stunningly uneventful that it would scarcely justify being celebrated in song were it not for Piaf's soaring, metallic voice, which, combining the vulgarity of the street with the divine tragedy of the human condition, transcends the banality and points us didactically towards heaven. At its most literal, 'Mon Dieu' is about a woman's desperation to hold on to an errant lover. But the voice—starting low down in her register and steadily climbing as she pleads with God to let her keep him a little longer—makes the prosaic if not blasphemous demand as moving as Christ's 'my God, why hast thou forsaken me?'

The religious dimension in Piaf's grand narrative is equally present in audience responses. Concert-goers often spoke of 'communion' between her and her audience and between audience members themselves. Some clearly felt they had experienced a form of transcendence when they saw her perform: Vassal describes her as 'taking her friends and her public with her on a quest for the absolute that ultimately led to God'.[43] Jean-François Noël's 1950 review bears the almost existentialist headline 'Édith Piaf utters before God the very cry of the earth'. And he goes on: 'Édith Piaf represents the fall of the angel at its basest and its greatest. [...] Her story is simple: it starts with love and ends with death.'[44] At the same time, as Noël hints, her perceived spiritual meanings actually hinge on a dialectic between the sacred and the profane, saint and sinner. Again like Christ, she is deemed to know and understand our lowest instincts for having experienced them, but through her transcendent voice, she raises us up and gives us hope of redemption. Her greatest power, writes Vassal, was the power of transfiguration.[45]

This brings us to a feature of the imagined Piaf we haven't touched on. Despite all these elements of iconicity, tragedy and spirituality, her public image in the 1950s was actually more mixed than this might suggest. National beatification in her lifetime didn't obliterate the negative, deterministic readings in evidence during the Occupation. According to Vassal, Piaf in part brought this on herself, as many stars would do subsequently, by courting the most popular newspapers and magazines, not least Vassal's own, *France-Dimanche*. He vindicates his and Noli's pursuit of Piaf in the late 1950s by claiming he was merely her accomplice in wooing the media. He insists that even Piaf's own motive for doing so was honourable: to get through to Mr and Mrs Average, who valued emotion above anything.[46] But her plan did have a downside. By 1960, her addictions were sufficiently well known for her to be briefly cited in a warning about drug abuse, particularly the new phenomenon of 'happy pills'.[47] As we saw earlier, the theme of ugliness resurfaced in the media's fascination with her physical decay, as paparazzi grew desperate for photos of her on her sick bed or better still her death bed. Her sexual activities, especially with married men, were also widely covered and deplored.

Once more, the affair with Cerdan was the catalyst here. When the couple flew back to Orly on the same plane in December 1948, Piaf used a different exit and, caught out by a journalist, was reportedly abusive and had someone smash the camera. 'The lady once called it "la vie en rose"!' *L'Aurore* loftily commented. 'A good shower wouldn't do her any harm...'[48] A string of other scandals would accompany her to her death. At the age of 46 but looking much older, she married the 26-year-old Théo Sarapo, the latest of her protégés. The man-eater and marriage-wrecker now became the cradle-snatcher, with some in the media presenting their relationship as abhorrent or embarrassing. She was becoming everything we understand today by the celebrity, beneficiary and victim of Morin's starification.

As French national television developed in the 1950s, she started appearing in variety shows like *Le Théâtre XYZ* in 1951 and *La Joie de vivre*, a series recorded live at the Alhambra and given over to the life of an invited celebrity, in which she would appear several times in the 1950s as well as being the star guest herself in April 1954. Televised entertainments like this projected yet another Piaf: fun-loving, giggly, at ease with herself and the public. In 1951, she played the lead alongside Eddie Constantine in a light-hearted musical written for her by the boulevard playwright Marcel Achard, *La P'tite Lili*, which had a successful run at the ABC, despite being interrupted soon after opening by one of her health scares. She also appeared in more films, including *Si Versailles m'était conté*, *Boum sur Paris* with Jacques Pills, and Jean Renoir's *French Cancan*, all three released in 1954.

With Piaf's regular contracts in America, the French media also began to relish her showbiz associations: her appearances on the *Ed Sullivan Show* and the Hollywood personalities or top politicians queuing up to see her perform. Her close friendship with Marlene Dietrich thrilled French gossip columnists. Dietrich was a witness at Piaf's marriage in 1952 in New York to Pills and was pictured attending to Piaf's footwear like a dutiful bridesmaid. Both of Piaf's weddings in fact attracted huge media attention: what she wore, how she felt, how the bridegroom comported himself. While her marriage to Sarapo would offend the guardians of propriety, her first, to Pills, was presented in the complicitous style of today's celebrity magazines: 'Édith Piaf and Jacques Pills fly off to seventh heaven', ran one headline as the couple flew out to New York.[49] Text and image would present the newlyweds in domestic situations, as mature adults working or relaxing together, with a discreetly starry lifestyle and a happy, companionable marriage. In these ways, Piaf was a forerunner of global celebrity culture, which in those days rarely included Europeans. In her wake would follow Bardot, Sophia Loren, the Beatles, Aznavour, Julio Iglesias and more.

Yet her actual work in the 1950s wasn't unequivocally admired. Although 1951 and 1952 saw her awarded two prestigious prizes, for 'Le Chevalier de Paris' (The Knight of Paris, Vannier and Philippe-Gérard, 1950)[50] and for 'Padam' respectively, her revival with Pills of Cocteau's *Le Bel Indifférent* in April 1953 at the esteemed Théâtre Marigny, associated with the prestigious Renaud-Barrault company, was judged mawkish and disappointing. *Le Monde* suggested gently that she was becoming bourgeois.[51] It's impossible to gauge how far any coolness towards her was an aesthetic or a moral judgment. By 1953, she was addicted to cortisone and morphine, as well as taking sleeping pills, and went into rehab for the first time. Alcoholism was also a problem, causing her that same year to be heckled at the Casino de Royat for being drunk on stage, an incident she recalls with mortification in *Ma vie*.[52] Nor was everything entirely rosy in the United States. While she was still a regular at the Versailles, Barrier negotiated a booking in Las Vegas in 1955. When the promoters met her, they changed their minds, honouring the contract but only on the condition she didn't perform.[53]

So how far did this negative side of her reputation and the episodic decline in the quality of her work affect the art discourse which had accumulated round the nation's favourite tragedian? While in Piaf's hands *la chanson française* was becoming a new middlebrow and her work continued to be cast as popular tragedy, in her later years she increasingly drifted into melodrama, or what we might think of today as soap opera. It was Piaf herself, as she became more conscious of her mortality, who nudged public perceptions in that direction by taking the conflation of singing and being to the point of caricature. The more the media represented her as morally decadent, the harder she tried not so much to counter that image but to re-work it epically, polishing up the Piaf she would leave behind. This was an audible subtext in her later interviews, especially a series of three televised encounters with Pierre Desgraupes from 1959 to 1962.

Her answers to Desgraupes's po-faced questioning are noticeably unhesitating, as if well rehearsed, which in a sense they are because she has spent a lifetime concocting them. This is no forensic interrogation exposing a concealed Piaf: it's a choreographed *pas de deux* and Piaf's self-conscious responses are those of the consummate pro. She lives her songs and exists only to sing. She gives of herself unstintingly to her beloved audience. She ceases to belong to herself when she sings because she enters an alternative state of consciousness. Life for her is a battle that she always wins. She sees things through, no matter the cost to herself. Without love we are nothing—a line from 'La Goualante du pauvre Jean' (The sad song of poor John, Rouzaud-Monnot, 1954).[54] She has a mysterious sixth sense when it comes to recognising talent where others fail to see it. And, most plangent of all, she has no regrets.[55] This expert self-exposure is just as apparent in her two autobiographies. And her compliant songwriters plough the same furrow with equal nous, culminating triumphantly in 'Non, je ne regrette rien', whose lyric by Vaucaire reflects the recent interviews.

In the interviews as in the song, tragedy tips into melodrama through an excess of knowingness. The press are complicit, as with her divorce from Pills in 1956 after four years, portrayed as a perfect love condemned only by her inexorable misfortune. The Piaf factory—the media, friends like Cocteau with a gift for the lyrical soundbite, her writers, and most of all herself—goes into overdrive, turning her life into something between Racine and *EastEnders*. This is the *chanson réaliste* of the first half of the twentieth century passed through the star system of the second. Édith Piaf as popular diva.

The term 'diva' in English, from the Italian for 'opera singer' and 'goddess', is used today indiscriminately to denote any female star deemed 'raunchy' or 'feisty', those two key lexical components of diva discourse. But it carries more specific, less casual connotations when applied to earlier generations of women. Although much younger than Piaf, Brigitte Bardot is a useful comparison since the two are France's best-known female stars of the twentieth century. They met after one of Piaf's Olympia concerts and by all accounts got on well.[56] Certainly, there are similarities between them, alongside the obvious differences. Both were iconic French women of the 1950s and have remained so ever since. Both liberated themselves from social prescriptions of female sexuality and, by doing so, attracted moral indignation tinged with repressed envy. The gender identity of each is also characterised, as Diana Holmes argues of Bardot, by a central contradiction: as emancipatory figures for women, whose 'performance of femininity implicitly claimed the right to a sexual and social independence hitherto identified as masculine' and yet who encouraged an essentially conservative view by 'imply[ing] in the end that "women's liberation boiled down to (hetero)sexual promiscuity"'.[57] But the two are most notably different from each other by virtue of the commodification of their bodies. Bardot's body is 'delectably consumable' and made for pleasure, primarily her own.[58] Piaf's, modestly clothed in black from the outset, is made for tragedy: it signifies pain and mourning.

Nor does Bardot's persona have self-destruction at its core. In this respect, more apt comparisons can be found in two other twentieth-century popular divas: Billie Holiday, born the same year as Piaf, and Judy Garland, slightly younger. Piaf is often bracketed with both, and the three together, even today, form a global pantheon of tragic women who followed a pattern: immensely talented, demanding, fearsome and hard to live with, but flawed, needy, vulnerable and ultimately destroyed—popular reconfigurations of the classical tragic heroine. But unlike Garland or Holiday, who functioned within an Anglophone entertainment culture, Piaf is working with—and on—the very different cultural parameters of *la chanson française*. She in fact occupies an emerging discursive space in which popular culture aspires to the classical. In her, we intuit that the tragic destiny of the aristocratic heroes and heroines of classical or neo-classical drama, a destiny which destroys but elevates them, may equally destroy and elevate the humble, who are just as capable, in their own fashion, of rising to the challenges of the human condition at its most awesome. She proposes a democracy of suffering.

At the height of her powers, and in the intensity of the emotions she performs, the imagined Piaf in fact places in the public domain a particular conception of popular art: an art that elicits direct, emotional identification and projection. As Deniot puts it, a song is 'popular' when the suffering of its creator meets the suffering of others.[59] Prefiguring the role of celebrities and soaps today, the diva as Piaf embodies it has a dual function. It structures, dramatises and transfigures ordinary, anonymous experience. And in so doing, it relieves us of the responsibility of living: by legitimating the popular ideology of destiny, persuading us of the irresistible power of fate. But the problem for Piaf was that this particular conception of the popular led straight back to the *chanson réaliste*. When Bardot and Piaf briefly crossed paths at the Olympia, they stood together at a crossroads. Bardot, nearly 20 years younger, was preparing the way for today's sexualised representations of the mass-cultural diva; Piaf, whether she meant to or not, was irrevocably looking backwards to the *chanson réaliste*, her nemesis. Having voluntarily fashioned herself in that mode in the 1930s, she had by now found that there was no going back.

It's perfectly true that she poeticised the realist song and turned it into an intense, moving vehicle which transcended the kind of weepy lament that had been characterised in the mid-1930s as 'the most inane form of the romantic' ('la forme la plus niaise du romanesque').[60] And as we saw earlier, she did try to avoid being labelled in this way from 1943, claiming to want to sing about happy things. The occasional journalist would even see her point, like Émile Vuillermoz in 1953: 'A realist, Édith Piaf? What a mistake!' ('Réaliste, Édith Piaf? Quelle erreur!'). Yes, he goes on, she does assume the rasping voice of a market greengrocer and rummage in the bins of humanity. But what she fishes out of them are 'dreams and more dreams [...] This is all pure romanticism, barely disguised.'[61] However, her realism also existed in the media's infatuation with marketable labels and in their laziness about abandoning them, however empty they might be. 'Our top realist singer' ('Notre première chanteuse réaliste'), exclaimed *France-Soir* in 1948,[62] even though her American experience had already redefined her. And in the same paper seven years later, after her first Olympia appearance: 'Édith Piaf, the grand lady of French chanson, is indisputably our top realist singer.'[63] And there was much the same reluctance to ditch realism among the French public, it would seem. Canetti once observed, 'the public preferred her realist repertoire which, it's true, was better suited to her voice and her weakly little figure'.[64] Again, we encounter the view that realism becomes her: her staged body and the grain of her voice lend themselves to it. And whatever she would sing subsequently, her voice would always contain within it, for anyone old enough to remember, that pre-war cultural memory. 'Just three notes and she once more becomes the thing she always wanted to escape from: the sad little bird who was born in the street.'[65]

Be that as it may, realism was still up to a point a choice. She is drawn irresistibly back to it, however much she may want to reject or transform it. Reflecting on her show in 1948 at the ABC, a reviewer argues that the 'persistent vogue for Édith Piaf' is the result of her thinking a good deal about her act: 'Her intelligence lies in her having knowingly remained what she was when she started out: a poor little kid. To those gut reactions, those cries of thwarted hope, that revolt of the scorned and unfortunate, she has been able, by labour and talent, to give a nuance, a resonance which generated emotion.'[66] She certainly continued to sing realist songs old and new late into her career and her songwriters continued to collude with her in this vein: 'Marie la Française' (Marie the French girl, Larue and Philippe-Gérard, 1956),[67] for example, with its familiar tale of drunken sailors and a prostitute, this time a French expat living in Sydney but nostalgic for home, who dies there while her old mother back in working-class Paris believes she is happily married somewhere 'in the Americas'.[68] Then of course there was Renoir's film *French Cancan* (1954), which cast her as Eugénie Buffet, precursor of the *chanson réaliste*. And just as importantly, from the death of Cerdan and the conversion of 'Hymne à l'amour' into autobiography, Piaf herself more resolutely ploughed the furrow of identification with her tragic songs, to the point of writing her life story with Noli through the lens of the *chanson réaliste*. So however much she may balk at being labelled realist, the form pursues her as a shadow and a temptation. And the cultural analogies that later position her alongside Garland and Holiday, not to mention Mary Magdalene, only reinforce this destiny. The 1940s were the high point of Piaf's re-invention of realism as a more universal tragic form.[69] Little wonder, then, that she should find it hard to let go of it entirely throughout the 1950s, especially as fans at concerts wanted to hear old favourites and she would usually oblige.

During that period, the notion that *la chanson française* was a distinctive national artefact had developed around her and Piaf was working to perpetuate it by coaching a new generation of singers. The once child-like novice had become the experienced ancestor. The programme for her first Olympia show in January 1955 spelt this out: 'She has transformed chanson, and numerous artists owe her what is best about them.'[70] Those who had made their names by working with her as writers, composers or singers—Asso, Monnot, Contet, Émer, Montand, Constantine, Aznavour, Gilbert Bécaud—were now established or rising stars in the chanson firmament. But her desire to mould the future was also a resistance to change. Already, with her revival of *Le Bel Indifférent* at the Marigny with Pills, there was a sense that she was repeating herself. And she too recognised the fact that, with chanson changing round her, her job was to stay true to her invented self via what she called 'the tradition of the character'. Of course there has to be change, she once commented: 'But I always keep to a sort of tradition. I want to remain what I am and develop within the character I have created. I don't want to change to a different one.'[71]

Her long absences in the Americas—an uninterrupted 14 months from March 1955 to May 1956 followed by another stay from September 1956 to August 1957—distanced her from new musical developments at home. While she was away, the death in January 1956 of Mistinguett, a defining presence since 1895, symbolised the changes afoot, partly brought about by the successes on stage or celluloid of Piaf's own protégés, most notably Montand, Aznavour, the Compagnons and Constantine in his film roles as Lemmy Caution.[72] The dynamic styling of Bécaud at his live shows was causing a prophetic frenzy among the young. The emergence of the singer-songwriter and the associated career of Gréco as a Left Bank Piaf[73] heralded a new, more poetic or intellectual middlebrow that made Piaf's undiluted emotionalism seem like melodrama. More exotic and commercial women singers like Dalida (her massive hit 'Bambino' came out in 1956) and Gloria Lasso were also breaking through. And the pre-pop ways of doing things that she and her team still followed were being swept away by professionalisation and industrialisation. The slow dislocation of that team, with Chauvigny's illness, Monnot's death and Piaf's own deterioration, poignantly symbolised the fact that the seemingly stable, intimately Franco-French world of chanson was finite.

Commenting on her show in Tours in November 1957, a lone journalist dared to wonder whether Piaf's continuing loyalty to 'the romanticism of the streets, ports and stations of which Carco and Mac Orlan celebrated the miseries and the joys' is really likely to appeal to today's youth as much as yesterday's.[74] This turned out to be an especially pertinent question.

PART III

AFTERLIVES

CHAPTER 7

Losing Piaf

'ONE FINE EVENING she'll leave us, and the *chanson française* will have lost its *raison d'être*', a journalist mournfully predicted a decade before her death on 10 October 1963.[1] We need to think about the meanings of that death, for French chanson and more widely. In a sense, she quit the scene at the best possible moment. France's abrupt experience of decolonisation, migration, consumerism and the baby boom marked the end of a conception of chanson that had been evolving since Bruant and had reached its apogee in the 1950s, just before the advent of pop and rock. As we've seen, this was the golden age of both the singer-poet and the *interprète*. Most of them—Barbara, Brassens, Brel, Ferré, Gréco, Montand and the posthumous Piaf—would survive the pop revolution that ushered in the Beatles, Dylan, Hardy, Sylvie Vartan, Sheila and Hallyday. But we have to ask whether Piaf, older than Brel and Barbara by almost a generation and imprisoned in the realist tradition, would have done so had she lived.

Her last years weren't happy ones. A full decade before she died, a doctor had privately described her as a 'living corpse'.[2] Her health continued to deteriorate, making the years 1958 to 1960 peculiarly harrowing. Three car accidents in less than a year weakened her further. She was taken ill on stage several times and was in and out of operating theatres with serious conditions. During her gruelling French tour in late 1959, dubbed her 'suicide tour' in the press, she had to leave the stage during a concert in Maubeuge and collapsed straight after the last show of the tour in Dreux. In the first of her televised interviews with Pierre Desgraupes, recorded just two days before, her speech was slurred, she wrung her hands constantly and she looked vulnerable.[3] Often, she wasn't expected to survive, and when she did the media called it a miracle. Her concerts were by now major events, with crowds drawn there to celebrate her survival but also, secretly, to witness her dying—the ultimate authenticity. She knew this perfectly well, acknowledging that if a show didn't sell out, she only had to fall ill on stage and the punters would come running.[4] If she really did love her public as individuals as she often claimed, she had no illusions about it as a crowd. For Danielle Bonel, Piaf's attitude to fans was encapsulated by her friend Pierre Brasseur: 'Love the parts we play or the songs we sing, but don't concern yourself with the people who play the parts or sing the songs.'[5] And yet Piaf positively encouraged audiences to concern themselves with the person behind the songs, occasionally with disturbing consequences when fans obsessively projected their difficult lives on to her. A young woman working at Les Halles market wrote in January 1961 pleading with her to help her become a realist singer, calling her 'dear darling mummy' ('Chère Maman chérie'), and calling herself Édith Marcelle Piaf.[6]

Despite her physical decline, Piaf did look to the future and recognise the changing times. She acquired a younger entourage, among them the musician and composer Francis Lai, the singer-songwriter from Quebec Claude Léveillée, the future film-maker Claude Berri, her new arranger Noël Commaret, and the aspiring singer Claude Figus. She had started working with new lyricists, too, like Michel Rivgauche, René Rouzaud and Jacques Plante, and with the composer Charles Dumont. For some years, Piaf had also been including more upbeat numbers in her set, like 'La Goualante du pauvre Jean', a big hit in the USA, 'Milord', and even a French version of a mildly rock'n'roll song by the famous writing duo Jerry Leiber and Mike Stoller, 'Black Denim Trousers and Motorcycle Boots', recorded by the Cheers in 1955, which became 'L'Homme à la moto'.[7] It's also in this context of attempted renewal that we can better understand a new signature song that would become her most iconic.

In the standard biography, the three dark years from 1958 to 1960 came to an end when, with her health problems seemingly in remission, she made a surprise comeback at the end of December 1960 with a triumphant return to the Olympia that lasted from the premiere on the 29th to the following April. Piaf had minutely prepared for it, personally managing lighting, sound, curtain falls and the position of each musician.[8] The renaissance was assisted, symbolised and mythified by 'Non, je ne regrette rien' ('No Regrets' in English), brought to her by Michel Vaucaire and Charles Dumont the previous October.[9] It's difficult now to recapture what it signified when she first performed it, so imbricated is it with what the world knows about her second marriage, her death and her afterlives. It's usually assumed to be her swansong, like Sinatra's 'My Way'. In both, the narrative voice is imagined to be that of the singer reflecting with melancholy, courage and defiance on a life and career that are practically over.[10] Age has apparently given the singer the serenity and wisdom to weigh up their life. Yet although both singer-protagonists are able to assess their strengths and weaknesses with equal realism, Sinatra's standpoint is in the end quite different from Piaf's. His assessment of his life is entirely retrospective. He has nothing left to do but be proud of having done things his way, without futile regrets. Two-thirds of the Piaf song proceed along similar lines: lyric, melody and vocal are freighted with the audience's memory of the singer's experiences and those of every doomed street girl she has ever sung about. But the song ends with a *coup de théâtre*. For she has found a new lover and it's this, not clinical self-assessment in eternity's antechamber, which explains why she has no regrets about her past. This unexpected vision of a glistening highway to the future provides a marketable climax, though it's something of a let-down for anyone who assumes the song is a stagey valediction.

Olympia audiences nonetheless loved it and the whole set. The official premiere, on 2 January 1961, was an unmissable ceremonial attended by Arletty, Louis Armstrong, Lucienne Boyer, Brassens, Claude Chabrol, Dalida, Alain Delon, Duke Ellington, Paul Newman, Romy Schneider, Roger Vadim and other celebrities. No doubt because everyone had accepted that she was finished and because she still looked frail, the applause and the chanting of her name when she first appeared would go on for ten minutes before she could start, coupled with cries of familiarity and encouragement: 'Édith we love you', 'you're back!', 'Bravo, Édith', 'Hi, darling'.[11] Noli, watching from the wings, witnessed an auditorium transported by collective hysteria.[12] The media went into overdrive, the religious imagery habitually wheeled out to describe her performances now expanded to accommodate resurrection and redemption: 'From one song to the next—or rather, from one litany to the next, because there really was something religious in this perpetual "Hymn to Love"—the audience's ardour intensified. [...] That evening, Piaf tasted the delights of beatification. This was Édith raised from the dead, miraculously saved, beseeched and glorified by the faithful. Édith as Mary Magdalene'.[13]

But the adulation Édith received didn't continue unalloyed after the Olympia triumph. Her health failed again in 1961 and it was noted that her performances, when she could get through them, weren't always up to par. Her voice would falter sometimes or she would forget the words. Her very last appearance at the Olympia in September 1962 received ecstatic applause from the crowd, which included Montand and Simone Signoret, Sacha Distel, Gainsbourg, and a weeping Johnny Hallyday seated in the front row. But her new songs, her voice and her delivery were criticised. Catherine Charbon's witty but merciless review for the *Tribune de Genève* was especially telling.

Having decided to see her live for the first time on the recommendation of friends, Charbon was a double outsider, observing Piaf from Switzerland but also from a different generation. She was expecting a 'magical show', 'a pagan mass'. But she ended up wondering what all the fuss was about. Piaf was out of tune and her 11 new songs, still in the realist style in Charbon's judgment, left her cold: 'I've got nothing against ladies of the night, but listening to them vent their distress for half an hour is a bit too accusatory and exhausting, especially when they wander about in cathedrals demanding that God immediately give them back their boyfriend.'[14] Charbon's irony bears witness to a whole change of culture. Hers is a new mindset that just can't relate to what Piaf means. And the very fact that friends have explained to her that 'this is what Piaf is' suggests that even they are now at a remove from her realism. Piaf was ceasing to signify culturally in the way she had always done. The meaning that remained was a packaged nostalgia, not the organic, forward-facing nostalgia she had represented during the Occupation. Some liked the package, others didn't; she was no longer the universal paradigm of an age and a nation.

Nor was Charbon alone in criticising Piaf's material. Despite producing some exceptional new compositions like 'Non, je ne regrette rien', her latest lyricists were generally manufacturing off-the-peg Piaf. 'Le Petit Brouillard' (A bit of fog, Plante-Lai, 1962)[15] harks back to the crime scenario of 'Paris-Méditerranée'; 'Emporte-moi' (Take me away, Plante-Lai,

1962)[16] is reminiscent in subject matter of both 'L'Accordéoniste' and 'Elle fréquentait la rue Pigalle'; several repeat the festive-tragic structure of 'La Foule'. Or the songs were driven, as rising young singer Claude Nougaro put it, by 'a sort of obsession with one kind of love' ('une sorte de monomanie d'un certain amour').[17] Piaf too was at fault here, as with her lyric for 'Roulez tambours' (Roll, drums, roll, Piaf-Lai, 1962).[18] References to Pearl Harbor and Hiroshima briefly hint at some vague engagement with reality, but she soon drifts off into less explicable evocations of Napoleon and the battle of Jericho. The song's bewildering message seems to be that the thunder of drums should be heard for love, not war. Similarly, 'Le Droit d'aimer' (The right to love, Nyel-Lai, 1962)[19] has her defiantly giving notice that, whatever price she has to pay—there are vague allusions to the 'laws' of 'men' and even crucifixion—nothing and nobody will stop her being in love, though a listener today might be baffled why anyone would actually want to, since only the context of her second marriage, referred to in the song, really explains it.[20]

On 9 October 1962, a year and a day before her death, she married the hairdresser and aspiring singer Théo Sarapo, whom she had met the previous January and was now, inevitably, coaching to be a singer. He was 20 years her junior and towered above her, healthy, dark and good-looking. On the evening of the wedding, they appeared together at the Olympia, where she sang 'Le Droit d'aimer' and asked the audience outright if she had the right to love; they obediently answered yes.[21] After her years of physical decline, this latest whirlwind romance was another instance of life imitating art, for their relationship was carefully constructed to reflect the narrative of rebirth in 'Non, je ne regrette rien'. As another song written for her by Émer, 'À quoi ça sert l'amour?' (What's love for?, 1963),[22] which she performed as a duo with Sarapo at the Olympia, insisted: he was her 'first' and last love, though the reality was rather different.

For traditionalists in 1962, a woman marrying a man young enough to be her son was morally shocking and plain embarrassing. Fans and celebrity-watchers turned out in their thousands to see the newlyweds, who appeared on the balcony of the city hall like royalty.[23] Piaf had defiantly made a public occasion of the event, and this, added to her duetting with him on 'À quoi ça sert l'amour?' that evening, was her mistake. 'The strangest marriage of the century', headlined *Paris Jour*.[24]

Another source crudely asked: 'How can a little old woman, skinny and pitiful with a ravaged face and round shoulders, get a good-looking bloke of 26, who's full of life?'[25] For the acerbic Charbon, the duet with Sarapo was indecent: 'you feel like having a quiet word with her about privacy in the boudoir and the opacity of drawn curtains'.[26] The old collaborationist distaste for Piaf also resurfaced. François Brigneau—past member of the Vichy militia and future founding member with Jean-Marie Le Pen of the National Front—had a similar reaction to the marriage, but his comments in *L'Aurore* were all the more caustic given their appearance of generosity. Piaf is a great star, Brigneau began encouragingly, and older women have long taken younger lovers. But like Charbon he takes exception to her indiscretion. Her fault in his eyes would seem to be not her appetite for vigorous young men but her infringement of a code: women should recognise that such affairs are an embarrassment and keep them quiet. Artists of course need audiences, he concludes; but it's unfortunate that an artist of Piaf's calibre should 'consider it appropriate to invite them into her bedroom'.[27]

Shortly before the wedding, the novelist Jean d'Ormesson wrote an abrasive piece entitled 'Piaf: an obscenity', which was actually less vitriolic than this title suggested.[28] He too appreciates her as a nostalgic singer. We grew up with her 'naturalist romanticism', he reminisces, we learnt how to love through her songs and also, in a sense, we discovered poetry: 'I have a strong feeling she is our Villon.' De Gaulle, Bardot and she make up our 'little national mythology'.[29] What he's critical of is her extreme mediatisation and her complicity with it. The obscenity is the way people are waiting for her to die, but he's aware of the self-invention which has made her court this morbid publicity. After giving them so much, 'it is quite natural that she should also ask for much in return, to help her build her personal mythology'.[30] Even so, he concedes that those who are primarily to blame for the obscenity can be found on our side of the stage: 'What is immoral, what is frightful, what is obscene in you, is other people. A press, a public, a society, a people, have the stars they deserve. And I am not entirely sure that ours have deserved Édith Piaf.'[31] What d'Ormesson puts his finger on is the lure of the media that the dying Piaf, like others before and after her, was submitting to.

Despite Sarapo's gentle attentiveness right up to her death, Piaf as usual tired of him fairly quickly once she'd done all she could to turn him into a singer. It was also rumoured that their marriage was never consummated.[32] 'Théo had had his day', reveals Danielle Bonel. 'And he knew it.'[33] Yet for Piaf, fact seldom got in the way of a good fiction, and appearances were maintained. After all, she was by this time busy working on her posterity. Hence her second autobiography, *Ma vie* (*My Life*), where Théo is represented in the last few chapters in saintly terms and her love for him as wild and foolish but irresistible.

Ma vie bears the unmistakeable stamp of *France-Dimanche*, where much of it first appeared. Some of it is quite frank, particularly where she talks about her self-loathing. The prospect of death also hangs over the opening pages. The book is meant to be her 'confession', possibly her last, but it's a curious one. She admits to seeking absolution, yet when she finds herself in the great beyond, she tells us, she won't be repenting but repeating 'Non, je ne regrette rien'. She has lived a terrible life but also a marvellous one because she has known love: the love of life, men, friends and her public, 'the people for whom I've sung, even to the furthest limits of my strength, the people for whom I'd like to die on stage, at the end of one last song'. Transparently, she is setting up her death as an exquisitely melancholic last scene in a melodrama and her readers are none too subtly elbowed into having the right response when it happens: 'All that crowd who'll follow me, I hope, on the last day, for I don't like being alone.'[34]

Throughout the book, Piaf has this same watchful eye on the mirror, checking how she looks in the gaze of the reader, for whom she clearly has plans. As she narrates her life under Noli's guidance, she emphasises the place of astrology, portents, misfortune, her 'demons' and her destiny, making sure her slower readers fully comprehend her last meanings—her life has higher significance, she deserves our pity, and she is ultimately without blame: 'despite my age, I've remained a poor, over-credulous girl, pursuing eternally the same dream: wanting to be happy, wanting to be loved! Life has always managed to sully anything wonderful for me.'[35] She falls in love with a dashing legionnaire but sacrifices him for the sake of her daughter: 'I lost that legionnaire, surely because I wasn't destined for happiness?'[36] Faced with so pitiful a question mark, we can only concur and weep. She also wants us to confirm her self-abnegating sainthood. 'If someone has done me harm, I [always] let them remain anonymous' ('J'accorde toujours l'anonymat à ceux qui m'ont fait du mal'). 'Nothing has ever given me purer delight than being able to give without expecting anything in return' ('Rien ne m'a jamais procuré de joie plus pure que de pouvoir donner sans rien attendre en retour').³⁷ And, narrating her life as ever through the lens of the *chanson réaliste*, now updated in the style of the 'true confessions' magazine, she drapes herself in a seductive veil of popular fiction. The book, then, isn't a confession in any conventional sense. What she's pitching for isn't a passport to heaven but narrative eternity here on earth. And that can best be achieved, it would seem, through pre-emptive self-mythification.

After the remission of 1960, her health worsened again. She went on performing with Sarapo, undertaking in February and March 1963 an engagement at Bobino, where she had first appeared in 1938. Her shows there were moving occasions. Lucien Vaimber, the chiropractor who during the 'suicide tour' of 1959 had often helped her get back on stage and stopped her misuse of medicines and drugs, was in attendance at every show.³⁸ She looked diminished but was still able to put on a respectable performance. Audiences wept and applauded. The comic singer Marie Bizet saw her for the last time at one of these Bobino shows: 'When she appeared on stage, I sobbed, it hurt me so much to see her in that ruined state. She was unsteady, emaciated. Then she started singing and the miracle occurred. The crowd went wild. People were on their feet, jumping up and down, crying. An unforgettable sight!'³⁹ Not everyone was quite so moved. As she lay dying in autumn 1963, she received a number of hate letters. Referring to her disdainfully as both 'Madame "La Môme"' and 'Madame Sarah-pot' (Sarapo), one letter dated 24 September 1963 read: 'You're starting to get on our nerves with all your shtick about love and screwing! When someone makes the kind of "racket" you do—because it isn't singing—they at least have the good grace not to force us to keep hearing it'.⁴⁰ Another alluded to her presumed recreational use of morphine, cocaine and alcohol and fulminated about her supposedly criminal past: 'What crook got you out of prison and made you a star, when you were singing on the pavement with the kind of voice (!!!) that could drive dogs away?'⁴¹

Her last performance in Paris was at a cinema on 28 March 1963 and her last ever live appearance came days later, at the Lille opera house on the 30th and 31st, only half full due to a transport strike. Days later, on 7 April, she made her last recording, the song 'L'Homme de Berlin' (The man from Berlin, Vendôme-Lai, 1963).⁴² On the 10th, weighing only 66 pounds (30 kilos), she was rushed into a clinic in Paris and went into a coma. A month and a half later, on 31 May, she had recovered enough to fly to the South of France to convalesce. Staying in three different villas and gradually divesting herself of the hangers-on whose partying would often tempt her to abandon her strict diet and relapse into a hepatic coma, she ended up in the small village of Plascassier near Grasse. Théo was filming in Paris and only came down at weekends.

That summer saw a melancholy procession of faces from her past: Asso, Émer, Contet, Bourgeat, Dumont, Aznavour, all sensing that they would be seeing her for the last time. Cocteau, seriously ill himself after several heart attacks, rang and wrote regularly. Her half-sister Denise Gassion and Simone Berteaut turned up. Gassion was turned away and the more persistent Berteaut allowed in only cursorily. When Piaf died on Thursday, 10 October, sometime between midday and 1pm, she was accompanied only by her nurse, Simone Margantin, and the ever-faithful Danielle, though the two subsequently gave conflicting accounts of which of them had attended her last moments.[43] Sarapo and Barrier flew down immediately and that evening her body, accompanied by Théo and Margantin, was furtively driven back to Paris by ambulance in accordance with her wish to die there. With a doctor's complicity, it was announced she had died at home at the Boulevard Lannes, at 7am on Friday the 11th. Symbol of the people's Paris, she was long believed to have passed away in the city's arms. This was her very last invention. The re-inventions were now free to proceed untroubled.

This began immediately. Her body was embalmed and clothed in one of her black stage dresses, with a rose in one hand and an orchid in the other.[44] Sarapo did her hair and make-up. She was laid in a coffin with a small window so visitors could see her one last time. Faces from her past again came to say goodbye, including Tino Rossi, Andrée Bigard, Denise Gassion and Aznavour. The falsification of the date of her death made it appear to coincide with Jean Cocteau's on the 11th. In reality, he died about 24 hours after Édith, following his radio tribute to her, apparently pre-recorded. The French and foreign press could thus headline that her death had killed him, alongside, in *Le Parisien*'s case, a photo of her body with her jaw tied up.[45] In all likelihood, Cocteau was already at death's door, but the melodrama of a mystical tryst was too tempting to pass up: the poet and the call girl, the avant-garde genius and the music-hall singer, highbrow and lowbrow.

Other headlines spoke more plainly: 'Piaf is dead: Paris weeps'. 'Piaf's heart has stopped beating: an authentic flower of the streets'.[46] National radio replaced its usual programming with coverage of her passing. The Anglophone press was a little more dispassionate. For the *Guardian's* Philip Hope-Wallace, she was 'nothing much to look at, a woman of the people with Parisian overtones, but her animation, her passion, and sheer animal distress were extraordinary'.[47] The *Sunday Times* said her voice sounded like 'a cracked church bell and sometimes as if it were torn out of her entrails'.[48] The *New York Times's* obituary detailed her career, with some inaccuracies, but also noted the warmth and depth of her voice, and the power she had 'to cast a compelling emotional spell over an audience, particularly a French audience. She was their darling, and they worshipped her'.[49]

As would happen in Britain years later with the death of Princess Diana, public reactions in France became more extravagant once the news was properly digested and the press had cranked itself into action. *Paris Match*—typically, though it wasn't alone—produced two illustrated commemorative editions.[50] Never known to skimp on emotion, *Match* depicts Piaf at one of her last concerts as resembling 'a dead little girl in an orphan's dress, with her crucifix on a chain as if for her first communion. Her eyes, intensely blue and dazzled by the projectors, were imploring. She was asking our forgiveness for being so small, so weak, so ill'.[51] And, in case we're not yet weeping, we're told she was planning to release a Christmas song 'for all the children of the world'.[52] *France-Dimanche*, which had pursued her so relentlessly in life, produced its own feature on her death, including a letter containing a soap-operatic 'last confession', though its authenticity has never been established.[53] Tributes were shown before the main feature at Gaumont cinemas for the rest of the year.[54] Marcel Blistène managed to produce a short but highly emotional book, *Au revoir Édith*,[55] drafted just before and just after her funeral and published only a week later—his haste palpable in the eccentric punctuation and numerous typos.

The general public, too, reacted swiftly. Clamouring outside her apartment on the Boulevard Lannes as soon as her death was announced, they were in the end allowed in to pay their respects. An estimated

100,000 people did so, waiting for several hours in a 500-metre queue along the boulevard that lasted until the funeral on the 14th: 'They have all come. All the friends she never knew. Those who had applauded her on stage, heard her on the radio, or played her records. Men and women of all conditions, young and old, communing in a similar fervour with that little woman in whom each of them recognised the best part of themselves, the heart.'[56] Many in the queue were women, some weeping and a handful willing to tell reporters how they felt. 'Poor Édith, we loved her so', said one. 'I'm here because I loved her', said another. And a third: 'She was a woman of the people, like me, like us. She sang with her heart.' All three were in tears.[57] The Foreign Legion sent the president of its association to pay homage: by the coffin, he left the Legion's insignia, in the company of a rosary and a fluffy bunny.[58] Other visitors must have come with different motives, since many of Piaf's personal effects went missing during those 72 hours.

On the day of the funeral, a reported two million onlookers behaved as Piaf had urged them to in *Ma vie*, lining the route of the funeral procession. The cortege included a motorcycle escort and eight limousines bearing wreaths: from the city council, the actors' union, the Foreign Legion, Dietrich, Fernandel, the Compagnons and many others.[59] With the traffic lights switched off by order of the prefect, her friend Louis Amade, it wound its way from the upmarket 16th *arrondissement* in the west through Piaf's native Belleville to Père Lachaise in the east, where an estimated 40,000 waited, including numerous celebrities and the media. The police were outnumbered: barriers were overturned, onlookers fell to the ground in grief or by accident, chaos descended. People grumbled at chancers refusing to queue or pushing. Graves were knocked over as spectators stampeded to spot celebrities, and, in one account, Bruno Coquatrix was jostled into the open grave.[60] The people's Paris that Édith had always represented bustled, cursed and gossiped, claiming an implausibly intimate knowledge of her private life.

Looking back at the funeral, Danielle Bonel would recall 'scenes that were pitiful and poignant', which, thirty years on, still seemed quite unreal. Surging out of the metro into the historic cemetery came prostitutes, well-to-do families, women with babies, workers who had abandoned their machines and offices, children and old people in their Sunday best.[61] As with Margaret Thatcher, this was in all but name a state funeral,[62] France's formal *adieu* to the once subversive body of Édith Piaf. The imagined Piaf, however, still had a long and healthy life ahead. In the days after her demise, analogies were sought to try to make sense of what she had meant to the French and the world, some already familiar, others new: Mary Magdalene, Sarah Bernhardt, Marilyn Monroe. Blistène even maintained she could have had the big-screen career of a Bette Davis or a Katharine Hepburn.[63]

One of the most familiar analogies was again popular fiction. An article entitled 'She lived for chanson' ('Elle vivait pour la chanson') recycles the tale of her being born in the street with the help of two policemen at 5am under a gas lamp. 'No popular novelist would have dared imagine such beginnings for a heroine. But in Édith's case, it wasn't a novel'.[64] Of course, we're certain now that, metaphorically, it was, but what's interesting is the recognition that her life is the stuff of cheap fiction. Born and growing up on the city's streets, she was for *Paris Match* a reincarnated Fleur de Marie, the street singer of Eugène Sue's serialised novel *Les Mystères de Paris*, published in the mid-nineteenth century. And for maximum pathos *Match* adds its own twist to another familiar chapter of her childhood. She lost her sight 'as if she had to be prevented from seeing this horrible world where children can be abandoned'.[65] Other literary allusions were to the desolate Fantine or her daughter Cosette from Hugo's *Les Misérables*.

The high–popular divide was often invoked in postmortem efforts to capture what she was, a value-laden concern to clear her of any unsavoury associations with lowbrow populism. 'She is the only one who hasn't dishonoured the word "popular"', wrote one journalist. 'She was the ultimate popular singer, the only one who managed to draw the crowds wherever she went, even outdoors.'[66] So while 'popular' here clearly means appealing to a wide constituency, the word 'dishonoured' implies a distinction between a discreditable mass appeal and one considered somehow more legitimate, more authentic. In his 'psychoanalysis' of her success, Jean Monteaux discriminates with similar confidence—and obfuscation—between 'the soul of the people' ('l'âme du peuple') and 'the popular soul' ('l'âme populaire'). The street in the songs of Chevalier, Monteaux maintains, very much represents the latter: 'it is popular with all the vulgarity that adjective contains' ('elle est populaire avec tout ce que l'adjectif comporte de vulgarité'). However, '[the street in Piaf] is "the people" with all the nobility that word contains. [...] For the people means her, you, the crowd, me. [...] The people no more comes from Belleville than from Passy, from France than from Germany: it is universal. And Édith Piaf is it.'[67] This is a fairly common kind of French discourse on the popular at this time, and indeed more recently. But it's empty republican rhetoric more than empirical observation. If 'the people' is nothing less than the universal human, to say that Piaf belongs to it is senseless, however good it sounds. A brief editorial on the funeral in *Candide* comes at the question more reflectively. 'Édith Piaf was a "popular" singer, the vast majority liked her; this might be why people refuse to use the word "genius" in her case.' But why, it goes on, should genius reside only in a pen or a brush? The emotion experienced when hearing a Piaf song has little to do with either lyrics or melody; it's to do with her voice: 'That was Piaf's genius.'[68] Or as Cocteau, who had referred to her transcendent genius as early as 1940, put it just before he died, 'that great voice of black velvet, magnifying everything she sang'.[69]

Reflections on Piaf and the popular also pointed out the ordinariness of much of her later material—a common theme in the postmortem assessments, as if her death had made it acceptable to speak of it. Even so, the ordinariness is usually redeemed by the alchemical properties of her voice in performance. 'A voice that could shatter any microphone' ('Une voix à casser tous les micros'), in the view of Claude Sarraute, 'harsh, vast, ripping into lamentably banal songs which a single movement of the finger could render poignant'.[70] Guermantes, *Le Figaro*'s columnist, describes it in familiar terms as the voice of the old working-class Paris ('la voix du faubourg') but explicates that label perceptively. The 'harshness of its timbre' ('la raucité du timbre') isn't so much an aesthetic as a moral attribute. The pain of a life closely resembling that of her realist narratives gives the voice a broken quality which invests the 'obvious poverty' of the songs with a singular intensity. Seeing Piaf on stage, 'you were really plunged into a working-class universe, one which is still sensitive to timeless feelings, which gathers round street singers, an accordion, an accident, a misfortune or a celebrity'.[71]

All of these features add up to a makeshift theory of the popular voice. It lacks the refinement of the classical; it's the voice of naked emotion; and it speaks to those who instinctively aggregate in public places to listen or gawp. But, condescending though it is, this isn't a disparaging view.

For that voice, embodied in Piaf's physical demeanour, is fully capable of tragic vision: 'The poor Kid from the Boulevard of Crime took on the mask and gestures of a Greek tragedian. A popular singer reviving classical tragedy is pretty exceptional in the music hall of today. So it matters little that she sang cheap, facile songs.'[72] Popular tragedy in chanson is deemed to emerge from the qualities not of the writing but of the performance. And those qualities include the formal 'imperfections' of the popular voice relative to the classical. Imperfection, in fact, is what makes possible a specifically popular tragic in chanson. Piaf is the diva of the everyday.

Tragedy in Piaf is also identified with pathos, the affective rather than the cognitive. For Blistène, she found the way to audiences' hearts by saying what they themselves couldn't express.[73] Others saw her as casting a spell over audiences in a kind of therapeutic hypnosis. For the *Journal de Genève*, her songs work because they administer a shot of passion which people don't have enough of in their everyday lives.[74] And, as we saw earlier, some, like Monteaux, take the view that the audience's intellect is switched off at a Piaf performance. We don't have to accept this premise, particularly where the songs of Asso, Contet and Émer are concerned—or accept that tragic vision can be achieved without cognition. But Monteaux does confirm that lyrical banality was irrelevant to the virtual hysteria at her later shows. Reason, moderation, restraint—qualities perceived as classically French—are deliberately played down in performance in favour of visceral, uninhibited affect. Monteaux thus helps us distinguish between, on the one hand, popular chanson as embodied by Piaf, who sets out to elicit unadulterated feeling, and, on the other, the great postwar singer-songwriters who sought a finer balance between sentiment and cognition.

Another recurrent theme of the commentaries straight after her death is that her power to evoke such feeling made her unique and irreplaceable. After Damia, wrote Sarraute, there was Piaf, but today there's nobody to ensure her succession: 'She will remain, in our memory, a unique, irreplaceable and tragic little figurehead of French chanson.'[75] For Gilbert Bécaud, she won't be replaced or equalled because she is 'too personal, too strong' ('parce que trop personnelle, trop forte'). This was brought home to him when he tried to persuade her to adapt to jazz as Judy Garland had done, but she was too fixated on her own melodic style.[76] To a large extent, these were kindlier versions of the twilight-of-the-gods discourse which could already be glimpsed in her last years but which, with her now safely out of the way, could be made explicit. Irreplaceability was a polite way of saying that she had had her day. For the emerging singer Claude Nougaro, 'it's a whole chapter in the history of the chanson tradition that's changing and disappearing'.[77] And for Maurice Chevalier she was '*the* realist singer of an age' ('*la* chanteuse réaliste d'une époque') which he clearly sees as over, though he does add that she will be remembered through young singers who will follow her lead.[78] More candidly, an unnamed young female singer commented: 'In her style, she was a very great singer, I'm sure. Apart from "Milord", I didn't like her songs, I'm from a different time'.[79] Some even acknowledged that her death was timely, as her career would inevitably have declined.

There can be little doubt about this, and not only because of her health. Popular music was simply moving on as technology and commerce intervened ever more. On one trip to the USA she saw the young Presley on the *Ed Sullivan Show* and recognised the threat to chanson his kind of music posed: 'Goodness me, I never heard anything like it! If we want to keep going, we're going to have to put up a fight.'[80] It wasn't that she disliked rock'n'roll, though occasional claims over the years that, had she lived, she would have crossed over into rock or pop[81] are outlandish to say the least, as Bécaud's tale about jazz confirms. Rather, the timing of her death was symbolic. She disappeared just as the teen revolution was brought fully to the attention of the adult French population by the riotous open-air concert at the Place de la Nation in June 1963,[82] as if she had to discreetly stand down before that revolution could proceed without a backward glance.

But if she did represent the end of an era for *la chanson française*, it wasn't of course the end of French chanson itself, only of one conception of it, albeit the one that still lingers abroad. Her death heralded a generational shift *within* French chanson, as new singers and songwriters learnt to adapt to the multiple idioms deriving from rock'n'roll. And commentators on her passing seemed aware of this, varnishing her life and songs with quick-dry nostalgia.

Combat's Michel Perez, writing only days after her death, details the multiple Piafs that have existed: the realist, the romantic, the 'less personal' Piaf of her Compagnons phase, and the defiant Piaf of these last months. And he insists that, as these will live on, her physical departure is ultimately unimportant. The true Piaf will forever be that of 1942–43, when she influenced popular sensibility: the Piaf of wooden soles on women's shoes and lovelorn typists being chatted up by good-looking lads. This, he predicts, is the Piaf we'll remember, even when we have forgotten her life story.[83] Accordingly, those who, like another obituarist, Jean-Roger Rebierre, had been young when she was young still wept when she sang in her old style, just as they had in the 1930s, though now they are weeping for their lost youth. Yet, although Rebierre admits that the Piaf of today is 'a character from a different time' ('un personnage d'un autre temps'), his generation can't for all that think of her as old-fashioned. On the contrary, they feel sorry for those who are too young to thrill to such 'heart-rending nostalgia' ('nostalgie déchirante').[84] What is happening here is that, upon her death, Piaf—whose 1930s realist songs marked the dawn of a new sensibility, a loosening of bourgeois sexual mores—is already slipping beyond fashion and being discursively inducted into French folk culture, historicised yet timeless. Filleted and mummified by nostalgia, she is being boxed into a tradition.

Now safely beyond any further transgressions, she could also more easily be represented as a secular saint. One poignant aspect of her funeral was that, despite her faith, the Catholic Church denied her a mass. This was supposedly because she was divorced and had remarried in the Greek Orthodox tradition.[85] But beyond this rather convenient formality it isn't difficult to sense—as furious friends did—that it was her sinful past that was the real obstacle. The *Osservatore Romano*, unofficial paper of the Vatican, spoke of her amorous excesses ('égarements sentimentaux') and those of the arts world generally, comparing her to 'another idol of prefabricated pleasure: Marilyn Monroe, whose fame ended with a tube of barbiturate'.[86] This was a further meaning she acquired at the time of her death: sinner and religious pariah, though it was only half the story. When a priest was asked by *France-Soir* for a reaction to her passing and curtly responded that neither Piaf nor chanson was deserving of comment, another man of the cloth, objecting publicly to this remark, pointed out the profoundly spiritual significance of her music: 'Those who have been held spellbound for two whole hours by this little scrap of a woman with her unattractive appearance can never forget the sincerity of the cries of passion, pain and hope that she tore from the very depths of her being'.[87] Despite delivering that one last jibe at her looks, he implies that the humanity and authenticity of her art redeem her spiritually.

For many, in fact, her meanings as sinner and pariah made her all the more of a tragic heroine. Popular-cultural beatification ensued, as with the glossy commemorative editions that soon started appearing in the press. Monteaux evokes the mystical yet earthly nature of her faith and cites a churchman telling him, unexpectedly no doubt, that she would have made an admirable nun.[88] After her funeral, *France-Observateur* commented wryly that because her 'frenzy' and 'rage' were genuine, because this 'sick and ugly little woman' ('petite femme laide et infirme') was truly possessed, '100,000 people processed religiously before her remains; and now here she is, Saint Édith. I don't think this will happen to Sylvie Vartan'.[89] A number of others spoke of her performances as experiences of almost religious exaltation. Indeed, one priest, Monseigneur Martin, who joined the funeral procession on the 14th after having obtained permission to spend the night watching over her mortal remains, disclosed that her voice had saved him from suicide when he had lost his faith.[90]

The overall impact of her death seems to have been the assemblage, consolidation and ratification of meanings she had acquired piecemeal and sometimes only implicitly in life. Her greatness and her emotive power, her tragic, popular-cultural, quasi-religious and other meanings, were all foregrounded, while negative representations slipped quietly away or were transformed into positive ones by the halo of nostalgia. It's this halo that triggered and has subsequently shaped the various afterlives she has had since 1963. With her consignment to the earth, all the carefully fabricated representations of her over the previous 30 years could now come together in a polysemic bouquet. Like a lost balloon, the public Piaf, released from its flesh-and-blood source, became a free-floating signifier, autonomous and infinitely malleable. And as it drifted further away in time from its historical source, it lent itself all the more to creative recounting and re-invention.

CHAPTER 8

Remembering Piaf

'Piaf can't die... She won't ever die... She's gone, that's
all'

(Marcel Blistène)[1]

I N OCTOBER 2012, the American singer Lady Gaga was reported to
have bought up Piaf memorabilia which included clothes, shoes, letters
and even toenail clippings. She was also said to be trying to buy the rights
to some Piaf songs so she could sample them. 'Gaga sees a lot of herself
in Édith', asserted one insider. 'She, too, was a rebellious character in
her era.'[2] The equation is improbable, but it does illustrate how symbolic
Piaf has become. Still world-famous, she is a sacred reference for singers
young and old, male and female, French and otherwise. French TV news,
covering at length the fiftieth anniversary of her death in October 2013,
explained: 'She remains a giant in the hearts of the French [...]. After
half a century, she might have been forgotten, but that's not the case at
all.'[3] The question is why.

Decennial and even quinquennial commemorations of her passing
have become stock events in the French cultural calendar, and on such
occasions books about her roll off the presses relentlessly. The forms the
jubilees take are generally similar, but they are interesting for what they
can tell us about how the imagined Piaf has managed to survive for 50
years in her absence and how she's become an international currency.
These are the issues I want to tackle here. I'll trace how a modern

'commemorative consciousness'[4]—the mentality that makes us solemnly remember the likes of Churchill and Kennedy or the start of the Great War—has come to bear on Piaf, at home and abroad. In the next chapter, I'll consider what she has come to mean in the process of remembrance.

In France, rituals of remembrance were established quite rapidly, initially as a result of personal sentiment. The impressionistic recollections in Blistène's *Au revoir Édith* set the agenda. Like a number of his successors, he claimed a special relationship, as old friend and confidant. His book, structured only by grief and reminiscence, is all superlatives: her intuitive artistry, the infatuated responses of her audiences, her adorable personality and unstinting generosity. 'She understood it all', he enthused, 'she got it, and what her life as a poor kid hadn't taught her she'd picked up herself, by intuition [...]. She loved only beauty, in all its forms, in art, in the people round her, in nature.'[5] Published only days after her death, this is the first hagiography and a seminal one. With a handful of other acolytes, Blistène became a fierce guardian of her memory, and as a result the first anniversary of her death was mired in controversy over Pierre Desgraupes's television special *La Mort d'Édith Piaf* (The death of Édith Piaf), made with the assistance of the Bonels. Accused of being morbid and exploitative, it launched what Burke calls 'a struggle over the meaning of Piaf's life'.[6]

By that first anniversary, she was already being cast as a glorious anachronism. Esteemed music writer Guy Érismann, reluctantly consigning her to the past, felt obliged to wonder: 'What place will posterity grant Édith Piaf?' ('Quelle place la postérité accordera-t-elle à Édith Piaf?') But he seemed to know the answer already: 'A year ago already ... only a year and it seems a long time. [...] Fashion has swept away that way of loudly proclaiming, in a booming voice, the secret combination of heart and belly [...]. What will she be in 10, 20, 50 years, when, after the stage lights, the lights of memory have also gone out?'[7] The question was apt. Despite the rise of *yéyé*, a few talented young singers were launched as new Piafs. In 1965, a TV talent show pitched Mireille Mathieu against Georgette Lemaire. Mathieu won and subsequently established herself independently, but has never quite shuffled off the image of a Piaf impersonator; and few ever felt that she or Lemaire genuinely came close to the real thing. The 'end of an era' discourse, in which Piaf was deemed unique and irreplaceable, seemed to be confirmed, which meant that dedicated Piaf fans could only cling to the memory of her greatness, a life raft in a sea of mediocrity. So how did we get from such gloomy forecasts to her worldwide iconicity today?

One simple explanation is the sheer tenacity of those fans. The Association of Friends of Édith Piaf was set up in 1967 by a handful of people who had known and loved her: Blistène, Coquatrix, the actor Michel Simon and Bernard Marchois, a dedicated fan who had been introduced to Piaf as a 17-year-old in 1958. Their explicit intent was to halt the creeping oblivion they sensed had already begun. They set about doing so largely by maintaining Blistène's hagiographic narrative. The Association launched its first major celebration at the Théâtre du Marais (formerly the historic Concert PACRA) in 1968, five years after her death, attended by acquaintances like Charles Dumont, who would go on to be a fixture in the memory business, long after the death of Blistène in 1991. Her unissued last recording, 'L'Homme de Berlin', was played and a giant photo of her displayed. The music writer and film-maker Claude Fléouter also produced a TV programme, *Édith Piaf*, which aired on 9 October on the first channel. Later that month, on the 29th, just days after the death of Raymond Asso, the Association mounted a second anniversary gala, at Bobino. All three occasions were reminders to her followers not to forget. That they worked is illustrated by the dozens of poems and letters sent to the Association from the 1960s to the 1990s, particularly for the anniversaries,[8] which I will come back to in the next chapter.

Another explanatory factor was the publication of Simone Berteaut's notorious memoir, *Piaf*, in September 1969,[9] which became the year's bestseller alongside Henri Charrière's *Papillon*, selling 165,000 copies in just three weeks. The book caused a furore, not least because of its author's claim to be Piaf's half-sister. Stars like Montand spoke angrily of lies and half-truths; Piaf's real half-sister Denise (working on a rival book at the time) and brother or half-brother Herbert even attempted to sue Berteaut, without success. The Association, too, objected to her version of events. Blistène, its president, organised a debate in October that year entitled 'The true face of Édith Piaf', a face which, he complained, had already been sufficiently obscured by scurrilous accounts even before Berteaut's book. This was a revealing remark. Berteaut certainly did present the young Piaf in a crude, unflattering light, often emphasising the promiscuous sex and heroic drinking. The Association clearly saw its mission as being to clean up this image and divert attention towards her art. The public, meanwhile, was divided, between those appalled by Berteaut's blasphemy and those who felt her revelations hadn't gone far enough.

With hindsight, the real impact of the book was to refresh public interest. Berteaut inflected the imagined Piaf in contentious terms that made the world wonder anew who la Môme really was. She became a tantalising mystery, to be addressed through ruthless detective work or spicy revelation. The memoir acted as an irritant, stimulating an inexhaustible series of other books but also, over the years, films, plays, documentaries, tributes and even songs, all drawn to her mystique. And each of these has helped maintain the flame, intertextually perpetuating the kind of archetypal narrative that characterises all myths while adding new layers of meaning in tune with the zeitgeist. It's against this backcloth that the anniversaries should be understood.

The tenth anniversary in 1973 was the real starting point. As with most public anniversaries, one of its motives was commercial. It offered an opportunity to repackage old recordings, produce newspaper copy and TV documentaries, and publish more memoirs, like Noli's *Piaf secrète*. But commerce alone doesn't explain the anniversary phenomenon in Piaf's case. None of these activities would have come about if the imagined Piaf wasn't already being turned into a moral signifier. Victor Franco, who had once interviewed her as she came out of hospital, recounts in *Jours de France* her life in a popular-fictional style while at the same time magnifying the momentousness of the interview itself. He had expected to see a person wrecked by illness; and yet throughout the encounter, 'I saw her smile, a smile that spoke of joy, innocence, youth and, more than anything else, the ferocious will not to be vanquished. What a wonderful lesson in courage I received that day!'[10] In a letter to his local newspaper, a teenager confided that her death had coincided with his seventh birthday. Now 17, he is a passionate fan and member of the Association and he speaks of her with all the fervour of adolescence: 'this little bird who loved life too much and whose only fault is to have left us much too soon'.[11]

Another factor helping explain the response to the tenth anniversary is that, shortly before, André Malraux's decade as minister of cultural affairs (1959–69) had seen a concerted effort to preserve France's cultural heritage. And although at the time chanson didn't come within the ministry's purview, the initiative did over time contribute to a wider commemorative consciousness. Since 1973, Piaf has by increments been patrimonialised as a public institution, worked into cultural memory as part of the story that France tells its people. And the anniversaries have played a significant part in this.

The Association, Berteaut and the 1973 anniversary, then, established the terms of a posthumous grand narrative, a blueprint for remembrance of Piaf as an embodiment of popular art, love, heroism and the nation's past. And the succession of anniversaries since then indicates a periodic need to revisit this narrative and place it back in public circulation. This would sometimes happen outside the normal five- or ten-year intervals, both nationally and internationally. In December 1972, the first feature film about her life was announced, entitled simply *Piaf*, based on Berteaut's book. This was originally to be a Warner production with the title role played by Liza Minelli, who commented that Piaf reminded her of her mother, Judy Garland.[12] There was even talk of Ken Russell directing it. In the end, Warner decided it was too risky financially and left the project to a French director, Guy Casaril, who cast the little-known Brigitte Ariel in the lead role. Casaril focused on Piaf's struggle to the top in the 1930s, ending with her first performance at the ABC in 1937, where, anachronistically, she sings 'L'Accordéoniste'. Finally released in France in 1974, the film flopped,[13] but it did testify to a tendency to evoke or represent Piaf in works of the imagination.

Piaf had already become an inspiration for songs and singers. Léo Ferré, who had struggled to persuade her to record his material, nevertheless included a moving though un-idealised tribute, 'A une chanteuse morte' (To a dead singer), on his 1967 album. He describes her voice as being like birds singing with bleeding throats and he dubs her a Wagner of the streets. But his disparaging allusion in the song to Johnny Stark, manager of the 'new Piaf' Mireille Mathieu and a powerful figure in the French music industry, prompted the head of Ferré's record company, Eddie Barclay, to destroy the first 5000 copies pressed and release a new version of the album three months later without the track, to Ferré's fury.[14] In 1969, the singer Serge Lama, reacting to Berteaut's book, wrote and performed 'Édith', with music by Maxime Leforestier. The song impugns the money made by Berteaut when Piaf herself had (supposedly) died penniless. In 1977, Catherine Ribeiro brought out a tribute album of Piaf songs, *Blues de Piaf* (Piaf's blues), while Claude Nougaro recorded his own song, 'Comme une Piaf',[15] in which he yearns to be a male Piaf having the same emotional impact on his audience as she did. Allain Leprest, who, like Lama, acknowledged Piaf's influence, recorded his own song in 1986 called 'Édith', which focuses on her grave at Père Lachaise, re-imagined as a music hall.

But sung representations of her weren't limited to France. Joni Mitchell's 'Edith and the Kingpin' (1975), a shady tale of dependency between a young woman and her pimp or drug dealer, was, she later revealed, inspired by Édith, one of her influences, though neither the narrative nor the period portrayed in the song matches very well. The following year, Elton John's album *Blue Moves* included 'Cage the Songbird', with lyrics by his long-term collaborator Bernie Taupin inspired by Piaf's death, again with none of the specificity of Ferré's lyric, or indeed of their own tribute to Marilyn Monroe in 1973, 'Candle in the Wind'.

Of variable quality, such songs are somewhat contrived opportunities for the singers concerned to claim a place in the national chanson pantheon or to demonstrate their sensitivity and eclectic tastes. But they did contribute to Piaf's iconicisation. In the songs of Mitchell, John and Nougaro, Piaf isn't really the subject but an accommodating metaphor. By the 1970s the posthumous Piaf was being sentimentalised and quasi-fictionalised as a figure of cultural memory. But these songs also reminded France that the imagined Piaf was a transatlantic phenomenon, and this, like her first trips to New York, reflected back an image of her global cultural significance which was duly internalised. The transnational ping pong became self-perpetuating as the years went by and contributed to her patrimonialisation.

Nineteen seventy-seven, the year of Nougaro's and Ribeiro's records, turned out to be a busy one for cultural representations of Piaf at home and abroad, despite the absence of a neat anniversary. The fourteenth of February saw a musical by David Cohen, *Édith Piaf: A Remembrance*, staged at the Playhouse on West 48th Street, New York City, the venue where her American career had begun 30 years before, featuring Juliette Koka as Piaf. The very next day, in the UK, the Canadian comic actor Libby Morris, a familiar face on British TV at the time, launched her production, *Édith Piaf, je vous aime: A Musical Tribute*, at the King's Head Theatre, Islington, which transferred in June to the Shaftesbury Theatre in London's West End. The same year, Grace Jones brought out a disco version of 'La Vie en rose' on her first album, *Portfolio*, on Island Records. In France, Pathé Marconi issued a live album of Piaf's second Carnegie Hall concert in January 1957; and Bernard Marchois opened the tiny Édith Piaf museum consisting only of two rooms in his own flat in the 11th *arrondissement*, filled with memorabilia including a life-size two-dimensional model of her alongside a giant teddy bear of the same height bought for her by Sarapo. Still functioning today—only by appointment and on certain days of the week—the museum receives no public funding but is financed solely by the subscriptions of those in the Association.[16]

Marchois saw the museum as a necessity because Piaf songs were no longer being broadcast, though the press around this time often gave the impression that her voice was still being regularly heard on air, and not just in shows given over to nostalgia. Perhaps, though, Marchois's pessimism had more to do with a perception that the star being remembered was not the flesh-and-blood woman he had known, for throughout the 1980s the imagined Piaf continued to prove semiologically accommodating.

A new generation of fans, journalists and creators, often without the experience of Piaf live that Marchois's generation had, was in fact appropriating her on their own terms. The French singer Jack Mels performed a one-man show in April 1979 entitled *Piaf parmi nous* (Piaf still with us). Three years later, a popular-theatre company, La Chenille, was touring an innovative production entitled *Piaf ou qui j'aurai été* (Piaf, or who I was), by French author and playwright René Escudié. The action takes place against an historical backcloth of four politically sensitive moments in her lifetime which marked out her ascent: the right-wing uprising of 6 February 1934; the Popular Front of May 1936, the Occupation and the Liberation. Creative appropriations were also cropping up outside France as the twentieth anniversary approached. In Tokyo, where there's a substantial liking for *la chanson française*, the gay singer, writer, actor and drag artist Akihiro Miwa put on a spectacle in 1980 called *Amour et chanson: une vie. Histoire d'Édith Piaf* (Love and chanson: a life. A history of Édith Piaf), which became a huge success, while the singer France Normand performed *Hommage à la Piaf* at the Cabaret 1390, in Montreal's lively rue Sainte-Catherine district. By then, Pam Gems's powerful play *Piaf* had disseminated her story more widely in the Anglophone world. After opening at the Royal Shakespeare Company in Stratford upon Avon in 1978, featuring remarkable performances by Jane Lapotaire as Piaf and Zoë Wanamaker as a Berteaut figure named Toine, it transferred to London's Donmar Warehouse and toured, before moving to Broadway in 1981, where it won a Tony Award, and the following year Quebec City. In 1982, Piaf was being remembered from Texas (*Ladies and Gentlemen, Édith Piaf!*) to Kentucky (*Piaf: La Vie! L'Amour!*).[17]

By the 1983 anniversary, then, Piaf was at the centre of a thriving nostalgia industry, selling more records by that time than many successful living singers. Record companies were also churning out compilations for younger consumers, not to mention occasional new material like the Carnegie Hall concert album. Another stimulus to the ongoing interest was the post-punk, independently produced 'alternative rock' movement. This included bands who, immersed in the Anglo-American rock idioms of the previous 20 years, were also, in the DIY spirit of punk, searching for a sound and style that reflected the increasingly diverse, hybrid culture they had grown up with in France. Stretching from the late 1970s singer-songwriter Renaud to the more aggressively punk Garçons Bouchers and their label Boucherie Production, or the more eclectic Les Têtes Raides, the movement gave birth to the 'neo-realist chanson', which culminated in 1992 in the release of an album of updated covers of Piaf and Fréhel songs entitled *Ma grand'mere est une rockeuse* (my granny is a rocker), which included 'Bravo pour le clown' by Les Betty Boop and 'J'ai dansé avec l'amour' by Les Wampas. As Barbara Lebrun points out, there was a conscious attempt here to reconnect with a French popular heritage by reviving the realist canon 'as a relevant model for contemporary protest, full of vitality, anger and rebellion', though Lebrun astutely adds that these predominantly male performers tended 'to idealize the personal lives and performance styles of dead female artists, drawing sometimes far-fetched connections between the realist genre and their own, present, "alternative" aspirations.'[18]

Ironically, given these aspirations, their efforts formed part of the wider tendency to patrimonialise Piaf. This had begun quite modestly in 1966 with an official plaque over the doorway of 72 rue de Belleville after a subscription campaign mounted by *France-Dimanche*. It was taken an important step further with the Piaf museum ten years later. By its very nature, a museum, even a private one, confers status; it signifies the formal recognition of a social and cultural value, an existing or potential public interest. And although Marchois's archive still hasn't received official support, it has been woven de facto into a wider web of public recognition. In 1971, the cinema in Bernay, the town where Édith had spent time in her grandmother's brothel, was renamed Le Piaf, and the historical building has today been restored to its original function as a theatre. The Bernay municipality also named a street after her in 1988. The first municipality to do so, however, was further east: Chalon sur Saône, in 1979. The previous year, the Paris city council had agreed to rename a little square in the 20th *arrondissement*, not far from where Piaf was born, the Place Édith Piaf, though this wasn't inaugurated until September 1981, by mayor and future president Jacques Chirac. Twelve months later, the square was adorned with a small monument by the sculptor Jacques Devilliers, representing Piaf's face and hands, in the presence of Blistène for the Association and the sculptor himself. That evening, a free chanson concert was held, during which the Édith Piaf prize was awarded. At the nearby Café Édith Piaf, Friday night was Piaf night, with singing and dancing to an accordion from 7pm.

All this precursory activity helped make the 1983 anniversary more substantial and catalytic than its predecessor ten years before. Festivities took place across France. Some ten books about her came out that year. A *Reader's Digest* box set of eight LPs was summoned up, *Le Monde d'Édith Piaf*. In late March, a mass was held for the singer, which would become a regular anniversary event, no doubt to make up for her not being granted a religious funeral. This was followed by a gala in a marquee which included a screening of Blistène's *Étoile sans lumière* and a concert of stars doing Piaf in their various styles. The celluloid Piaf in fact became a bone of contention the following month, when Claude Lelouch's new film, *Édith et Marcel*,[19] featuring Marcel Cerdan Junior playing his father, was released. Lelouch had arranged a grand screening at the Forum des Halles, which turned out to clash with the Association's big anniversary exhibition, 'Édith Piaf, vingt ans déjà' (Édith Piaf, twenty years already), also at the Forum. With its 6000 members each paying 60 francs (around £6) for membership, the Association was in a position to mount a major event which included performances, lectures and round-table discussions with the likes of Herbert Gassion, Barrier, Dumont, Bécaud, Aznavour, Montand and Constantine. A total of 120,000 people attended over the three weeks of the exhibition. But there were also to be screenings of all Piaf's films. Protesting vigorously about the competition, Lelouch managed to have the Piaf showings moved.

For the actual anniversary in October, the deputy mayor of the 20th district and a representative of the Association laid flowers at her grave in the company of Théo's parents, as their son was also buried there. On 11 October at Saint-Eustache, the church near the Forum des Halles and the Pompidou Centre, a solemn concert in memory of both Piaf and Cocteau took place at which 200 choristers sang Dumont's 'Mon Dieu'.[20] Twenty years after her demise, then, an avatar of Piaf was being kept in circulation by converging elements: commerce, nostalgia, patrimonialisation and a new kind of art discourse which treated her life as suited to imaginative re-interpretation. 'For many', wrote Jean-Pierre Mogui early that year, '1983 will be the Year of Piaf',[21] though it was actually the twenty-fifth anniversary in 1988 that was publicly given that designation. That year, the Académie Charles Cros, formal yardstick of quality in the French music industry, awarded her the 'Prix patrimoine' (heritage prize).[22]

The anniversaries of 1988, 1993 and 2003 each in their way echoed and escalated the routines of memorialisation and patrimonialisation established by their predecessors. *Le Monde* pertinently said of the French on the thirtieth anniversary: 'We all have something of Piaf within our hearts. [...] We celebrate, we commemorate, it's an obsession with us.'[23] The obsession can perhaps be a little better understood in the context of what by this time was becoming known, after Primo Levi, as the 'duty of memory'. This notion concerns the recognition of society's moral imperative to remember atrocious suffering inflicted in the past, particularly the Holocaust and Vichy's complicity with it. But the notion of commemoration as a duty seems also to have trickled down to reach less cataclysmic events and individuals associated with suffering in some form. One reason why Piaf is memorialised much more assiduously than other entertainers of her era may therefore be the narratives of tragedy that have steadily been built round her.

Each decennial celebration has, however, taken the narrated Piaf a little further away from personal recollection, as the commemoration duties of those who had known her have steadily fallen to those who had not. Public remembrance of her has therefore become more intertextual, mediated through past documentaries, tributes, press coverage and anniversaries. As such it has also become less focused on Piaf the woman and more driven by other motives. In 1988, for example, Belleville held a 13-day celebration. It began solemnly enough on the day of her death at the St-Jean-Baptiste church, now the obligatory anniversary venue, where the equally statutory Charles Dumont sang 'Mon Dieu', recognised as virtually a sacred text despite its secular content. But the celebrations also included the laying out of five new paths in the Parc des Buttes, and the inauguration of a trophy, 'Édith Piaf-Nostalgie, chanson de la rue' (street song). There was intense rivalry between TV channels to get first access to archival material as yet unseen.[24] In October, a whole week of Pascal Sevran's TV show on TF1, *La Chance aux chansons*, was devoted to her, and the same channel, very recently privatised, commissioned an Ipsos poll which revealed that the nation's favourite Piaf song (61%) was 'Non, je ne regrette rien' and that 34 percent of the population now owned between one and three Piaf records.[25] For anyone who didn't, Pathé Marconi brought out a nine-disc box set of her 'complete' recorded works, though a tenth was somehow produced for the 1993 anniversary. In the States, a *Tribute to Édith Piaf* album on Amherst Records came out the following year using the familiar ploy of having celebrities of the moment perform the songs, even though these versions, by artists not generally in the Piaf style, did little to illuminate the originals. Yet another musical was staged in Chicago entitled *The Lady and the Sparrow*, which brought to life the parallels between Piaf and Billie Holiday.

At the end of this twenty-fifth anniversary year, the Ministry of Culture happened to be carrying out its periodic survey of French cultural practices. In one section, respondents were asked to state which of 66 personalities from the arts and entertainment, going back several centuries, they were familiar with. Piaf came top with a score of 94%, equal with the film star Jean-Paul Belmondo and the comic actor Louis de Funès. She beat Brassens (92%), Bardot and Hallyday (both at 91%), Gainsbourg (87%) and the hugely popular Renaud (82%), and by a wide margin Madonna (79%), Molière (74%) and Mozart (73%), to say nothing

of Rodin (45%), Iron Maiden (18%), Samuel Beckett (17%) and Pina
Bausch (2%).[26]

The fortieth anniversary, in 2003, demonstrates the commemorative
inflation that had steadily been taking place since 1973. Now officially a
national treasure, she was represented creatively in three significant ways.
A major exhibition, 'La Môme de Paris', exploring her importance to
the city was organised at City Hall. It proved immensely popular, with
queues snaking round the building and people jostling for a view in
the overcrowded display rooms. Second, a new documentary was made,
Sans amour on n'est rien du tout.[27] Like others, it cleaves faithfully to the
imagined Piaf and tends to rehash the same photos and clips. It does,
however, note with some acuity just how far she had come as a nationally
signifying icon: since the day of her death, 'she has continued to grow
and invade our universe [...] the adjective that suits her best: "living"'.[28]
And, third, a full-length statue, by Lisbeth Delisle, was finally erected
at the Place Édith Piaf, causing some controversy, as it was scarcely
flattering, suggesting a misshapenness that recalled old discourses on
her ugliness. In addition to these three representations, books about her
of course continued to appear and yet another play, though an excellent
one, *Piaf: L'Ombre de la rue* (Piaf: shadow of the streets), was staged at
the Theatre Essaion.

Repetitive though the anniversaries have become, the fiftieth in 2013
deserves a little more attention because of its sheer scale as well as the
symbolism of a half-century threshold. By then, Dahan's *La Môme* had
been released to international acclaim, earning an Oscar, a César (the
French equivalent), a BAFTA and a Golden Globe for its star Marion
Cotillard. It prompted a fresh surge of interest in Piaf, especially as yet
another memoir by someone who knew her, Ginou Richer, her one-time
secretary and a character in Dahan's film, was published that February.[29]
I'll return to the film in the following chapter, but its importance here
is that, rather than seeking to break new biographical ground, its *raison
d'être* was essentially reiterative and commemorative, in just the same way
as the anniversaries and the various tribute shows. Like them, it applauds
the imagined Piaf by telling the same well-rehearsed stories, largely
dependent on Berteaut's and Piaf's fabrications. In essence, it 'prints the
legend' for a new generation and crowns her patrimonial status, as the
2013 anniversary would do.

The events taking place to mark the half-century were exceptional primarily for their quantity. Only state commemorations of the great figures of French literature normally generate so much cultural activity. There were exhibitions and shows throughout the year. Existing shows, like Jacques Pessis and Nathalie Lermitte's *Piaf: une vie en rose et noir* (A life in pink and black, Théâtre Daunou), which had already toured the world, were revived, old documentaries like *Sans amour on n'est rien du tout* were dusted off and new ones were concocted, notably *Piaf intime* (The private Piaf), based on Marc Bonel's collection of home cine film. In the anniversary week itself, there was daily news coverage on all the main terrestrial channels, which also broadcast numerous programmes. The public channel France 2 screened Blistène's *Étoile sans lumière*. Special issues of news magazines were produced, like *Le Point*'s 'Piaf: a French destiny'.[30] A Belleville group calling itself the Comité Piaf, which brought together the Association of Friends and a number of local businesses, organised a four-day Piaf festival promoting Belleville. This included the usual memorial mass, relayed on giant screens and broadcast on TV. In another service, held at the Église Saint-Pierre d'Arène, close to where she had died, the officiating priest, Gil Florini, gave stylish renditions of 'Mon Dieu' and 'Non, je ne regrette rien' as if he were a singer, while his congregation joined in sonorously as if the songs were hymns. These numbers, he said afterwards, expressed 'a real humanity'; and clearly this justified for him their being performed in a place of worship.[31] Dumont, composer of both songs and by now the indispensable cheerleader on these occasions, offered his own 'Homage to Édith Piaf' at the Espace Cardin in Paris in October and Hugues Vassal mounted several commemorative events based round his photos.[32] Mireille Mathieu's record company re-released her album *Mireille Mathieu chante [sings] Piaf* as it had for earlier anniversaries, each time with a different sleeve.

There were events and news coverage in other countries too, including the UK. Various Piaf tribute acts, among them Eve Loiseau and Christine Bovill, had been touring Britain for some time but reshaped their publicity around the fiftieth anniversary. In London, described by Mayor Boris Johnson as France's sixth-largest city because of its substantial French population, the Southbank Centre hosted *Piaf the concert* featuring a script by Jane Lapotaire and live memories from Sarapo's sister, Christie Laume. But the most telling occasion was part of a major international tour by French singer Patricia Kaas, who chose London's Albert Hall to launch her album *Kaas chante Piaf,* on 5 November 2012.[33]

Kaas is another singer to have once been launched as the new Piaf, though on the strength more of her modest origins than of her singing style, which is of another age. Her tour was spectacular, containing some remarkable re-workings of songs, a number of them lesser known, with startlingly dramatic musical settings by the Polish film composer Abel Korzeniowski, who also conducted the Royal Symphony Orchestra on their pre-recorded accompaniments. 'I didn't want merely to copy Piaf's songs', said Kaas, 'as there is no way of bettering her, so I have given a different interpretation, trying to reflect her emotion but with a contemporary twist.'[34] Certainly, Kaas's obliquely biographical mise en scène re-theatricalised the songs, and at times the concert came to resemble a play, with lighting effects, actor-dancers and Kaas singing in costume against a constantly changing video backdrop. When she performed 'Les Amants d'un jour' (Lovers for a day, Delécluse-Senlis-Monnot, 1956),[35] she was thrust into a chair and interrogated by two sinister men in an oblique evocation of Piaf's interrogation after Leplée's murder. For 'La Belle Histoire d'amour' (The beautiful love story, Piaf-Dumont, 1960),[36] which Piaf had penned with Cerdan's death in mind, Kaas wore boxing gloves while the video behind her showed a real boxing match where a fighter was being badly beaten. Piaf here was as much a fictional character as in Gems's play and Dahan's film.

The London show ended with a recording of Piaf singing 'Hymne à l'amour'. The scene was staged unmistakeably as a state ceremonial and a liturgy. All the cast came on stage and stood solemnly, not quite to attention but heads tilted slightly upwards, while the screen showed a collage of pictures of Piaf. In the rhetoric of the scene, this was a moment of communion in which Piaf's secular hymn to love became a religious incantation and Piaf herself became the people's saint. Herself transfigured by the liturgy, Kaas received three standing ovations. These were certainly for her astonishing performance but also for her turning Piaf into a world heritage site.

A celebration of Piaf in New York a month before Kaas's London show was of a quite different tenor. In September, the French annual music festival Francofolies moved there with a special homage to Piaf at the Beacon Theatre, broadcast at home on France 2, and fronted by a comedian, François-Xavier Demaison.[37] Here, variety and amiability very much prevailed over solemnity. The line-up was impressive to an extent. While stars such as Harry Connick Junior, Madeleine Peyroux, Beth Ditto, Charles Dumont and Julien Clerc were well known, some of the participants—Camélia Jordana, Zaz, Nolwenn Leroy, Cœur de Pirate—were less so outside the Francophone world, especially those who were winners of reality talent contests. The best-known French star in the USA, Charles Aznavour, had dropped out at the last minute. And as had happened at past anniversary concerts, some of the songs were un-illuminatingly re-interpreted, particularly when they were transformed into R'n'B numbers. As a respectful homage like Kaas's to a revered patrimonial figure, the Francofolies event was questionable, but what did come over unmistakeably was the inexpungible imprint Piaf had made on the songs, confirming that French notion that a song is 'created' when it's first performed. More reverential, perhaps, and certainly more reminiscent of her historic past in that city was a momentary vox pop shown on French TV news where a man in a New York street admitted that whenever he hears a Piaf song, he's moved to kiss his wife.[38]

In Britain, the leader of Her Majesty's Opposition in 2013, Ed Miliband, chose 'Non, je ne regrette rien' as his final choice among eight records to have on a desert island,[39] though he was not by any means the first British politician to allude to the song. Piaf's standing in contemporary Britain is in fact an interesting case, simply because her songs hadn't inspired a great deal of interest there in her lifetime other than discretely, as with 'Milord' and 'No Regrets'. She sold relatively few records and didn't ever tour in the UK. The British didn't pay well and Piaf was simply not in demand there.[40] Additionally, despite her love of British royalty, she could also be disdainful of the British themselves, who, she claimed, didn't understand her.[41] Posthumously, though, she has become as much of a cult as in the States. Aside from the ongoing marketing of her records, the success of Gems's drama no doubt played a significant role in this. Then, in the 1980s, the two biographies by British writers, Crosland in 1985 and Bret in 1988, helped the process along. Since then, a growing public taste for popular-music histories has led to regular retrospectives about her on stage, radio and TV.

Her posthumous significance in Britain reflects a different relationship with France from America's, though in both countries it has to do with caricatures of Frenchness. Her cult status in the UK should partly be set against the rise of sybaritic Francophilia: middle-class tourists who regularly pop over to France, perhaps because they have their own little rustic place in the Dordogne or Provence, snapped up for a pittance given the disparity in property prices. They go for the climate, the wine, the cheese and to an extent the chansons, in short for the imagined France of Peter Mayle.[42] But Piaf is also part of the discovery in British popular culture of chanson, perceived as a more serious, more ambitious form of popular music than pop. Some singers and songwriters—Barb Jungr, Leon Rosselson, Des de Moor—explicitly draw on chanson in their own efforts to foreground expressive lyrics. Others, like David Bowie and Marc Almond, seem attracted to its drama and virtuosity, or to a campness it doesn't usually have for the French themselves. But whatever the reasons, Piaf has become a cherished signifier for the Europhile Briton. This was nicely illustrated in 2008 when the high-street optometry chain Specsavers decided to use a clip of her singing 'Non, je ne regrette rien' in a flippant TV advert for spectacles. This was a measure of the cultural standing she now enjoyed in the UK but also of the affection she and the song were held in, because the advert became the ninth most complained about that year, forcing the chain to justify itself.[43]

Globally, too, Piaf's patrimonial status is a given, especially in the entertainment world, where she goes on being reappropriated multifariously. English-language covers of her songs have been commonplace for many years. Rising singers looking for distinction and credibility often reference her as the object of their admiration. The late Jeff Buckley recorded an English adaptation of 'Je n'en connais pas la fin'. Ben Harper wrote his 'When She Believes' as a tribute to her, though there are no specific allusions to her. The young English singer Anna Calvi has declared that she prefers Piaf to pop.[44] Numerous films have used Piaf songs as soundtracks, notably *La Haine* and *Inception*. There is even a Montreal-based underwear chain called La Vie en rose.

In France itself, the same processes of musical remembrance and reappropriation apply, famously exemplified in Gainsbourg's homoerotic version of 'Mon légionnaire'. Juliette, who has recorded 'L'Homme à la moto', was identified as a new Piaf when her career began and so too more recently was the young singer Zaz, though the connection again seems tenuous. Various tribute acts still tour France, like Évelyne Chancel with her show *Piaf mon amour*. But the most significant occurrences from a cultural-historical perspective are those that consolidate her place in the pantheon of national heroes and heroines. In 1990, a series of stamps was issued commemorating 100 years of *la chanson française*, one of which portrayed a colourful drawing of a rather vampish Piaf. In 2012, a joint France–USA initiative produced a pair of stamps for use in both countries depicting Piaf and Miles Davis. And for the fiftieth anniversary, a collector's strip of four stamps was produced, with a short biographical text headed 'La Môme de Belleville' on the back. During Nicolas Sarkozy's presidency (2007–12), a questionnaire was introduced to test migrants' knowledge of French history. One multiple-choice question asked whether Édith Piaf is a singer, a cycling champion or a bird specialist.

Under Sarkozy's successor, François Hollande, the annual Fête de la musique, a nationwide celebration of music-making created by the Ministry of Culture in 1982, adopted Piaf as its special theme in 2013. Clearly convinced of her importance to cultural diplomacy, a ministerial communiqué announced, 'A mythical figure in French chanson, crossing borders and epochs, she will give the Fête de la Musique a joyful energy for audiences both in France and abroad.'[45] Hollande also asked various political figures for suggestions for famous French women whose remains might be transferred to the national mausoleum, the Panthéon, a largely male preserve. The junior minister for the aged, Michèle Delaunay, suggested Piaf, 'so that the people get into the Panthéon' ('pour faire entrer le peuple au Panthéon').[46]

However controversial, even subversive, she had been in life, particularly in the eyes of the Church and certain sections of public opinion, the imagined Piaf in death has manifestly become a comfortably installed heritage figure, proudly brandished as an emblem both of France's historical cultural values and of a new France expansively at ease with popular culture. Alongside, and not entirely distinct from, her ongoing commercial potential, it's this self-congratulatory patrimonialisation that accounts for the inexhaustible desire to celebrate her life by marking her death. But patrimonialisation raises a teleological issue. Since her departure, we're left only with public representations of her: Berteaut's book, Dahan's film, the anniversary celebrations. And the more books, films, documentaries and spectaculars we acquire, the more the public image of Piaf becomes refracted through them, just as they themselves are refracted through earlier representations. The imagined Piaf today, then, is an intertext. Certainly, we have recordings of the songs as she performed them. But given that these are heard today through 50 years of accumulated narratives, it's above all her narrated self that we hear. The Piaf that France has kept alive, remembered and heritagised for its own purposes for half a century is in fact this mediated, constantly re-imagined self. What it has come to mean today is the issue I want to tackle in the final chapter.

CHAPTER 9

Performing Piaf

I F W E S E A R C H B A C K over the 50 years of commemoration, one thing that stands out is that Piaf's posthumous meanings and uses derive more from her life than from her work, although the two still can't be properly separated. One obvious meaning she carries is the damaged star.[1] Hence her ongoing association with Garland and Holiday. As the number of TV documentaries on the three, separately or together,[2] suggests, the celebrity culture of the twenty-first century seems hungry for such icons, perhaps because it has difficulty throwing up damaged stars of its own that the public cares about for very long, and because celebrity is different from stardom. The reality show has played its part here. The logic of the reality format is to deconstruct fame, allowing us to see a flimsy mask of celebrity being manufactured then worn. We know the flaws before we register the fame, so there's none of the dramatic disclosure that there was with historically validated stars like Piaf or Holiday, who have gained our admiration, pity and fear because the tragic flaws underpinning their art were gradually exposed after the advent of fame. Piaf's self-invention offers a particularly elaborate version of this. Damaged since childhood, she was bent on constructing a public self that she controlled and could disappear beneath. But she also allowed the world to discover as much of the damage as she wanted us to know, while concealing its truly intimate nature. This strategy of self-protection through self-projection is close in some ways to the social psychology of Facebook, Twitter and the selfie: the desire for the inner life to be hidden beneath a remote-controlled outer one. The Facebook self, like the public Piaf, isn't a complete invention, removed from the private one: rather, the private self is embellished, made more socially acceptable, and perhaps more liveable too.

This points to another posthumous meaning, which is her claimed relevance for modern times. Much of the anniversary discourse over the years has involved passionate assertions about her undying appeal, even for the young. It has regularly been claimed that the majority (75% to 80%) of the Association of Friends' members are under 40, even today according to Marchois.[3] In 1988, the French journal of teachers of French as a foreign language confidently asserted, 25 years after her death, that her themes still speak to young people's desires and sorrows: 'Her message is not weakened by time; it transcends it'.[4] This might be the wishful thinking of the well-meaning pedagogue, but it would seem not, or not entirely. Since the 1960s, young fans too have insisted they aren't alone among their generation in adoring her. The romantic 17-year-old cited in the last chapter believes her survival has to do with love: 'Édith Piaf is one of only a few artists to encounter such posthumous success and for as long as there are loving hearts, the world will remember.'[5]

By 1988, this kind of fervour is still going strong. Much is made of the 100,000 records she sells every year. A new women's magazine, *Voici*, is convinced that she lives on in the hearts of the French and that, rather than being old-fashioned or nostalgic, she is the 'idol' of thousands of young people, though the use of 'idol' in her case sounds culturally inept.[6] Nor is any evidence adduced other than an unnamed poll showing that 56 percent of 18- to 24-year-olds declared she was important to them, the same proportion as for their grandparents' generation at 55 percent. Several young members of the Association are also interviewed in *Voici*. Éric, aged 26, loves the Piaf museum and comments rather tellingly: 'She's my friend, I don't have any others'. Nelly (22), Stéphane (16) and Régis (28) have been brought together by their love of Piaf and have now adopted the nickname 'the Piafs', as if they were a band. They insist she isn't a bygone myth: 'Her songs reflect everyday life, you never get tired of her voice', says Régis.[7] They spend their spare time tracking down unpublished documents or writing to people who knew her so as to make her seem more real. Yet it's still difficult to accept that these young fans are representative of their generation. In the 1988 survey of cultural practices, only 35 percent of 15- to 24-year-olds said they listened to French hits from before 1980 while a notional '110 percent'[8] revealed they listened to French hits from today. As Stéphane admitted to *Voici* in 1988, he doesn't talk about Piaf to his friends, as they are only interested in contemporary stars like Jean-Jacques Goldman and they dismiss her as outmoded.[9] Certainly, the pop sensibility of the time, with Madonna and Michael Jackson at their global peak, was a long way from hers: 'Her art', Jean Macabiès wistfully acknowledged in 1981, 'has become as distant and as foreign to us as that of the flatulist and the comic soldier of grandpa's day'.[10] Also revealing is a series of interviews in 1983, where a new generation of singers, contemporaries of Goldman (though he wasn't included here), who identified with *la nouvelle chanson française* but who had made their peace with rock, were asked how they felt about Piaf.[11] Most had never seen her live, but they recognised the power and inimitability of her performance and her cultural status as an historical model. But there's still a touch of showbiz tokenism in their genuflexions, for they also note the generational difference and don't actually see themselves as influenced by her.

The Association's archive of fan mail and poems from the 1960s to the 1990s sheds some further light on the question of her relevance, though the age of the contributors is rarely indicated. The archive exposes three decades of devoted, even obsessional fandom. The quality of the poems varies considerably and the letters sometimes betray a poor grasp of grammar. Such cases suggest authors from modest backgrounds who are expressing deeply held if occasionally bizarre emotions. Many of the poems are structured around binaries of light and dark, joy and suffering, regret and gratitude, grandeur and misery: that tiny, frail body and the vast, magnificent voice bursting from it. One recurrent motif is that Piaf didn't die: the little sparrow simply flew away. Bird imagery is abundant, occasionally in eccentric combinations with messianic metaphors, as in one case where a bird is depicted carrying a heavy cross before crucifixion. In other cases, Piaf is shown as restoring the poet's faith in a dark hour, as accepting to die for our sakes, or as still watching over us as we grieve. One of the poems assures us that if we kneel by the grave shared by Édith and Théo we will hear them talking affectionately to each other. Another expresses abandonment and loss at her departure but anticipates her return. Her voice is said to be like a church bell, telling us that love makes life beautiful amidst the misery. A few of the poems and letters are decorated visually, with a coloured border in felt tip, for example, or a pen

drawing of Piaf; others are acrostics of her name. Sentimentality, spirituality, redemption, consolation: all of these meanings remain present in
her fans' imaginations, long after her death. She is the people's Messiah.

In truth, the arguments for and against her continuing relevance
both need to be nuanced. Popular though she clearly still was in France
by the 1990s, including with an unknown number of young people, it
was for a music that was indisputably historical and nostalgic. And yet,
as French cultural tastes since the 'music boom' of the 1970s became
more eclectic and omnivorous,[12] retro became fashionable in the 1980s,
as with the neo-realist chanson. In the end, the question of relevance
has in fact to be approached through the binary of *la chanson française*
and commercial pop, which in turn is bound up with authenticity. The
discourse on the posthumous Piaf is underwritten by a duality between
the authenticity of chanson and the inauthenticity of pop. This had set
in by the first anniversary, when her passing was being seen as the end
of an era and observers were remarking on the gap between her style
and *yéyé*. In most cases, that gap was regretted. Two decades on from
1964, the same chanson–pop binary is still discernible. The young people
interviewed in *Voici* see Piaf's distinctiveness not as old-fashioned but
as a laudable authenticity that pop stars of the day like Madonna and
Jackson simply don't have. 'At least she wasn't synthetic!' ('Elle, au moins,
ce n'était pas du synthétique!'), grumbles Régis.[13] It's the absence of 1980s
pop irony that he and the other interviewees appreciate, her uninhibited
embrace of raw emotion.

They weren't alone. In 1977, when both rock and chanson were still
coloured by the protest ideology of 1968, *Le Point*'s Monique Lefebvre
noted with dismay that Piaf's kind of full-throated sincerity was out of
fashion:

> She delivered no message. She didn't come over as 'intellectual'.
> She shouted, cried, laughed, living out on stage the ordinary
> moments, the ordinary love affairs, the ordinary misfortunes
> and the great joys. Inimitable, unequalled because she was
> never phoney. [...] Listen to her be herself. And give yourself
> permission to be like her, conjugating the verb 'to love' without
> sniggering at the melodrama. She knew the value of sincerity.[14]

Clearly, for Lefebvre, the point has been reached where post-1968 music lovers actually need to be educated in how to listen to her. It's also noticeable around this time how much factual error is creeping into media coverage. Names are misspelt; the year of her death is given wrongly; she is thought to have married Cerdan; and so on. Like King Arthur, the 'real' Piaf is slowly drifting out to Avalon, leaving behind only uncertain legends of heroic struggles. Increasingly mythified, she is turning into a metaphor.

It's hard to generalise about what she represents metaphorically, not least because she is of course invested with untold private meanings. But we can discern at least three shared meanings. First, she stands for France's place in the world, or more accurately its mystique for outsiders. As one TV news source commented in 2013: '50 years on from her demise, she remains *the* French voice'.[15] If we try to tease out what this means, one reason why she has survived is that she has come to embody France's cultural memory of the Occupation: its self-image as an historical survivor in a global sea of troubles and in particular a bastion of democratic resistance: 'Piaf had that ability to sum up the character of occupied and post-war France—a nation that was going through hell but still singing'.[16] Indeed, singing becomes an integral and flattering part of this self-image. Like Édith facing down illness, it's how France triumphs over adversity. 'Everything ends with songs' ('tout finit par des chansons'), the French adage goes. Hence the special status of *la chanson française*. But also, crucially, she was one of the few to export and consolidate that self-image throughout the wider world, particularly America.

Similarly, of course, again at home and abroad, she symbolises a mythical popular Paris. Considering the thousands who turned out for her funeral, Noli observes: 'Paris was paying homage to its most authentic representative. In her, all these women and men recognised themselves and were burying one of their own.'[17] And mayor of the city Jacques Chirac called her 'this great artist who incarnated with so much passion and truth the soul of the people of Paris'.[18] Each articulation of this local symbolism confirms and solidifies the myth further. When Dahan's film came out, one commentator enthused that Piaf 'is Paris, she is a France that's joyful, cheeky, miserable and eternal. America, i.e. the entire world, is singing "La Vie en rose"'.[19] And of course the more the world sings it, the more France comes to symbolise *la vie en rose* globally: the land where life is lived more intensely through wine, love and song; where *la joie de vivre* is a defining characteristic of Frenchness.

More specifically, Piaf has come to signify again what she signified at the start: a Paris vanishing beneath rampant urbanisation. As one columnist noted on the twentieth anniversary, if you turn from her resting place at Père Lachaise and look up towards her native Belleville, 'it's still the Ménilmontant of the old days. Village Paris, despite the invasion of concrete. Not far from the too new apartment blocks, there are three-storey houses with washing at the windows and straw chairs on the pavement. Just the right setting for la Môme.'[20] Today, there's even an 'audio walk' available introducing visitors to Piaf's Paris. In the Anglophone world particularly, she contributes, as does Chevalier and to an extent Trenet, to the Paris that British holidaymakers and American grand tourists look for in vain: the first city envisaged for a romantic spring break, the Montmartre of bohemian artists and saucy cabarets, the literary Montparnasse where in the 1970s one could still see Sartre and de Beauvoir having a working lunch at the Coupole. Part of her appeal for Anglophones is the scent wafting from her like Gauloise smoke of the imagined Paris.

There is, though, a paradox in all this. Anglophone representations still follow French ones in emphasising that she is the voice of the capital's gritty urban realities. And yet the songs Anglophones know best in English—'La Vie en rose', 'Hymn to Love', 'No Regrets'—have none of that grittiness: they have been delocalised into the global love song, where 'arms' can be happily rhymed with 'charms' and 'years' with 'tears'. This is partly an effect of transnational adaptation, although these same songs lack local specificity in the French originals too. French listeners can at least, if they choose, invest the later songs with recollections of her earlier grittiness. Those limited to the English versions can't, though somehow they still manage to find in them the local as well as the global. The imagined Piaf can play strange tricks.

A second metaphoric meaning concerns gender at several levels. Her public image is saturated with expectations of femininity, as we've seen. The pre-war realist form was one in which 'the serious issues in life and love appeared to emerge only from the hearts of women', whereas male singers at that time mostly sang light-hearted or caricaturally working-class material like Chevalier's, or were romantic crooners in the

Tino Rossi mould.[21] Piaf's persona is in fact a palimpsest of representations of women, from oppression to indomitable spiritedness. Put schematically, oppression is more visible in the early songs, at a time when, as Vincendeau points out, the realist genre is defined by women being represented metonymically by the prostitute, 'available, controlled and exchanged by men'.[22] Resilience and spiritedness are more features of her later work, and her later life, when she personally controlled her career and tenaciously faced down illness. Vassal reveals that after every relapse she would summon him to take a photo as she was convalescing, designed to depict her as irrepressible, making yet another courageous comeback.[23] Yet resilience and courage feature above all in *posthumous* interpretations of her life and work, flowing no doubt from the keynote 'Non, je ne regrette rien'. Again, analogies with Garland and Holiday have often sprung to mind, this trinity having become an intertext—consciously or unconsciously but very often in dilute form—for more recent women singers: the Grace Jones of 'La Vie en rose', the Barbara Streisand–Donna Summer duo of 'Enough Is Enough' and the Gloria Gaynor of 'I Will Survive'.

Piaf's association with indomitability in the teeth of hardship and oppression may also help explain her appeal in gay cultures. There's little to suggest same-sex interests in Piaf herself, with her professed liking for legionnaires, sailors and muscular sportsmen and her general dislike of other women. Dietrich's daughter, Maria Riva, did suggest a sexual relationship between her mother and Édith—supported by a photo of a kiss on the mouth between them but flatly denied by Danielle Bonel.[24] But Piaf did have a significant number of gay admirers over the years, starting with Leplée and Cocteau. And she has posthumously become a gay icon. For the twentieth anniversary of her death, an article in the monthly magazine *Gai-Pied* gave a long list of all the things she had come to mean from childhood until death, concluding with a reference to the adoption of 'La Vie en rose' as a Gay Pride anthem, and the coda 'you are all this and more besides. Piaf you will remain in our hearts. Édith, I love you.'[25]

A number of drag artists across the world have also adopted the Piaf persona, equal in number, apparently, to those drawn to Elvis. In Tokyo, the gay singer Akihiro Miwa, whose *Amour et chanson* show 13 years previously had, as we saw, been a triumph, has continued to powerfully interpret her work. For the thirtieth anniversary, he put on a lavish spectacle in French covering 'Milord', 'La Foule', 'L'Accordéoniste' and 'Hymne à l'amour'.[26] His tribute in drag seems to have avoided ironic distance, just as this was absent in Piaf's own emotional directness. Indeed, the drama of Piaf's life and songs and her associations with resilience and power have proven posthumously suggestive as a metaphor for the fluidity and social constructedness of gender.

Yet although she has been adopted as an emblem of particular sectors of society, she has also become—and this is her third metaphoric level—universally emblematic of the human condition: love, joy, suffering, decline and death. And her songs, important though they are, make up only part of this narrative today. The universal symbolism of her life experience appears again and again in posthumous assessments. On the first anniversary of her passing, the artist Carzou commented, 'for me, she was more than a singer, she was the soul, the mirror, the living reflection of human misery, the poignant cry of suffering, the image of our solitude and our distress'.[27] Timelessness, too, is built into this teleological meaning, as in those evaluations that insist she is above fashion and has eternal appeal.

Morin maintains that stars exist because we have a deep cultural need for them,[28] and this is the key to the imagined Piaf's universality. She is both totem and talisman: worshipped because she wards off evil. Like a lightning rod, she draws our pain and suffers in our stead. At the same time, she reflects back at us an idealised image of suffering. She intensifies but also aestheticises it, making it more endurable. In death as in life, there's a lexis of magic surrounding her. Magic is of course a cliché in descriptions of popular singers' impact, but in her case it carries a special weight, suggesting a preternatural power of enchantment and possession that can't be rationally explained. This was present in and perhaps even prompted by Cocteau's first attempts to capture that power, as when he describes her voice on stage as a wave of black velvet: 'This warm wave submerges us, passes through us, enters us. The trick has worked. Édith Piaf, like the nightingale invisible on its branch, is herself about to become invisible.'[29] In an attempt to better understand this 'trick' in the context of Dahan's film, *Le Point* quotes this passage from Cocteau and then goes on: 'For there is magic afoot here, in this charm, where nostalgia, the fog of invented memories, snatches of literature (Zola), bad soap opera and pure tragedy are all mixed together, with the whole sublimated by the singing. The miracle is that the charm still works. Something to do with the collective imagination no doubt.'[30]

Such evocations of her place in an ineffable French imaginary or collective unconscious have become common, particular at anniversaries. At the time of the twentieth, the singer Jean Guidoni, for example, remarked: 'Édith Piaf is part of French culture in the fullest sense, or rather she belongs to a collective unconscious of the people. She's a giant, a monument, an image that clings to France. [...] A bit like an ancient fantasy.'[31] Another singer, Michel Jonasz, drifts into related psychic territory when he admits how difficult it is to speak about her live performances without sounding banal, because she touched a sixth sense. As a 14-year-old, Jonasz had been taken to see her live, and he describes the unexpected psychological intensity of the experience. It wasn't his ears and eyes that were assailed; it was 'something else. You spluttered, she made you shake. It was like a massive trauma.'[32] Half-concealed in the cliché of 'magic', then, is the idea that she appeals to a French sensibility buried deep, beyond words, an unconscious zone which she alone can reach. Vaguely Jungian allusions of this kind can of course flow too easily from the keyboards of journalists, but their widespread recurrence does seem significant. Richard Dyer in his study of film stars is doubtful about the notion of a collective unconscious in such contexts, as it appears essentialist, suggesting 'a supra-individual, quasi-metaphysical human consciousness (rather than people having in common the codes of the culture they live in)'.[33] He is doubtless right, but even if we draw the line at a collective unconscious and think instead, like Dyer, in terms of shared cultural codes, we can still place her among those codes: the collective representations that French people consciously or pre-reflexively share and that compose a cultural sensibility and heritage.

We encounter here the notion of cultural memory, which is useful for describing the process by which Piaf has been systematically patrimonialised. Jan Assmann has identified several defining characteristics of cultural, or 'collective', memory, two of which are especially helpful. First, it concretises identity: it 'preserves the store of knowledge from which a group derives an awareness of its unity and its peculiarity'. Second, it works by 'reconstruction', by which Assmann means that 'it always relates its knowledge to an actual and contemporary situation'.[34] Both of these apply to the ways Piaf has been commemorated. Her life, pared down and purged so as to form an exemplary narrative, has become a fragment of the meta-narrative of France, but its meaning is always being deferred, or in Assmann's terms 'reconstructed' in relation to the present, by the succession of documentaries, films and above all anniversaries. This is how we can better understand Dahan's film. It doesn't propose a new understanding of Piaf but plays with her existing narrative, renewing and refreshing it filmically for a new generation. Dahan is thus complicit in her patrimonialisation. But her constant 'reconstruction' is also transnational. The constant revising and updating of her life narrative is both temporal and spatial, as she circulates as a global as well as national signifier. Hence her different meanings abroad, which, as I have suggested, aren't discrete, alternative meanings or cultural 'misunderstandings': they actually re-circulate, revising and deferring her French meanings.

This symbolic function in cultural memory points to one of Piaf's most significant afterlife meanings: her performability. We've often seen how since the start of her career her life has been construed as popular fiction. This is because narratives of her life have been artfully structured by signs, symmetries, ironies and pathos that have helped generate meanings posthumously. Much of what makes the Piaf story a global myth is in fact its geometry. The arc of her life appears to be described by an implacable destiny worthy of Greek tragedy or by some invisible Pirandellian dramatist. Even the minor characters like the Bonels are dimly aware of being players in a drama. As we know, Piaf herself was largely inventing or underscoring this geometry. So too were the Bonels, who after her death became the self-appointed gatekeepers of her meanings. 'Today, the legends have to be destroyed', writes Danielle. 'All of them. A clean sweep.'[35] They saw it as their duty to clean up the Piaf narrative for posterity. And part of the editorial work they undertook was to reframe her in tragic terms, depicting her stumbling and getting up again when the gods had condemned her. Dumont, Vassal, Noli and Marchois all in their ways did the same.

This patterning of the Piaf narrative has a dramatic potential that creators in various arts have recognised. Starting with the very early music-hall posters of Charles Kiffer and the paintings of Douglas Davis in her lifetime, journalists, singers like Wainwright and Kaas, songwriters like Nougaro and Leprest, playwrights, directors, tribute acts, documentarists, film-makers and cartoonists[36] have all responded accordingly. This is barely surprising given that so much creative work had already been done for them by Piaf and her other inventors. So those seeking to recreate her since her death have been making meanings from meanings already made, often long ago. Film-makers and dramatists in particular have recognised that her life as narrated is structured like a play or script, one which re-imagines her as tragic heroine, a Mother Courage for our times. This is what links Lelouch, Dahan and Gems.

The commercial success of Gems's play in the late 1970s and again in 2008 probably owes more to the eponymous performances of Jane Lapotaire and Elena Roger respectively than to the script, which, as critics agreed, was too rapid and fragmented for audiences to gain real emotional purchase on the characters. But from our point of view, its significance lies in its recognition of and contribution to the nature of Piaf as role, imagined and imaginable and therefore performable. Fragments of her known story and an assembly of mostly invented though vaguely recognisable minor characters are stitched together in a pacy and racy 90 minutes, interspersed with songs taken out of chronological order. The result is a gritty and rather two-dimensional picture of a coarse, funny, randy and cynical cockney who ends up a junkie shooting up before our eyes. Gems interprets Piaf's experience as a woman's struggle to triumph in a man's world that brutalises and manipulates her. Her very vulgarity is a product of that struggle and a form of resistance.[37] Resistance is there in her ripe, resilient wit and her wilful refusal to conform to a code of female sexual decorum. But we see very little of the other facets of Piaf's personality: her longing for romance and tenderness or her religiosity. And the Cerdan episode is dealt with summarily in just one scene. This isn't really bio-drama, then. Rather, a few of the best-known aspects of the Piaf story are rewoven into a dramatic parable expressing the playwright's own concerns. The play is ultimately a cultural translation for Anglophones of the Piaf myth.

As for the cinematic Piaf, why did Dahan succeed commercially when an experienced popular-film-maker like Lelouch struggled to do so? The cinematographic differences between the two films are beyond the scope of this book. But Lelouch opted to interweave an invented love story with that of Édith and Marcel, in which the female lover was played by Évelyne Bouix, who was also playing Piaf. This mirroring was no doubt part of the problem, as it baffled some and made the film long to little discernible effect. Others maintain that neither Bouix as Piaf nor the inexperienced Cerdan Junior—brought in at the last minute after the suicide of the star originally cast, Patrick Dewaere—was entirely convincing in their role.[38] But Dahan, as well as a shrewd pre-release advertising campaign, also had the benefit of a greater temporal distance from the original. Direct memories of Piaf were fading by the start of the new millennium and the upcoming generation of music fans and filmgoers was less familiar with her life story. Dahan, therefore, was able to introduce them afresh to the tragic patterning of that life. But he also opted to approach tragedy as melodrama. *Le Monde*'s film critic complained: 'the directing doesn't skimp on effects and the soundtrack thoroughly exploits the timbre of a heart-rending voice. This is the choice Dahan has made: a film that's popular, sentimental and dramatic.'[39] In particular, he accentuated the pathos. The child actor depicting Édith in her girlhood is innocently wide-eyed. The story of the doll Louis Gassion bought his daughter as a reward when she first sang with him—the only sign of paternal tenderness we see in the film—is drawn out. Leplée's murder and Momone's forcible separation from Édith when she is at her most vulnerable have all the weeping and screaming of a modern soap. 'La Foule' and 'Mon Dieu' are used as emotive underpinnings of the narrative, and the closing scene of Piaf singing 'Non, je ne regrette rien' nudges us into submitting to her greatness. Her biography is also smoothed over somewhat. Unlike in Lelouch's film, we see nothing of her activities during the Occupation; nor do we see any sign of casual sex, for Marcel is constructed as her one true love. Mediated by the songs and accumulated past narratives, this is a film not about Piaf but about her legend.

Dahan had one other advantage, which was that by 2007 Piaf was now more regally enthroned in cultural memory than when Lelouch's film was made. This was already evident in and assisted by the 1996 stage musical *Piaf je t'aime*, directed by Jacques Darcy and with Nathalie Cerda as Piaf. The production attracted over 200,000 spectators at the Cirque d'Hiver and Cerda won an award as theatrical revelation of the year. Darcy then revived the show shortly after the release of *La Môme*, at the Olympia itself, with Marie Orlandi in the title role, where it was again a success. The show itself follows the familiar pattern of the bio-musical, composed of a series of snapshots from Piaf's life. But it's the way the 1996 production described itself that interests us here. The 'Foreword' that featured in its printed programme recognises the growth of Piaf's fame since her death and her current ubiquity, but it regrets that no show 'of any importance' has been put on in France, while 'more or less made-up versions' ('des versions plus ou moins fantaisistes') have been staged in London, Moscow, Canada and Brazil. No doubt, Gems's play is a target here, and also possibly Morris's (1977), with its almost identical title, or Patsy Gallant's Montreal show *Piaf: Love Conquers All* (1992). At any rate, such shows are dismissed as giving only a 'negative, deformed, caricatural image of one of the greatest interpreters of la Chanson Française'. As these initial capitals reveal, for the producers of the French show the sanctity of national cultural memory is at stake here. And, yet again, we have a representation of Piaf that promises to get at a truth deemed uniquely tragic: 'Her destiny was exceptional, constantly marked by the inexplicable, the strange, the irrational, bearing the secret seal of tragedy. There's something esoteric about Édith's life. Fate caught up with her at every crossroads of her life, guiding her from love to fame, a fame which is being perpetuated.'[40] There are several elements to unpack here. First, the tragic weight of destiny in the Piaf narrative is entirely taken for granted, as if it were plain fact. Second, only a French interpretation is deemed capable of representing this, judging by the placing of the above statements immediately after the reference to all those foreign productions which have missed the point. Third, a grave mission now falls to *Piaf je t'aime*: 'retracing that life in the form of a show bringing out the destiny of a little creature born of the street, glorified by the street, and who, like a priestess destined forever to worship love, turns her singing into incantation'.[41] The assumption is that her life *needs* to be more faithfully performed, by a French production of integrity and seriousness which doesn't 'deform' it or present it 'negatively' as 'foreigners' have. This is because of what that life signifies: it is at once a metaphor of the tragic human condition and yet uniquely 'esoteric'. So heroic a task seems oddly portentous for a musical, but it does indicate the deeply serious place that Piaf occupies by the turn of the century in French cultural memory. And once again we glimpse the importance accorded to cleansing the world's image of her. There is clearly no realist intent here, no forensic evaluation of an equivocal life, any more than in Dahan's film. The Piaf the show is concerned with is a vital human archetype, a hieratic artefact to be celebrated, worshipped.

One conclusion to be drawn about Piaf's significance is that the meanings we attribute to her today are mostly posthumously generated. Death, commemoration and artistic representation have at least stabilised her meanings enough to make it seemingly easier to sift through her experiences and see their shape and the forces controlling them. The iconic status of 'Non, je ne regrette rien' offers a good example. Musically conventional, the song's lyric is also a banal tale of someone putting the past behind them because they have found new love. But its worldwide popularity today is a result of tragic hindsight. We know that the new life the song promises lyrically, and musically in the rising cadences and the closing crescendo, soon became a reality for Piaf herself with her redemptive relationship with the young, healthy, caring Sarapo. But we also know that the gods were actually toying with her. Soon after happiness bloomed, it was crushed by illness and death. Now this of course is, by all accounts, a misrepresentation of their actual relationship, but that's something the average listener to the song doesn't know and doesn't want to know. Whatever other meanings we may find in Piaf's life, the one we cleave to most is tragedy.

Conclusion

I BEGAN THIS BOOK by suggesting the improbability of our ever knowing who the 'real', private Piaf was, since any apparent truths about her beyond a handful of factual certainties are part and parcel of an imagined, narrated Piaf. My overarching assumption has also been that, although she was undoubtedly a great singer and performer, this alone can't explain the singular place the public Piaf has retained in French and global memory, a whole century after her birth. Hence the need for a cultural history, investigating what this public, imagined Piaf has come to mean in the course of that century.

One thread running through the book has been that what we today understand by Édith Piaf was an invention from the start. While acquaintances have busied themselves trying to reveal the Piaf they thought they knew, and biographers a real Piaf hidden from view, both have largely passed over her importance as a cultural artefact generated by both production and reception. This artefact was methodically produced and placed in circulation in the second half of the 1930s. Once out there, it was refined or re-invented for the rest of her life, a production process she increasingly took charge of. So, if there is a real Piaf, it's perhaps Piaf narrator of the self, 'controller of [her] own *mise-en-scène*'.[1] Her publics, meanwhile, at home and abroad, appropriated and re-imagined this production in their own terms and for their own purposes, lending it unforeseen meanings and uses. At home, she became a national symbol of romance, class, gender, identity, decadence or renewal, popular culture and the human condition. Internationally, too, she meant all of these things but refracted through an outsider's perception of chanson, France and Frenchness. Since her death, she has been further re-imagined for over half a century, in a suite of afterlives. These later meanings have never eradicated the earlier ones. Beneath the broken star or the patrimonial icon, the frail Parisian waif is still visible. Piaf today, then, is a complex palimpsest of narratives, beneath which the original is unrecoverable.[2]

A second concern has been to show that the imagined trajectory of her life is structured like a tragedy. It begins with her meteoric rise from nothing between 1935 and 1945 and culminates in national and international apotheosis from 1945 to the early 1950s. This is followed by irresistible decline and death. This downward curve of the arc is interrupted for an instant by one last triumph at the Olympia in December 1960 and one last great self-affirmation with 'Non, je ne regrette rien', the song she is most identified with internationally. But as death approaches, her populist version of *la chanson française*, adapted from the elderly *chanson réaliste*, begins to be outrun by newer versions, from her 'existentialist' rival Juliette Gréco and the poetic singer-songwriters, to rock'n'roll and *yéyé*. This doesn't diminish her reputation but it does make it more ambivalent, as she appears to be offering repeat performances of the old Piaf more than genuinely renewing herself. By October 1963, there's a discernible sense that musically as well as physically her time is up. Death, however, becomes her. Her afterlives eliminate the ambivalence and she is gradually transfigured into an extratemporal, patrimonial, quasi-fictional trope of global popular culture, to be regularly celebrated. This is where she stands today, encrusted with meanings as never before.

The cultural history of Piaf also sheds light on issues concerning French culture in the last and present centuries. She represents a key transition in the development of popular music and popular culture in France. She began singing professionally at a time when the French music industry was in its infancy. Radio, recording and the microphone were still new but developing. The music economy from which she emerged—the *chanson réaliste*, the distribution of popular songs via street singers and the selling of *petits formats*—still bore traces of the nineteenth century. This is the economy in which her meanings were forged, in which she made sense. 'Amateurism' is a word best avoided here, but for most of her career she lacked the slick professionalism of today's stars. And she remained first and foremost a live performer, from the street to Carnegie

Hall and the Olympia. Her studio recordings attempted to capture the intensity and uniqueness of the live experience, rather than aiming to exploit the full technological resources of the recording studio. Rehearsals for both often took place in her own flat, unscheduled and impromptu, in front of a motley crew of friends and hangers-on, rather than in the sophisticated concert venues or purpose-built facilities of today.[3] Her post-1945 team, competent and successful as it was, still largely operated by an informal division of labour within which associates and friends could scarcely be distinguished.

Nevertheless, the situation by the end of her life was quite different from that of her beginnings. The collective nature of her work, which would become standard in the second half of the twentieth century, took her away from the romantic individualism of the lone street singer that had been the original basis for the development of her repertoire and performance style, towards something closer to what Howard Becker theorises as an 'art world':[4] collective interactions, both institutional and discursive, that produce and give meaning to a work of art. With the rise of the vinyl album and single in the 1950s and the protracted emergence of television, a French star system had developed, in music as in cinema, and she was one of the first French singers to be gilded by it. Asso's meticulous work with her on performance and image prefigures that system, and the later media interest in her private life, an indispensable feature of 'starification', testifies to her eventual enrolment in it.

Piaf's career also bears witness to the importance America assumed for the postwar French music industry, since, like Chevalier before her, she had to succeed there in order to develop a fully global profile. To an extent, she represents the Americanisation of French popular music, in that jazz influences appear in her work almost from the beginning, though much less than with a Trenet or a Montand. After her remarkable successes in America, she sought to become an international torch singer by avoiding the sociological and national positioning of her early work. And yet she continued to embody what would become a widespread endeavour, right up to today, to somehow preserve a Frenchness in chanson, whatever that might mean, in her case by cleaving to big emotions and taking song immensely seriously.

On one level, then, she both exemplifies the development in France of mass culture and contributes to its processes of fabrication and star-making. Through her, we can see how the notion of the popular evolved during 30 crucial years in the cultural history of France, from the 1930s to the 1960s. As I've argued elsewhere,[5] 'popular' culture as understood at the time of the 'Popular' Front subsequently shifts, just as it does in Piaf's career, from the particular to the universal, so that a 'popular' song is no longer understood as one which emerges authentically from working-class or rural particularisms but as one that is industrially produced and distributed and appreciated by a sociologically mixed 'mass' public. Since Piaf's death, of course, that second sense has been transformed in turn by the ever greater segmentation of tastes.

Equally, Piaf helped change national and international perceptions of French chanson by developing a style and discourse which legitimate the popular song as a specifically French art form. In the 1930s and 1940s, alongside Trenet though differently from him, she developed a blueprint for the author-composer-singer model of the 1950s and 1960s with which *la chanson française* has so often been associated in global perceptions. We've seen how closely she involved herself in the composition and production of her repertoire and how she systematically constructed a chanson persona by singing songs that fitted her own experiences but also narrating those experiences to fit her songs.

What she also contributed to a chanson discourse were her quasi-artisanal production values. The improvised functioning of her creative team is one example. Her apparently unsophisticated, 'natural', though in truth studiously constructed appearance on stage is another. Far from the consummate entertainer harking back to the 1920s revue, she constructs herself and is constructed as a vulnerable lone figure who has come before us not to entertain but to bare her soul and who now finds herself in the spotlight, bewildered about why we should take any interest. Even when she was accompanied by a full orchestra, she astutely took the decision to conceal it behind the stage curtains. This sense of solitary, intimate communication with the audience would become part of the author-composer-singer trope in France, just as it would, though differently, with the early Dylan or Joni Mitchell. Peter Hawkins is right to detect Piaf's affective theatricality in Jacques Brel's full-on stage style.[6] But we can also recognise different dimensions of her in the more economical staging of Ferré, Brassens and Moustaki. Whoever else might be on stage with them, the rhetoric of singer-songwriters such as these is that they are here not just to give us a good night out but also to disclose, person to person, how they see the world.

But Piaf herself always keeps one foot firmly in music hall or variety. This can be heard in the pacy or sing-along renditions of songs like 'La Goualante du pauvre Jean', 'Bal dans ma rue' or 'A quoi ça sert, l'amour'. It can also be seen in the singing stars she helped launch, who in most cases retained a variety dimension, most obviously Montand, Constantine and Aznavour, often seen as France's Sinatra. The imagined Piaf in fact combines three of the main tropes of modern French chanson: the intimate singer-songwriter, usually male (though much less so today), the female singer performing gendered suffering, and the entertainer.

The tendency in France, from Mireille Mathieu in 1965 to Zaz in 2010, to launch young women singers as new Piafs points to one other crucial meaning: as a vector of national cultural memory. For Deniot, the fact that she continues to be referenced and reappropriated is indicative of a mythical status.[7] For Aznavour, she's a symbol of France in the same way as Jeanne d'Arc or Victor Hugo.[8] But perhaps, more precisely, she has become a *lieu de mémoire*, a site of memory. For Pierre Nora, sacred, ritualistic dimensions of collective memory once bound societies together as 'imagined communities'[9] but have now disappeared, particularly in a France obsessed, Nora believes, with progress and the future. Cultural memory, therefore, as a living process which keeps the past alive in the present, actually no longer exists. We're left with only history, a mere representation of the past which persistently labours to demythologise it and turn 'whatever it touches into prose'. Memory is 'a phenomenon of emotion and magic, [which] accommodates only those facts that suit it. [...] History, being an intellectual, nonreligious activity, calls for analysis and critical discourse.' Nora maintains that in the past the French practice of history had a 'didactic role in forming the national consciousness'.[10] But today's self-consciously critical history has challenged this mission. History, memory and nation are thus sundered. As a result, French society, nostalgic for this lost commonality, looks for ways of artificially reconstructing it. Hence sites of memory: '*Lieux de mémoire* are fundamentally vestiges, the ultimate embodiments of a commemorative consciousness that survives in a history which, having renounced memory, cries out for it.' They are fabricated exercises in nostalgia, arising out of a sense 'that we must create archives, mark anniversaries, organize celebrations, pronounce eulogies, and authenticate documents because such things no longer happen as a matter of course'.[11] And although sites of memory have a material reality, they are in fact 'pure signs', apparently existing outside history and open to an infinity of meanings.[12] This is where Piaf comes in.

What I have traced in the book is the process in which an imagined Piaf has steadily broken free of her material existence. The very first representations of her made meanings out of that very physicality: her stunted body, her supposed ugliness, her image as victim, and so on. But from 1945 her meanings slowly became more abstract. So, when she died, these meanings and the public self she had herself constructed easily lent her to being appropriated as a *lieu de mémoire*. This helps us understand why the French cling so tenaciously to her, commemorating her whenever the calendar allows and, in biography after biography, handing down her story like a folktale. I have underscored the way her performances gradually became emotional, ritualistic experiences in France. She can be seen as one of 'the rituals of a ritual-less society', as Nora puts it: 'fleeting incursions of the sacred into a disenchanted world'.[13] Representations of her life and work, and of her voice particularly, constantly introduce the sacred into the profane, the divine into the earthily human.[14] There are also the quasi-religious practices of fans, such as the attention paid to her grave, which is seldom unattended and always decorated with flowers, and the Piaf museum, packed tight with memorabilia.[15]

Nora's reconfiguring of cultural memory and cultural history has been challenged by other historians for appearing to be primarily applicable to French historiography. Certainly, Piaf's meanings in Britain and America are somewhat different from those in France, in part precisely because of her sacred significance in her home country. The ethnographic distance I referred to in the introduction, the 'stranger's gaze', as Michael Kelly calls it,[16] can perhaps serve as a counterweight in this respect. But if I have deconstructed her myth, it has been not with the intention of dethroning her or belittling the pleasure she gives but in order to examine how the Piaf imagined in France has functioned as a public narrative, and why an aura of sacredness surrounds her there, even to an extent in the work of scholars of chanson like Dutheil Pessin and Deniot. I've done so in fact in order to bring out the singularity of her national meanings in comparison with those she's acquired in the UK and USA.

Although not quite so sacred outside France, she nevertheless belongs among the great signifying myths of the twentieth century, those instantly recognisable icons, living or dead, of global culture: Dylan, Presley, John Lennon, Billie Holiday, Bardot, Marilyn Monroe. Like Bardot, she's one of only a few French nationals to achieve this status. Piaf, Holiday and Garland were international divas more powerfully than those celebrities to whom the term is so liberally applied in the twenty-first century, but they were also forerunners of celebrity culture. Piaf's life became a living soap opera and her posthumous myth remains so. Both her life and her myth embody what have today become familiar, populist representations of working-class women, as suffering, tragic but also 'brassy', 'feisty', giving as good as they get. In some respects, she is the Elsie Tanner or Roseanne Barr of chanson.

For both national and international audiences, life and song are ultimately indistinguishable in the imagined Piaf. The dispersed fragments of her lived experience only seem to come together in a signifying, mythical whole when that life is recreated in song. Her songs are of course about love, though in increasingly clichéd terms. But what have engaged and inspired audiences across the globe and across several generations are, I suspect, the other human preoccupations that love songs serve to stage and which I have tried to tease out: beauty and ugliness, gender and sexuality, men and women, privilege and underprivilege, destiny and misfortune, and the importance in our lives of festivity, music and song, which bring solace and pain in equal measure. Piaf's appeal lies both in the immediate emotions these preoccupations elicit when enriched and complexified by her uniquely plaintive voice and in the cathartic identification-projection that voice elicits.

There's a good deal more to be said about her meanings and uses. In writing this book, I have become especially aware that the gendering of Piaf is complex and requires a lot more exploration. The same applies to the postcolonial dimensions of her meanings, which I've only touched on. The palimpsest of her afterlives also needs to be unpicked further. How much longer will those afterlives continue? As I write, the celebrations of her centenary have only just begun, so it remains to be seen what they will reveal. But perhaps there are already minute signs that the earnest respect in which she's been held in France for over 50 years is changing, even, perhaps, diminishing. The majority of those who appreciate her today have only ever encountered her indirectly and in mediated form; and many are at a cultural remove from the kind of unashamed emotion she elicited in the 1930s, 1940s and 1950s. What was particularly striking about the New York Francofolies in September 2013, fronted by a comedian, was not just the youth of the performers earnestly trying to update her best-known numbers, but the self-conscious, reality-show atmosphere that prevailed there.[17] Rather than a sublime homage like Kaas's show, this was a festive, juvenescent, mildly irreverent occasion. No doubt Piaf was still recognised as an icon by the young performers involved, but she was also a pretext for self-positioning: for showing off their own talents and for being seen there in New York, under the bright lights of the world's gaze.

The imagined Piaf was certainly present at the event, albeit like an indulgent grandmother who'd let them use her front room for a party and was sitting discreetly in the back parlour while they had their fun. Every now and then, they'd bring her a drink and check she was OK, telling each other how amazing she was for her age and giggling just a little at her quaintness as they made their way back to the dancing. Somewhere, no doubt, in that amiably chaotic New York celebration of twenty-first-century Frenchness, Piaf's next afterlife was being minted.

Notes

Introduction

1   *Le Point*, 2015. Piaf also has her own Facebook page: https://www.facebook.com/edithpiafofficiel?rf=198136600367617.

2   Throughout the book, I'll use the French word 'chanson' without italics to represent the relatively common use of the term in English, in which it normally designates a style of popular song associated with France whose lyric is especially important and is often seen as dramatic, poetic or narrative. I will italicise *la chanson française*, *la chanson réaliste*, and so on, to distinguish specifically French uses of the term. The semantic distinctiveness of the latter will become clearer as the book progresses.

3   This book was virtually complete when, between 7 and 9 January 2015, there were terrorist attacks on the offices of the satirical magazine *Charlie Hebdo*, two police officers and a kosher supermarket. Seventeen of those attacked died, and three terrorists. Marches and other manifestations took place across France mobilising some four million people in all. In Paris, the songs broadcast along the route were also by Trenet ('Douce France') and Aznavour. Equally significantly, on the evening of the rally French public TV channels, concocting a live 'Soirée je suis Charlie', instinctively turned not only to cartooning and satire, the magazine's staples, but also to *la chanson française* (Alain Souchon, Julien Clerc, Catherine Ringer and Benjamin Biolay all performed, among others). The show was a not altogether comfortable mix of sobriety and variety. But by looking to singers to soothe and affirm the nation, it demonstrated the continuing symbolic weight of chanson even in today's culturally diverse France. This book will explore that weight further.

4   Monteaux, 1963, 16. As with this note, I use the author-date referencing system, though I avoid embedding bracketed notes in the text itself, for ease of reading. Full details of Monteaux and all other texts referred to are found in the references section at the end of the book.

5 'la fabrication psychologique de la vedette'. As here, the original French versions of all translated quotations are provided in the endnotes.

6 'Il ne peut pas être question d'un soupçon de fabrication dans le cas de Piaf. [...] Elle n'appartient qu'à elle-même.'

7 Bonini, 2008, 146.

8 Peterson, 1997.

9 'La nuit de son appel, j'ai compris qu'il y a une deuxième femme en elle. Une femme déboussolée par le succès, par l'argent, une femme qui s'impose par son talent, et, d'un autre côté, une pauvre malheureuse, un pauvre petit oiseau, une enfant privée de tendresse.' Bonels, 1993, 235.

10 'Personne ne peut raconter Piaf, car elle était différente pour chacun d'entre nous. On ne pouvait pas la cerner et elle entretenait à plaisir cette ambiguïté, se cherchant et se trouvant elle-même.' Quoted in Marchois, *La Vraie Piaf*, 2013, 253. The bulk of this volume consists of interviews organised by the Association des Amis d'Édith Piaf with various people who knew her. Many of the interviews originally appeared in Marchois, 1995, though new ones were added for the 2013 book. Curiously, there are discrepancies in wording between the two editions, though these are mostly minor. Marchois assured me in 2014 that the later volume reproduces the exact wording.

11 'Comment savoir qui était la vraie Édith Piaf? Elle a joué tellement de rôles. C'était un caméléon. Elle prenait le climat de l'homme du moment. Elle ne savait pas rester elle-même tout le temps. Je l'ai connue sous toutes ces formes. La vraie Édith était celle qui se retrouvait face à elle-même, quand elle n'avait plus de rôle à jouer et qu'elle se posait la question: "Qui suis-je?"'. Danielle Bonel in conversation with Bonini, 2008, 344.

12 English translation, Piaf, 1992, 9. 'Je serai morte, et on aura tant dit de moi, que personne ne saura vraiment qui j'aurai été'. Piaf, 1964, 7.

13 'Quant à ma vie privée, la véritable, personne ne la connaît. Les gens ne savent que ce que je veux bien dire.' Piaf quoted in Vassal, 2002, 141.

14 'Que représentait Édith Piaf pour avoir provoqué une telle adhésion populaire en France comme à l'étranger?' Mortaigne, 2007.

15 Bonels, 1993, 17.

16 Bret, 1988, 12. He later produced a second book, *Piaf: A Passionate Life* (Bret, 1998), drawing on and amplifying the first.

17 Crosland did produce an updated edition: Crosland, 2002.

18 Burke, 2011, xvii.

19 Burke, 2011, 229.

20 Vincendeau, 1987; Rifkin, 1995, which references Piaf across various chapters but particularly chapter 2; and Reader, 2003.

21 Dutheil Pessin, 2004.

22 'les cadres, à vocation généralisatrice, d'une analyse [...] de la scène du geste vocal'. Deniot, 2012a, 27–28.

23 'un "je" intrusif'; 'mon lien personnel à la chanson'; 'la subjectivité radicale comme sentier privilégié d'accès à l'intersubjectivité'. Deniot, 2012a, 39.

24 Dyer, 1998, 2.

25 See Loïc Vadelorge, 2011, 12. This standard definition is attributed to, among others, the French historians Pascal Ory and Roger Chartier. It also appears in elaborated form in Rioux and Sirinelli, 2002, 11.

26 Frith, 1998, 26. As regards cultural theory, it would certainly have been possible to analyse Piaf by referring to the now canonical French 'theorists' associated with French studies and cultural studies, from Barthes to Bourdieu, Derrida, Kristeva or Foucault. But there are dangers in doing so. Occasional French scholars use the Franglais term 'la *French theory*' to lampoon the Anglo-American reflex of turning to a small a group of French intellectuals (who in reality have little in common) as 'a badge of high intellectuality' (Mattelart and Neveu, 2003, 88), without feeling the need for any empirical investigation (for further discussion of this debate, see Holmes and Looseley, 2013, 5–6). A further risk is that such high theory may in all its density become more prominent than the subject to which it's being applied. In the particular case of a popular-cultural icon like Piaf, it seems paradoxical to produce a book that's inaccessible to all but the initiated. Hence my preference for a conceptual approach drawing on cultural history, which can offer a third way between the excesses of theoreticism and empiricism. The book certainly is theoretically informed and I will draw attention to this where necessary, though—I hope—as discreetly as possible.

27 Frith, 2011, 12.

28 'Aucune chanteuse plus que Piaf n'a autant mêlé sa vie et sa chanson, au point qu'il est impossible de les discerner l'une et l'autre.' Dutheil Pessin, 2004, 278.

29 Nora, 1996, 6.

30 Morel, 2011, 241.

31 'les cultures nationales se construisent autant à l'extérieur qu'à l'intérieur des frontières, […] la notion d'identité nationale est fondamentalement plurielle, mouvante et largement dépendante de phénomènes qui ont lieu au-delà des frontières de l'État-nation'. Tournès, 2011, 252.

32 Morel, 2011, 239. Among other contexts, the word 'passeur' was employed during the Occupation to designate those who led escapees to safety across France's borders.

33 'les comportements populaires peuvent être aussi riches de sens, aussi subtils que ceux des élites'. Neveu, 2011, 160.

34 Deniot, 2012a, 171.

35 I borrow the phrase 'ethnographic distance' from Charles Forsdick: see Looseley, 2013a, 19–28.

36 Looseley, 2013a, 19–28.

Chapter 1: Inventing la Môme

1 'Avec quelle monstruosité elle veut devenir autre chose'. Contet in conversation with Bonini, 2008, 97.
2 For the reasons pointed out in the introduction, the following biographical summary can only resort to accounts whose reliability is sometimes questionable. See Duclos and Martin, 1993, chapter 2, for an intelligent sifting of what is false, assumed or backed by documentary evidence. Belleret, 2013, chapter 1, also brings some new evidence to the story of her childhood.
3 Burke, 2011, 14.
4 Dillaz, 1991, 176–77.
5 Dillaz, 1991, 176–77; Looseley, 2003, 14–17; Looseley, 2013c, 55–58.
6 Dillaz, 1991, 177–79.
7 Guibert and Le Guern, 2011, 32.
8 On this trend and on the general commercialisation of cabarets in an attempt to compete for punters with the music halls, see Richard, 1991, 209–17.
9 French and English understandings of the word 'chanson' are certainly different, and capturing that difference is a long, complex and controversial business, which illustrates my points in the introduction about ethnographic distance. There is, though, a small but growing literature in English on the subject. See Looseley, 2003, chapter 4; and Looseley, 2013c. Also valuable are Lebrun, 2009 (see 'chanson' in her index), and Lebrun, 2012.
10 Looseley, 2013c, 57.
11 Deniot, 2012a, 302.
12 'une voix de cathédrale'. Laure quoted in Marchois, 2013, 295.
13 Belleret, 2013, 56.
14 Piaf, 2003 [1958], 81.
15 Marchois (1993, 13) is sure she began there on 25 October, as is Belleret (2013, 67), more or less. Marchois's compendium is the most readily accessible source of press cuttings on Piaf, many reproduced in their entirety, from the start of her career to the end of her life. Its main flaw is that the articles aren't always properly attributed and there are also a number of typographical errors.
16 For his account of her discovery, see Bleustein-Blanchet, 1964, 51.
17 For Canetti's own account of how he helped launch Piaf, see Canetti, 2008, 32–33. Canetti went on to be a major player in the development of the postwar French singer-songwriter, both at Polydor and Philips and at the Trois Baudets cabaret, which he set up in 1947, where the likes of Brel, Brassens, Ferré, Anne Sylvestre, Serge Gainsbourg and others made their names.
18 Piaf's mother died from drug abuse in 1944 and her father passed away the following year. Shortly after his death, Piaf bought a family plot at the historic Père Lachaise cemetery in the east of Paris, where she had his remains reburied.

She did the same for her daughter Marcelle and is herself buried there. She left her mother's remains where they were.

19 For example, her first dress-maker, Marinette Mousquès, stated: 'She wasn't very clean, drank like a trooper and had never seen a dentist' ('Elle n'était pas très propre, buvait comme un soldat et n'avait jamais vu un dentiste'). Quoted in Bonini, 2008, 108.

20 Belleret (2013, 55) is unconvinced by this tale.

21 Extract reproduced in Bleustein-Blanchet, 1964, 51.

22 'une petite bonne femme minable dans sa robe de quatre sous. L'air traqué de celle qui vient d'écoper une bonne dérouillée'. Rim quoted in Bonini, 2008, 103.

23 'ce petit bout de femme en robe plissée à la mode des filles des Halles et en chandail blanc […]. Elle faisait songer à toutes ses sœurs du pavé de Paris. Avec de la gouaille au bout des lèvres, elle fredonnait des chansons du bitume.' The journalist, who signed himself only 'Serge', is quoted in Bonini, 2008, 79, and, with slightly different wording, in Belleret, 2013, 458.

24 Rossi, undated: 'Un être imprévisible et difficilement compréhensible, dont l'humeur alternait bizarrement, passant tout à coup de la plus folle gaieté au désespoir le plus inconsolable'. Aznavour, 1980s: 'un enfant dictateur […] un être qui avait des réactions totalement infantiles'. Both are quoted in Bonini, 2008, 291 and 333 respectively.

25 The following arguments about Piaf's 'inventors' were sketched out in Looseley, 2013b, 234–46, but are more fully developed here.

26 Crosland, 2002, 38.

27 Frith, 1998, 169–71 *passim*.

28 Berteaut, 1973 [1969], 122. I have restored from Berteaut's original French the first double quotation marks round 'my', omitted by the translator. In her first autobiography, *Au bal de la chance* (Piaf, 2003 [1958]), translated as *The Wheel of Fortune* (Piaf, 2004, 81–88), Piaf tells the story quite differently, claiming among other things that Asso had written the lyric for her based on her affair with the legionnaire, which she had recounted to him. As the editor of *Au bal*, Marc Robine (Piaf, 2003 [1958], 84–85 n1), points out, this is false, since the song was written for Dubas, for whom he worked before he began working with Piaf. Duclos and Martin (1993, 88) suggest Asso may have been writing the song when he first met Piaf. This said, we can't be any more confident of the version recounted by Berteaut.

29 'Sa vie telle qu'elle me la servait était un mélange, subtil et habile, de Zola, de feuilleton pour cœur solitaire, d'Aristide Bruant, de roman à l'eau de rose.' Noli, 1973, 75.

30 Belleret, 2013, 38.

31 'Il y a du vrai, il y a du faux. Cela dépend comment on raconte les histoires.' Piaf quoted in Duclos and Martin, 1993, 179.

32 Noli, 1973, 75.

33 Bonels, 1993, 55.

34 'un chien perdu quelque part qui m'empêchera d'être heureuse'. Anouilh, 2008 [1942]. First staged in 1938. Piaf made frequent allusions to Anouilh's famous line in the late 1950s, after the actor Pierre Brasseur wrote a lyric for her entitled 'Et pourtant' (Brasseur-Émer, 1956), which ended with the line. See Saka, 1994, 245–46.

35 Bonel in conversation with Bonini, 2008, 102.

36 'ce ne fut pas non plus Zola'. Bonini, 2008, 102.

37 Giroud, 1952, 217.

38 'tout ce qu'elle fait dans le but de s'élever socialement, de s'élever dans la culture [...], ça nous laisse tous pantois!' Contet in conversation with Bonini, 2008, 97.

39 'Elle revêtait, pour chanter, une seconde personnalité, aussi tragique que la première pouvait être comique.' Gassion cited in Marchois, 2013, 223.

40 For her own summary of this repertoire, see Piaf, 2003 [1958], 42.

41 In French, to 'create' a song, a piece of music or a play commonly means to perform it for the first time.

42 Saka, 1994, 19–20. As here, first references to songs associated with Piaf will normally (unless syntax requires otherwise) be followed by a parenthesis giving first the lyricist, then the composer, then the date of publication of the score (e.g. Asso-Monnot, 1936). I will also refer the reader to the collected lyrics of her songs anthologised by Pierre Saka.

43 Piaf, 2003 [1958], 57–61. See also the account of the incident in Belleret, 2013, 72–73.

44 Deniot, 2012a, 51. The *café-concert* of the mid- to late nineteenth century was a rowdier forerunner of the music hall.

45 Vincendeau, 1987, 112.

46 Deniot (2012a, 43) suggests it was likely a music publisher's invention.

47 Dutheil Pessin, 2004, 39, 79.

48 Dutheil Pessin, 2004, 33.

49 Vincendeau, 1987, 108. Vincendeau evokes 'a voyeuristic obsession with the capital and in particular with the lives of its "lower" classes in which proletariat and underworld mingle'.

50 'The Paris celebrated by *chanson réaliste* constantly deplores its own demise'. Vincendeau, 1987, 110.

51 Vincendeau, 1987, 123.

52 'Elle interprétait des chansons réalistes avec une telle force, une telle intensité, que déjà elle nous arrachait les tripes. [...] Elle exprimait par ses chansons toutes ses misères de jeunesse.' Ketty quoted in Marchois, 2013, 262–63.

53 Deniot, 2012a, 132–33, 200.

54 Deniot, 2012a, 133, 142.

55 Deniot, 2012a, 148.

56 Deniot, 2012a, 133.

57 Deniot, 2012a, 133. On 'realist' authenticity, see also Vincendeau, 1987, 114–17.

58 'les ondes portent la voix poignante de notre chanteuse dans les chambres les plus intimes et cette voix se mélange à la vie d'une foule de personnes'. 'Je travaille avec Édith Piaf', 1940. Article reproduced in Marchois, 1993, 31–32 (quotation: 31). Marchois provides no source or precise date.

59 Dutheil Pessin, 2004, 292.

60 'Cette fille venue de la rue donne aux chansons de la rue la même poésie poignante, pénétrante et doucement vénéneuse que Carco à ses romans de la rue.' *Le Petit Parisien*, 1935, 7. Francis Carco (1886–1958) was a French novelist specialising in the Parisian street life of the period, especially Montmartre.

61 Saka, 1994, 81–82.

62 Letter of reminiscence written by Asso to Piaf shortly before her death, reproduced in Bonels, 1993, 210–11.

63 English translation (which I have slightly adapted), Piaf, 1992, 13. 'Ah! Comme je l'ai aimé, mon légionnaire. [...] Longtemps, je n'ai pas pu la chanter [the Asso song] sans frémir. C'est peut-être pour cela que la chantais si bien?' Piaf, 1964, 16–17.

64 There is in fact another version of the affair which suggests that he didn't die. As for the claim that Asso wrote the song based on her story, she doesn't, strictly speaking, say which song, though the implication is quite clearly that it was 'Mon légionnaire'. Several biographers, however, suggest it must have been 'Mon amant de la Coloniale.'

65 See Pénet, 2004, 749–884.

66 Piaf, 2003 [1958], 43.

67 Saka, 1994, 39–41.

68 Both *moineau* and the slang term *piaf* mean 'sparrow' in French.

69 Piaf, 2003 [1958], 50.

70 Press extracts by Asso reproduced in Marchois, 2013, 38.

71 As Piaf lay dying in the South of France, he wrote to her to reminisce and offer his help as head of the SACEM (Société des auteurs, compositeurs et éditeurs de musique). In the letter, he reveals that his song 'Elle fréquentait la rue Pigalle' had begun as a short story. Letter reproduced in Bonels, 1993, 210–11.

72 Piaf, 2003 [1958], 217–18. Her first Bobino appearance was in fact as part of a touring troupe called 'La Jeune Chanson' in 1936, before Asso became her manager. She may mean her first appearance alone, in February 1937.

73 Correspondence between Asso and Mousquès quoted in Bonini, 2008, 143–44. The original choice of a simple black dress as her stage outfit is claimed

by several people, including Bruno Coquatrix, who very briefly became her manager in 1936.

74 'Programme ABC: Pour la première fois La Mome Piaff [*sic*]', reproduced in Marchois, 1993, 15.

75 Interview with Piaf entitled 'L'Événement capital de leur carrière', *Le Matin*, 30 March 1947. Article reproduced in Marchois 1993, 56. Years later, she would tell the same story in her first autobiography, Piaf, 2003 [1958], 89–90.

76 Piaf, 2004, 46. '[D]ans ce "tour [de chant]" éblouissant, rien n'était laissé au hasard, à l'improvisation. Ni les jeux de physionomie, ni les gestes, ni les attitudes, ni les intonations.' Piaf, 2003 [1958], 90.

77 Bonels, 1993, 208.

78 'En deux ans, elle perdra son côté vulgaire pour évoluer et se métamorphoser. Son visage devint bouleversant de pureté. [...] Ce fut la naissance, la création, l'accouchement d'un nouvel être.' Asso quoted in Marchois, 2013, 39.

79 'Édith, c'était la chair de ma chair. Je l'ai faite. J'ai accouché d'elle, souffrances comprises'. *France-Soir*, 1969, 8.

80 Asso quoted in Marchois, 2013, 38 and 41 respectively.

81 English translation in Piaf, 1992, 23, though I have altered Crosland's translation somewhat. 'Je me vautrais dans la bêtise comme une sale petite bête dans la boue. Je m'y complaisais. Et dans la laideur aussi. [...] Raymond m'a transformée. Il m'a appris à devenir un être humain [...] [à devenir] une femme et une vedette, au lieu d'un phénomène dont on écoutait la voix comme on montre un animal rare dans un stand forain.' Piaf, 1964, 32.

82 'Comme tu dois souffrir pour m'écrire d'aussi vilaines choses, mais tu as raison, je suis bête, [...] et je me dégoûte, je n'ai plus confiance en moi, je ne suis rien en somme d'après ce que tu m'as écrit'. Piaf's letter to Asso, published by him after her death, quoted in Bonini, 2008, 142.

83 Piaf, 2003 [1958], 80.

84 Asso quoted by Piaf, 2003 [1958], 80. The following analysis of Asso's songs draws on Looseley, 2013b.

85 Saka, 1994: 'Browning', 69–70; 'Le Contrebandier', 23–25; 'Paris-Méditerranée', 74–75. For a more detailed analysis of 'Paris-Méditerranée', see Looseley, 2013b, 234–46.

86 Saka, 1994: 'Mon amant de la Coloniale', 57–58; 'Le Fanion de la Légion', 63–64. On this and other representations of the Legion in popular culture, see Cooper, 2006.

87 'c'était ma meilleure amie. Son talent, je n'en parlerai pas puisqu'il m'a aidé à être Édith Piaf!' Quoted in Marchois, 2013, 326.

88 'La Môme est morte! ... C'est Édith Piaf que vous allez entendre!' Quoted in Duclos and Martin, 1993, 136.

89 'La môme était charmante, certes et son succès justifié. Mais Édith Piaf et le triomphal accueil que le grand public fait maintenant à chacune de ses

chansons, c'est évidemment autre chose. C'est une artiste, une grande artiste.'
Marc Blanquet, 'La Môme Piaf est morte. Vive Édith Piaf!', *Le Journal*, 26
November 1937. Article reproduced (with no source given) in Marchois, 1993, 15.

90 Belleret, 2013, 99. See Saka, 1994, 44.

91 'elle gardait son éducation de jeunesse, malgré le luxe qui l'environnait
[…]. Moi, j'ai essayé de l'éduquer aux belles choses, à une hygiène de vie plus
conforme à mes goûts propres. […] A notre rencontre, j'ai exigé d'elle qu'elle
s'habille chez de grands couturiers et qu'elle ne se maquille pas à la ville comme
à la scène! Elle était très jolie vous savez et il suffisait de bien peu pour embellir
son joli visage. […] Avec moi, elle montait d'un échelon dans la classe sociale
et elle savait que cela lui était nécessaire.' Meurisse quoted in Marchois, 2013,
321–23.

92 'On a dit que c'était Asso qui l'avait formée. C'est vrai, mais c'est surtout
qu'elle comprenait ce qu'il disait.' Hureau quoted in Brierre, 2003, 43.

Chapter 2: Piaf and her public

1 See Fréjaville, 1943b, which reviews both shows.

2 'Le texte est dans une chanson ce qui m'intéresse d'abord'. Piaf, 2003 [1958],
105.

3 'Et puis cette voix, cette voix froide, de la couleur des huîtres qu'on ouvre
dans les paniers mouillés devant les bistros, cette voix indéfinissable, rauque et
ample, à la fois ordinaire et unique—mais unique—devrais-je écrire, cette voix
humide, enrhumée, encore enfantine et déjà désespérée vous prend au creux du
ventre, inexorablement, au moment ou vous n'y pensiez plus.' Régnier, 'Toujours
au Gerny's', 1936, no source or more precise date given. Article reproduced in
Marchois, 1993, 13.

4 '[cette voix qui] vous fait paraître sans rivales dans leur genre, et définitives
les paroles les plus stupides des chansons les plus bêtes et les plus connues'.
Régnier, 'Toujours au Gerny's', 1936, no source or more precise date given.
Article reproduced in Marchois, 1993, 13.

5 'C'est la voix d'une chanteuse des rues, sèche, avec des envolées soudaines.
Une voix âpre, sourde, qui se casse. Une voix de pauvresse qui rêve, d'enfant qui
s'émerveille.' 'Édith Piaf chante à L'Avenue', *Aujourd'hui*, 13 April 1941. Article
reproduced in Marchois, 1993, 33.

6 'Ce petit bout de femme chante de sa belle voix rauque "Le Légionnaire"
[*sic*], "Le Contrebandier", dix autres œuvres fortes, vêtue de sa robe en velours
noir, avec son visage blême, ses yeux mauves et fiévreux qui miment la détresse,
la douleur, la misère, l'amour, si atrocement bien qu'on a envie de rassurer, de
protéger cette enfant qui a l'air de subir tant de tristes choses!' 'Au théâtre de
l'ABC', *L'Intransigeant*, 3 April 1937. Article reproduced in Marchois, 1993, 15.

7 Barthes, 1977, 179–89.

8 'Elle arrive avec ses grands yeux lumineux et graves, avec sa robe noire si simple. Elle s'ouvre un passage entre les tables et monte sur une petite estrade [...]. Pas de sourire, pas de révérence. Pâle, grave [...], elle regarde la salle et il y a dans son regard quelque chose comme de la peur de la vie, la peur de qui connaît toutes les blessures du destin [...]. Sa voix, pleine d'une gravité qui se fait profonde, ouvre le rideau sur les plus pittoresques, mais aussi les plus tristes scènes du monde.' Salvador Reyes, of the Spanish publication *La Hora*, is quoted at length in Duclos and Martin, 1993, 156–57 (quotation: 157).

9 'A la fin de chaque chanson, quand l'enceinte s'emplit d'applaudissements, Édith Piaf reste muette, sans sourire, se mordant les lèvres et regardant en face d'elle avec un peu de l'animal blessé et un peu de la femme ardente.' Reyes quoted in Duclos and Martin, 1993, 157.

10 'la voici qui s'avance dans la lumière dure des projecteurs. Ses mains d'enfant à l'agonie, transparentes, presque inertes, se joignent sur son étroite poitrine, sur son gros front. Ses yeux où il y a toute l'épouvante et la détresse du pauvre monde deviennent immenses, et sa voix s'élève, d'abord plaintive, sourde, comme étranglée de larmes, puis elle s'amplifie, monte, devient un cri déchirant, rauque, interminable de bête blessée à mort.' 'Les Émissions', *Le Dimanche illustré*, 16 July 1943. Article reproduced in Marchois, 1993, 36.

11 Fargue, 1938, 512–14.

12 'Ne s'improvise pas qui veut, du jour au lendemain, remueur de tripes. Il y faut un certain passé, un certain regard, une longue fréquentation de paysages et de détresses.' Fargue, 1938, 513.

13 'Tout son art consiste à [...] devenir, elle-même, peu à peu, la plus forte et la plus sûre émotion de la mélodie.' Fargue, 1938, 513.

14 Barthes, 1977, 188.

15 Saka, 1994, 53–54.

16 Deniot, 2012a, 51–53.

17 Dutheil Pessin, 2004, 59–61.

18 Dutheil Pessin, 2004, 61–66.

19 'une catégorie chansonnière convertible'; 'une écorce dont nous pourrions aisément nous passer'. Both quotations in Deniot, 2012a, 55.

20 'les autres deviennent pitoyables—ceux qui écoutent—car elle concentre les peines de leurs âmes et elle les exprime. [...] Elle inspire le respect avec ses musiques du trottoir, avec ses "airs" que chacun fredonne et qui semblent nés du macadam. Oui, car le privilège de ces romances faciles, c'est qu'elles répondent à un appel secret de la foule et que la foule qui les répète s'imagine les inventer.' Cocteau, 'Je travaille avec Édith Piaf', 1940, unidentified article reproduced in Marchois, 1993, 32.

21 'un réalisme du jour qui rôde du côté de la Villette, grésille de la suie des cheminées d'usine et bourdonne de refrains chipés à la TSF du bistrot.' *L'Intransigeant*, 3 April 1937, quoted in Belleret, 2013, 117.

22 Asso interviewed in *France-Soir*, 30 September 1969, 8.

23 Burke, 2011, 17.

24 *Paris-Soir* (1936a, 1, 5, and 1936b, 1, 2, 3, 5) covered Leplée's murder in some detail, with photos of la Môme Piaf on both front pages.

25 Contet quoted in Marchois, 2013, 142.

26 'La Môme Piaf ne porte qu'un chandail assez pauvre et une robe toute simple; elle ne sait pas faire un geste, et le feu des projecteurs la gêne; elle ne sait pas saluer même; en vérité, elle ne sait rien...' *Le Petit Parisien*, 1935, 7.

27 'Elle n'a pas de robe du soir et, si elle sait saluer, c'est parce que je le lui ai appris hier.' Piaf, 2003 [1958], 47.

28 'de gens bien élevés qui se demandaient si leur hôte n'était pas subitement devenu fou. Des gens aussi qui, venus au cabaret pour oublier leurs soucis, n'étaient peut-être pas tellement contents qu'on leur rappelât qu'il y avait sur terre, et tout près de chez eux, [...] des fillettes comme moi, qui ne mangeaient jamais à leur faim et crevaient de misère. Avec mes pauvres nippes et mon visage de fantôme, je détonnais dans ce cadre élégant. Et s'ils s'en apercevaient, eux, j'en avais conscience, moi aussi.' Piaf, 2003 [1958], 47.

29 'Que voulez-vous, Messieurs les jurés, qu'en écoutant des chansons pareilles qui donnent le mauvais exemple, nos jeunes ne deviennent pas des voyous, des voleurs et ... des assassins!' Bonini, 2008, 78 n1.

30 Deniot, 2012a, 165–67.

31 'l'accent tour à tour gouailleur et chaleureux de la misère qui relève la tête'. Georges Devaise, 'Les Disques du mois: la Môme Piaf', 1937, no source or more precise date given. Article reproduced in Marchois, 1993, 14.

32 The night owls (Joullot-Dalbret, 1936). Saka, 1994, 27–28.

33 'Eh oui, elle beuglait. Mais quels beuglements! Toutes ces choses dans sa voix. Toute la misère du monde s'abattait sur toi [...]. C'était donc ça qu'ils entendaient, les mômes, ça qui leur faisait faire la moue? Merde! Moi, ça me laissait pantelant, sanglotant, les tripes à l'air.' Cavanna, 1988, 43.

34 Dutheil Pessin, 2004, 56.

35 'Une voix qui fait du mal comme le spectacle de l'injustice [...]. Une voix qui sent la misère ou l'émeute.' 'Les Émissions', *Le Dimanche illustré*, 16 July 1943. Article reproduced in Marchois, 1993, 36.

36 'Avez-vous entendu la Môme Piaf? C'est la voix de la révolte. La troubleuse d'ondes.' Jeanson quoted in Bonini, 2008, 138.

37 'est en forme de valse et c'est un accordéon qui le traîne; mais il n'y a pas à s'y tromper, c'est la même fleur étrange issue de la tristesse des pauvres, c'est le même charme poignant, le même cri d'amour pour la vie, de révolte contre la misère'. Reproduced in Vian, 1997, 218. The 45 rpm EP was released by Philips under the title *Chansons immortelles*.

38 'Mlle Piaf, ardente, indisciplinée, semble dressée sur une barricade d'où elle invective contre les injustes forces sociales.' 'Édith Piaf de nouveau à l'ABC

jusqu'au 4 décembre', 25 November 1937, no source given. Article reproduced in Marchois, 1993, 15.

39 Belleret, 2013, 112–13.

40 Asso wrote anti-Semitic articles for the collaborationist *La Gerbe* in 1941 and also attacked the rebellious youths known as 'zazous', according to Rifkin (1995, 171 n7) and Belleret (2013, 113, 225–26).

41 I draw here on my argument in Looseley, 2013c, 59–60. In fairness to Asso, his manager, Jean Richard, claimed that 'Le Fanion de la Légion' was the only song Asso ever repudiated and that it must have somehow slipped out in a 'moment of ideological weakness' ('un moment de faiblesse idéologique'). Richard quoted in Bonini, 2008, 148.

42 See Jackson, 2003, 102, and Cooper, 2006.

43 Saka, 1994, 65–66.

44 Bonini (2008, 273) is quite wrong to describe this song as a denunciation of colonialism. There's no suggestion that the black protagonist has been forced on to the boat and carried off. On the contrary, the portrayal of him as an inarticulate simpleton betrays the reflex racism of many at the time.

45 Recounted in Bonini, 2008, 365–66.

46 Saka, 1994, 90–91.

47 'Leplée connaissait les goûts de sa clientèle faisandée. Cette gosse du faubourg qu'il exhibait et faisait chanter de sa voix aigre sur la piste rouge du Gerny's, c'était le ragoût, le piment, le poivre, grâce auxquels les noceurs ataxiques se sentaient revivre.' Quoted in Bonini, 2008, 85.

48 'Elle fait se lever pour vous un monde d'images sans gaieté, mais non pas sans beauté: carrefours tristes où tournent des refrains, soirs d'octobre sur la ville, avec l'odeur des premiers brouillards et des premiers marrons, pavé de Paris luisant au crépuscule [...]. Il y a aussi les espaces désolés, les terrains vagues, les abandons, les quais, les ports... Toutes ces images tournent dans ses chansons, s'inscrivent dans cette voix qui vous prend aux mœlles.' 'Édith Piaf chante à L'Avenue', *Aujourd'hui*, 13 April 1941. Article reproduced in Marchois, 1993, 33.

49 'toutes ces voix de la rue, merveilleuses, [...] Ta voix, ta voix. Celle des copains qui ont mal, des copines qu'on plaque ou celles qui nous foutent dehors [...]. Tu es tout ça et tu l'as été tout de suite lorsque je t'ai vue pour la première fois'. Undated letter to Piaf reproduced in its entirety in Bonels, 1993, 42–45 (quotation: 44).

50 Saka, 1994, 15–17 and 39–41 respectively.

51 Saka, 1994, 48–50.

52 Saka, 1994, 45–46.

53 'Le seul mot qui puisse remplacer Paris, c'est le mot Piaf'. Dietrich is quoted by Pierre Hiégel in Marchois, 2013, 257.

54 Burke, 2011, 6.

55 Bonini, 2008, 278.

56 'Moi, elle ne m'a pas acceptée tout de suite. Je peux même dire qu'elle ne pouvait pas me blairer. J'étais blonde, bourgeoise, tout ce qu'elle détestait.' Bonini, 2008, 44.

57 Marchois, 2013, 374.

58 'Elle aimait voir l'homme se déchaîner dans toute sa masculinité'. Philippe-Gérard quoted in Brierre, 2003, 108.

59 Bonels, 1993, 16.

60 Saka, 1994, 91–93.

61 Vincendeau, 1987, 118.

62 Deniot, 2012a, 222.

63 Saka, 1994, 97–99. The song was completed in 1940 but apparently not published until 1942.

64 See Belleret, 2013, 122 n2.

65 'Elle a l'expérience précoce et quasi intuitive de celles qui, depuis plusieurs générations, ont souffert de faim, de froid et de solitude. Elle connaît par avance l'âpreté et l'égoïsme du mâle, et s'y soumet de bonne grâce puisque son désir n'a d'égal que l'esclavage féminin à l'assouvissement renouvelé de l'Espèce. 'Édith Piaf', *La Guerre*, 11 May 1944. Article reproduced in Marchois, 1993, 38.

66 Saka, 1994, 94.

67 See Deniot (2012a, 215–20) for a still of this moment and a close analysis of the performance in the film. At the time of writing, the whole scene is available on YouTube at www.youtube.com/watch?v=9spjtoKUqII (consulted 4 April 2015).

68 I draw here on my chapter in Lebrun and Lovecy, 2010, 132–34.

69 'ce besoin lancinant en moi, presque morbide, d'être aimée, d'autant plus aimée que je me trouvais laide, méprisable, si peu faite pour être aimée!' Piaf, 1964, 23.

70 Barrier quoted in Marchois, 2013, 48.

71 'Elle est petite, elle est laide, elle est tordue'. 'Les Émissions', *Le Dimanche illustré*, 16 July 1943. Article reproduced in Marchois, 1993, 36.

72 'Regardez cette petite personne dont les mains sont celles du lézard des ruines. Regardez son front de Bonaparte, ses yeux d'aveugle qui vient de retrouver la vue'. This well-known text has been widely reproduced. Here, I quote from Marchois, 2013, 125–27.

73 Simone de Tervagne, 'Portraits non retouchés: Édith Piaf', *Révolution nationale*, 15 July 1944. Article reproduced in Marchois, 1993, 38. I look at this text more closely in chapter 3.

74 On the whole significance of black, see Deniot (2012a, 261–65), which I borrow from here.

75 Deniot, 2012a, 284.

76 'j'ai un faible pour la môme Piaf! Elle agit sur moi comme une drogue. Je ne puis m'en passer! J'éprouve une invincible tendresse pour son visage blanc, pour ses doigts fins, pour son regard pathétique, pour sa petite silhouette couleur de nuit! Il faut l'écouter, certes, mais il faut surtout la contempler.' 'Au théâtre de l'ABC', *L'Intransigeant*, 3 April 1937. Article reproduced in Marchois, 1993, 15.

77 'Elle nous prend aux entrailles avec une douceur impérieuse. Sa voix chaude et âpre à la fois [...] fait vibrer nos fibres.' G. Joly, 'Édith Piaf à L'Étoile', *L'Aurore*, 13 February 1945. Article reproduced in Marchois, 1993, 51.

78 'Cette fille laide prend, quand elle est possédée par sa chanson, une étrange, une incroyable beauté'. 'Édith Piaf chante à L'Avenue', *Aujourd'hui*, 13 April 1941. Article reproduced in Marchois, 1993, 33. Brierre (2003, 52) attributes this article to *Marianne*.

79 'son allure de môme battue et de gosse qui a trop réfléchi'; 'Nulle adresse en elle, des dons et, les développant, une intelligence alertée'. Léon-Martin, 'A L'Européen: Édith Piaf', 1939. Article reproduced with no further source details in Marchois, 1993, 16.

80 'son intelligence de la scène, son intelligence tout court'. Pierre Francis, 'Marseille: Édith Piaf et Yves Montand au Théâtre des Variétés Casino du 18 au 30 avril'. Article reproduced in Marchois, 1993, 51–52 (quotation: 52).

81 'car en quelques secondes, cette jeune femme frêle avait imposé sa volonté au public qu'elle conduisait avec une sûre autorité par la gamme des sensations qu'elle voulait lui faire éprouver.' 'M.H.', 'Quelques instants avec la Môme Piaf', 26 August 1938. Article reproduced in Marchois, 1993, 16.

82 Dyer, 1998, 59.

83 Reader (2003, 205–33) draws a persuasive parallel with a better-known Flaubert creation, Emma Bovary.

84 'Tu attends avec impatience ma longue conversation avec Jésus. La voici. J'ai pleuré d'abord, j'ai beaucoup pleuré et après j'ai parlé. Je lui ai dit: "Empêche cette guerre." [...] Et puis j'ai regardé ses pieds, ses mains et sa figure remplis de souffrance. Enfin j'ai pensé à tout ce qu'il avait enduré sans en vouloir à personne.' Letter quoted in Duclos and Martin, 1993, 142–43 (quotation: 142).

85 'était aisément perceptible dans ses interprétations dont le caractère profane cédait souvent la place à des élans quasi religieux qui n'étaient pas sans parenté avec le Gospel. [...] Édith possédait un sens inné de la sacralisation qui donnait ampleur et noblesse aux sentiments qu'elle traduisait en musique.' Vassal, 2002, 101–02.

86 Cocteau, 1940, 'Je travaille avec Édith Piaf', unidentified article reproduced in Marchois, 1993, 32.

87 Quoted in Deniot, 2012a, 129.

Chapter 3: A singer at war

1 'La guerre fut une période de plénitude pour Piaf. Sans doute ne fut-elle jamais plus drôle, plus sûre de ses moyens et dans une meilleure forme physique.' Lange, 1979, 56.

2 Bensoussan, 2013, 89.

3 Lange, 1979, 56; Sizaire, 1996, 61.

4 Burke, 2011, 76.

5 Saka, 1994, 128–29.

6 Burke, 2011, 84.

7 Bret, 1988, 45–48 *passim.*

8 Martha Wainwright, 2009, *Sans fusils, ni souliers, à Paris.*

9 Belleret (2013, chapters 6–9) competently takes on this task, at least as far as it's currently possible to.

10 Belleret, 2013, 219–21. Bonini (2008, 170) also cites the report.

11 Belleret (2013) has consulted the records of the committee's work.

12 Bigard quoted in Marchois, 2013, 57.

13 Bonini, 2008, 170.

14 Guller's case is recounted in Bonini, 2008, 170.

15 Saka, 1994, 201–02 and 268–69 respectively.

16 Burke, 2011, 81.

17 For a gripping account of Glanzberg's eleventh-hour escape, see Freyeisen, 2006, 131–61.

18 Bonnat, 1944, 1.

19 Belleret, 2013, 240–50 *passim.* Brierre (2003, 61) confirms the lack of evidence to substantiate the story.

20 Desbœuf and Bigard are cited in Marchois, 2013, 176–77 and 57 respectively. No doubt the truth about the escapees will never be known. Desbœuf's account is remarkably precise. He maintains that she travelled with a troupe of some fifty people, which was never counted when she arrived. Undertaking 'seven or eight journeys', by which he presumably means visits to seven or eight camps, she would leave each camp with ten to fifteen escapees, armed with false papers. But since logically he could only be talking about her second German tour (the false identity papers could only have been passed on to prisoners on a return visit), even at the rate of fifteen escapees per visit, we still don't arrive at the '170 listed POWs' he speaks of. And the word 'listed' seems more likely to mean listed as POWs than listed as escapees helped by Piaf.

21 Bensoussan, 2013, 89.

22 She did receive thanks from the prisoners' aid organisation, and apparently a bouquet whenever she appeared in Marseille, though it isn't clear whether this was simply in gratitude for her touring Germany to lift prisoners' spirits.

23   Bonini, 2008, 195. Piaf had been asked to be 'godmother' of Stalag IIID, a common practice for entertainers during the war.

24   Contet cited in Duclos and Martin, 1993, 219.

25   Belleret, 2013, 285–87.

26   Berteaut, 1973 [1969], 193.

27   Berteaut, 1973 [1969], 193.

28   Belleret, 2013, 245. Bonini, 2008, 193–94.

29   Belleret, 2013, 247–48.

30   Belleret, 2013, 207. The STO (Service du travail obligatoire) was the compulsory labour service that forced many able-bodied Frenchmen to work in Germany, although a minority volunteered.

31   Belleret, 2013, 207.

32   Spotts, 2008, 209–10. He also claims, citing an official of the German propaganda department whom he doesn't name, that she acceded two or three times to Waechter's many requests that she sing to German troops in Paris.

33   Duclos and Martin, 1993, 214–15.

34   Freyeisen, 2006, 88–89.

35   Marchois, 2013, 159–60.

36   This anecdote from Dalban is cited from conversations with Bonini (see Bonini, 2008, 195).

37   'n'a guère boudé les facilités et le confort que lui procurait la situation dramatiquement contrastée de son pays'. Belleret, 2013, 227.

38   Berteaut, 1973 [1969], 173.

39   Lange, 1979, 56.

40   'Eh bien, merde alors! Si c'est ça l'Histoire, j'aime mieux la lire que la faire!' Quoted without attribution in Sizaire, 1996, 59.

41   'Accueil enthousiaste! Tout Paris m'attendait à la gare, les fleurs, la presse et tout. Je n'ai jamais vu un tel tamtam. C'était formidable! Il m'a fallu donner une conférence de presse au déjeuner. Comme si j'avais été une princesse!' Correspondence quoted in Freyeisen, 2006, 91.

42   'sa petite personne, toute menue et chétive'. Georges Dallain, 'Édith Piaf à "La Vie en rose"', *Le Petit Parisien*, 16 May 1943. Article reproduced in Marchois, 1993, 36.

43   D.-J. Mari, 'Comment avez-vous vu et entendu Édith Piaf?', *L'Éclaireur du soir*, 19 November. Article reproduced in Marchois, 1993, 34.

44   'ce petit bout de femme malingre, le visage crispé, le faciès douloureux sous la double flamme de ses mèches rousses et du projecteur dévorant. Ce qu'elle chante est pauvre, hanté d'images tristes qui sentent le dénuement moral et "le vice à bon marché." Cela ne correspond ni au climat moral du moment, ni au moindre idéal humain.' 'Le Perroquet au nid inauguré par Édith Piaf'. Article reproduced with no source indicated in Marchois, 1993, 36.

45   'Vingt chansons sur la misère, le vice et la mort … c'est beaucoup en ces

temps de misère et de mort'. 'Édith Piaf à la Salle Pleyel', *Soir*, 23 July 1944. Article reproduced in Marchois, 1993, 37.

46 'le physique souffreteux de cette petite personne aux yeux caves, à la grosse tête macabre, rentrée dans des épaules voûtées. Puisqu'on a cru bon de nous en imposer la vue, nous sommes libres, me semble-t-il, de dire qu'Édith Piaf serait sans doute utilisable au cinéma en qualité de "monstre"'. Vinneuil, 1941, 11.

47 'Elle incarne admirablement notre époque décadente [...]. Son corps menu, sa taille ratée, sa tête volumineuse, son front bosselé, son air malheureux, ses yeux pleins de détresse, tout y est [...]. Elle fait penser à une fin de race. Elle est un réquisitoire contre notre société, contre nos lois, contre nos institutions [...]. Normalement, Édith Piaf aurait dû devenir une chanteuse populaire, qui débite des rengaines au coin des rues et dans les foires. Par miracle, elle a échappé à ce destin. Et cela, grâce aux snobs, qui l'ont accaparée, applaudie, lancée [...]. Il y a même quelques cérébraux qui la trouvent belle, admirable'. Simone de Tervagne, 'Portraits non retouchés: Édith Piaf', *Révolution nationale*, 15 July 1944. Article reproduced in Marchois, 1993, 38.

48 'Et pourtant, faite comme elle est, elle aurait dû se contenter d'enregistrer des disques et de chanter à la radio. Mais non. Elle a osé faire du music-hall [...] Elle a même, un jour, osé paraître à l'écran [...] dans *Montmartre-sur-Seine*, de triste mémoire. Chaque fois que je repense à ce film, j'éprouve, malgré moi, une gêne infinie à la pensée qu'il pourrait aller à l'étranger et que des Suisses, par exemple, pourraient s'imaginer que cette "vedette" qui semble sortir d'un miroir déformant de Luna-Park représente la grâce et le charme de Paris. [...] Ah, décadence des décadences! [...] Comme me disait l'autre jour un vieux paysan bourbonnais: "Avec tout ce qu'on voit aujourd'hui; [*sic*] allez vous étonner qu'il y ait la guerre!"' Simone de Tervagne, 'Portraits non retouchés: Édith Piaf', *Révolution nationale*, 15 July 1944. Article reproduced in Marchois, 1993, 38.

49 'Elle chante? Non, elle revit les images touchantes, les romans populaires et désespérés de ses couplets. Elle a toujours l'air d'une môme, [...] Édith avait des larmes mal retenues dans la voix, et moi j'avais la chair de poule en entendant là les voix qui chantaient aux carrefours de ma jeunesse.' 'Édith Piaf chante chez "L'Aiglon" jusqu'au 3 octobre', *Aujourd'hui*, 22 September 1940. Article reproduced in Marchois, 1993, 32.

50 'Ces refrains sentent le caniveau, le trottoir, le coin de la rue [...], les vers de Baudelaire et la prose de Charles-Louis Philippe'. Vittorio Guerriero, 'Édith Piaf (Théâtre ABC)', *Panorama*, 24 June 1943. Article reproduced in Marchois, 1993, 36. Charles-Louis Philippe (1874–1909) was a French novelist who depicted working-class life.

51 'Édith Piaf n'est-elle pas en effet une des plus brillantes ambassadrices de la chanson et la chanson n'est-elle pas le plus sûr remède pour apaiser la nostalgie des cœurs épris de souvenirs? Là-bas, loin du beau pays de France qu'ils regrettent, elle évoquera pour eux tout ce qu'ils aspirent à retrouver et qu'ils n'ont pas oublié.' H.-D. Fauvet, 'Édith Piaf va chanter pour les prisonniers', *Paris Midi*, 9 August 1943. Article reproduced in Marchois, 1993, 37.

52 Burke, 2011, 88.

53 See Duclos and Martin, 1993, 197–98; and Belleret, 2013, 196.

54 *Vedettes*, 1943. Belleret (2013, 208) describes *Vedettes* as a collaborationist publication.

55 Belleret, 2013, 206. The statement from Piaf that he cites is from *Paris-Midi*, 9 August 1943.

56 See Belleret, 2013, 205; and *France Actualités*, 1943. *France Actualités* was a mouthpiece of Vichy, also broadcasting in the occupied zone.

57 Belleret, 2013, 242.

58 Saka, 1994, 119–20.

59 Quoted in Burke, 2011, 108.

60 Belleret, 2013, 235.

61 'Zazous' was the name given to a youth subculture during the Occupation, generally apolitical but nonetheless persecuted by the Vichy regime for its outlandish appearance and Americanophile musical tastes.

62 Le Chanois-Besse, 1942. Saka, 1994, 101–02.

63 For example, 'Le Roi a fait battre tambour' (The king has called for drums, traditional; Saka, 1994, 133–34) and 'Céline' (traditional; Saka, 1994, 134–36).

64 'il est arrivé ce miracle que ces solitudes s'épousent et composent un objet sonore par où la France s'exprime jusqu'à nous tirer des larmes.' Cocteau, 'Les Compagnons de la chanson', 24 May 1946. Article reproduced with no source given in Marchois, 1993, 53.

65 'Écoutez leurs voix s'allumer l'une à l'autre pareilles aux feux de la Saint-Jean, qui se communiquent de colline en colline. Écoutez-les se taire et se répondre. Écoutez-les s'éparpiller et se regrouper comme le mercure. Et répétez-vous qu'il est ridicule de plaindre la France alors qu'elle vous donne sans cesse et à l'improviste les preuves innombrables de ses secrets et de son pouvoir.' Cocteau, 'Les Compagnons de la chanson', 24 May 1946. Article reproduced with no source given in Marchois, 1993, 53.

66 Burke (2011, 110) also uses the nightingale metaphor, though it was Cocteau who originally described Piaf as 'comme le rossignol invisible, installé sur la branche' (like the nightingale invisible on its branch), quoted in Marchois, 2013, 126.

67 Vittorio Guerriero, 'Édith Piaf (Théâtre ABC)', *Panorama*, 24 June 1943. Article reproduced with no source given in Marchois, 1993, 36.

68 'la chanson triste qui est une délivrance pour ses pareilles, les filles aux rêves tout simples, aux déceptions toujours les mêmes, qui veulent qu'on leur dise leurs regrets et leurs peines, et que rien n'est de leur faute mais que la vie est ainsi faite.' Le Minotaure, 1946.

69 'Édith Piaf, c'est le cas rare, celle qui fait sortir les êtres d'eux-mêmes ou plutôt les force à rentrer en eux par un procédé bien voisin de l'état de transes'. Pierre Heuze, 'Édith Piaf jugée par le public de l'Européen', *Paris Midi*, 27 April 1941. Article reproduced with no source given in Marchois, 1993, 34.

Chapter 4: A new Piaf

1 Piaf-Louiguy, 1945 (Saka, 1994, 121–22). There is some uncertainty about the precise role of Louiguy as composer of the song.
2 'Un seul nom, et dans ce nom toute la chanson: Édith Piaf'. Blistène, 1963, 86–87. See also Belleret, 2013, 328.
3 See Ralph Harvey's 'Appendix 2: the chanteuses réalistes', in Crosland, 2002, 247–66.
4 'l'appel d'une poésie plus hautaine et plus dépouillée'; '[les] poètes les plus elliptiques et les plus raffinés'. Fargue, 1938, 512–14 (quotations: 513).
5 Billy quoted in Crosland, 2002, 73.
6 Canetti quoted in Marchois, 2013, 104.
7 Bonels, 1993, 142–43.
8 Émile Cerquant, 'De la môme Piaf… à Édith Piaf', *France-Soir*, 1 August. Article reproduced in Marchois, 1993, 52. See also Duclos and Martin, 1993, 233, for a brief account of this episode; and Belleret, 2013, 271, based on Cerquant.
9 'Édith Piaf est une coupable ancestrale. […] Le bon sens populaire grave les tables de la loi. Il dit le bien et le mal. Selon le bon sens populaire Édith Giovanna Gassion appartient à cette catégorie de femmes à qui l'on prédit qu'elles finiront sur l'échafaud.' Bonels, 1993, 207.
10 Société des auteurs, compositeurs et éditeurs de musique.
11 'puis brusquement c'est miraculeux, la chanson est en train de naître, avant même d'être écrite, avant d'être composée, elle "la sent".' Blistène, 1963, 42–43.
12 'Cette collaboration étroite avait pour but d'élaborer des chansons pleinement adaptées à son univers esthétique et affectif, ainsi qu'aux possibilités spécifiques de sa voix. Édith ne concevait pas autrement la création, chaque texte, chaque musique devant coïncider parfaitement avec sa personnalité, son caractère, sa sensibilité. Grâce à quoi, elle pouvait s'y investir cœur et âme.' Vassal, 2002, 67–68.
13 Saka, 1994, 253–55. Incorrectly listed as published in 1956.
14 'Voilà le point de départ. Tout doit tourner autour de ce mot. Toute la chanson est là.' Vassal, 2002, 68–69.
15 Émer quoted in Marchois, 2013, 199.
16 'Nous écrivons pour elle des balbutiements: elle en fait des cris, des appels, des prières.' Contet quoted in Lévy, 2003, 89.
17 'Où je me méfie, c'est quand je commence à devenir consciente de ce que

je fais dans une chanson, quand je sais que je la chante, quand je calcule des gestes, quand ils ont perdu la spontanéité qui les fait authentiques et "valables".' Piaf, 2003 [1958], 209.

18 Berteaut, 1973 [1969], 178.

19 I have modified here Ghislaine Boulanger's published English translation (Berteaut, 1973 [1969], 176) not because it is inaccurate but because in striving for readability it blurs somewhat Berteaut's exact words in French and those she attributes to Piaf: see Berteaut, 1969, 190.

20 'Et ça, voyez-vous, ça n'est pas Piaf. Le Public connaît trop ma vie... Je ne suis pas faite pour chanter la joie de vivre.' Quoted in Blistène, 1963, 117.

21 Berteaut, 1973 [1969], 130.

22 Berteaut, 1973 [1969], 177. I have modified very slightly the published English translation: see Berteaut, 1969, 191.

23 Belleret, 2013, 200.

24 Duclos and Martin, 1993, 174–75.

25 'Je ne suis pas une chanteuse réaliste! Je déteste ce genre. Je crée des chansons populaires. [...] J'aime les fleurs, les amours simples, la santé, la joie de vivre'. Quoted in Belleret, 2013, 200–01.

26 Saka, 1994, 121–22, 195–96 and 287–88 respectively.

27 Letter cited in Brierre, 2003, 91.

28 'c'est pour ça que je n'ai plus le droit d'être ignorante. On me prend au sérieux, eh bien, moi aussi il faut que je m'y prenne et pour cela je compte sur toi.' Letter cited in Bonini, 2008, 235.

29 Contet quoted in Marchois, 2013, 139.

30 'un vrai poète dans le plus périlleux des genres'. G. Joly, 'Édith Piaf à L'Étoile', *L'Aurore*, 13 February 1945. Article reproduced in Marchois, 1993, 51.

31 In his eighties, Contet himself would maintain that critics hadn't understood the humour intended in his lyrics; quoted in Brierre, 2003, 58–59.

32 This second title probably refers to the bluesy 'Le Brun et le blond' (Contet-Monnot, 1943).

33 'prennent leur place dans un répertoire qui évolue vers des nuances de sensibilité un peu moins simples, vers une poésie visionnaire, aux suggestions mystérieuses, presque magiques.' Fréjaville, 1943a, 6.

34 'dont l'exaltation presque démente a de quoi déconcerter des âmes simples insuffisamment initiés aux paroxysmes de l'imagination et aux excès de l'ivresse lyrique'; 'des émotions moins mêlées d'artifices littéraires'. Fréjaville, 1943a, 6.'

35 'n'essayez pas, Mademoiselle Piaf, de trop vous élever, ni de vouloir chanter plus haut que votre culture. Vous avez toute une foule de gens qui vous aiment parce que vous êtes simple, nature, et que vous avez eu des chansons aussi simples que vous, avec des mots que tout le monde pige. [...] N'allez pas les décevoir avec des chansons trop littéraires, qui deviendront de plus en plus nébuleuses, auxquelles vos spectateurs ne comprendront goutte.' Serge Weber,

'Mademoiselle Piaf: du 9 février au 8 mars', no source given, 15 February 1945. Article reproduced in Marchois, 1993, 51. In Marchois and one or two other sources, this name is given as Veber. I have been unable to verify either spelling definitively, though Serge Veber is the name of a scriptwriter who worked on Lacombe's *Montmartre-sur-Seine*. It seems unlikely that he would be writing such a brutal commentary on Piaf's performance.

36 'nous le savons fichtre bien que vous n'êtes pas jolie: nous en sommes même certains et ça nous est égal. Vous ne seriez pas ce que vous êtes si vous étiez jolie. La souffrance que vous incarnez pour nous n'a pas de traits réguliers. Elle est voûtée comme vous.' Serge Weber, 'Mademoiselle Piaf: du 9 février au 8 mars', no source cited, 15 February 1945. Article reproduced in Marchois, 1993, 51.

37 'L'art, d'une façon générale, s'adresse aux masses. L'art de la chanson plus encore que tout autre, ne s'adresse qu'aux masses. Si votre art de la chanson est sans définition, il ne peut toucher vraiment personne, ni la masse, ni l'élite'. Jean Wiener, 'Édith Piaf', *Spectateur*, 3 October 1945. Article reproduced in Marchois, 1993, 52.

38 'vous faites trop dans l'intellectuel, vous faites trop dans le "génial". Vos attitudes mêmes, qui savent être si bouleversantes, sont excessives, elles sont si chargées d'intention, qu'elles ne portent plus.' Jean Wiener, 'Édith Piaf', *Spectateur*, 3 October 1945. Article reproduced in Marchois, 1993, 52.

39 Saka, 1994, 110–12.

40 English translations: Piaf, 2004, and Piaf, 1992, respectively.

41 My own translation. For the published translation, see Piaf, 1992, 12. 'Cela ressemble à un roman-feuilleton, un peu trop facile, je sais. Mais toute ma vie ressemble à un feuilleton presque incroyable'. Piaf, 1964, 15.

42 Saka, 1994, 85–86. This song was unpublished according to Saka, but Piaf did record it.

43 Saka, 1994, 34–36.

44 Saka, 1994, 152–53.

45 Saka, 1994, 106–107.

46 Reiner, 1999, 111.

47 'l'aide à se libérer de la musique de ses hommes'. Reiner, 1999, 111.

48 Brierre, 2003, 47.

49 Noli, 1973, 38.

50 The Bonels (1993, 35) recount that Piaf did manage to get her young protégés onto the influential TV programme *L'École des vedettes*, which would launch Johnny Hallyday, among others. But her show wasn't a success.

51 Margantin quoted in Marchois, 2013, 315.

52 Bonels, 1993, 167.

53 Bonini, 2008, 223.

54 'Je suis la plus grande bienfaitrice du music-hall. On manque de vedettes? Eh bien, moi, j'en fabrique. Voici la recette.' 'Piaf: "Voici comment mes secrétaires font fortune"', *Paris Jour*, 27 March 1962. Article reproduced in Marchois, 1993, 130.

55   Deniot, 2012a, 72–73.

56   The quotation from Hirschi is in Deniot, 2012a, 73 n147, from *Jacques Brel, chant contre silence*, Paris: Nizet, 1995.

Chapter 5: High art, low culture: Piaf and la chanson française

1   'En 2013 on célébrera le centenaire de la naissance de Charles Trenet, que l'on considère unanimement comme le précurseur des *auteurs-compositeurs-interprètes* [...]. Dans son sillage, au cours des années cinquante et soixante, des auteurs tels que Brassens, Brel, Ferré, Gainsbourg, Ferrat, Aznavour, Moustaki, Barbara, Bécaud, Vian [...] ont diffusé la chanson française dans le monde entier, et ont contribué à une extraordinaire rencontre—voire une fusion—entre *musique* et *littérature.*' Fondazione Sapegno, 2013.

2   'Créer une chanson, c'est faire vivre un personnage. Comment y parvenir si les paroles sont médiocres, même si la musique est bonne?' Piaf, 2003 [1958], 106.

3   Drott, 2011, 104–05 (quotation: 105).

4   'Auteur' is in fact a masculine noun in French which didn't have a feminine form (other than the antiquated *une autrice*) until one was created (*une auteure*) relatively recently.

5   Looseley, 2003, 68–69.

6   Louis Terrentrov, 'Édith Piaf à l'ABC', *L'Auto*, 30 October 1942. Article reproduced in Marchois, 1993, 35.

7   'S'il est un nom qui évoque pour nous la chanson française et la gratitude des foules, c'est bien celui de cette émouvante vedette'. L. B., 'Édith Piaf aux Variétés avec Yves Montand', *Victoire tendance*, 25 November 1944. Article reproduced in Marchois, 1993, 38.

8   'la souplesse et la solidité d'un talent dirigé par l'intelligence, qui ne doit plus tout à la nature, qui sait désormais bien ce qu'il veut et où il va'. Fréjaville quoted in Duclos and Martin, 1993, 191–92.

9   Holbane/Giroud quoted in Duclos and Martin, 1993, 192.

10   Frith, 1998, 26, 36–42.

11   ABC programme reproduced in Marchois, 1993, 15.

12   'Une fois par siècle se révèle un instrument parfait traducteur de la poésie populaire. Édith Piaf est cela. C'est aussi, tout simplement, une grande artiste.' 'Édith Piaf chante chez "L'Aiglon" jusqu'au 3 octobre', *Aujourd'hui*, 22 September 1940. Article reproduced in Marchois, 1993, 32.

13   Ferré quoted in (among others) Belleret, 2013, 173.

14   'elle se dépasse, elle dépasse ses chansons, elle en dépasse la musique et les paroles. Elle nous dépasse.' Cocteau quoted in Marchois, 2013, 125–27.

15 For a discussion of the nation as an imagined community, see Anderson, 2006. For examples of this leftover folk discourse, see my chapters 1 and 2 above.

16 See, for example, http://www.ina.fr/video/I04084451/moustaki-et-piaf-video.html (consulted 27 August 2015).

17 'Il faut être résolu à être soi-même, et à n'être que soi-même'. Piaf, 2003 [1958], 104.

18 Deniot, 2012a, 132–34. Deniot herself (73 n147) refers to Hirschi, *Jacques Brel: chant contre silence*, Paris: Nizet, 1995.

19 'l'identification directe aux bonheurs et malheurs de l'interprète'. Deniot, 2012a, 133.

20 Deniot, 2012a, 53.

21 'alors je sais ce que je dis. Et on a besoin de savoir ce qu'on dit quand on chante pour le faire comprendre aux autres et pour que les autres vous comprennent.' Piaf quoted in Deniot, 2012a, 171.

22 Serge Weber, 'Mademoiselle Piaf', no source cited, 15 February 1945. Article reproduced in Marchois, 1993, 51.

23 'la vraie petite Piaf, chaude et simple, de dans le temps.' Jean Wiener, 'Édith Piaf', *Spectateur*, 3 October 1945. Article reproduced in Marchois, 1993, 52.

24 Looseley, 2003, chapter 4.

25 'Édith Piaf nous fit atteindre l'ineffable au même titre, bien que dans des genres différents—qu'un Chaliapine, un Walter Gieseking, une Marian Anderson, un Yehudi Menuhin, une Michèle Morgan ou un Jean-Louis Barrault!' Obaldia, 1946.

26 Saka, 1994, 82–83.

27 'une des plus grandes vertus de notre peuple, je veux dire: le génie de la spontanéité'. Obaldia, 1946.

28 Kuisel, 1993, 2–3.

29 On both Chevalier and Trenet in America, see Singer, 2013, 111–12.

30 Conversation with Bonel cited in Bonini, 2008, 240–41.

31 Brierre, 2003, 82.

32 Burke (2011, 119) cites the critic George Jean Nathan describing her voice as 'cultivat[ing] the pitch and tone of gulpy despair'.

33 *New York Herald Tribune*, 1947, 21.

34 Taubman, 1947, 92.

35 Bonini, 2008, 256–67.

36 Chapman, 1947. Raquel Meller (1888–1962) was a Spanish singer and film star who had toured America before the Second World War.

37 Quoted in Burke, 2011, 120.

38 Atkinson, 1947, 30.

39 Zolberg, interview with author, September 2010. Zolberg cannot remember exactly which performance she witnessed.

40 'N'y lisait-on pas, en conclusion, que, s'il me laissait repartir sur cet échec

immérité, le public américain aurait fait la preuve de son incompétence et de sa stupidité?' Piaf, 2003 [1958], 138–39. My translation. For the published translation, see Piaf, 1992, 83.

41 Article reproduced in Thomson, 2002, 144–45. Thomson's original article appeared as 'La "Môme" Piaf', *New York Herald Tribune*, 9 November 1947, 1 and 6 of section 5 of the paper, though the front-page reference only consists of a cartoon of Piaf and the Compagnons entitled 'Edith Piaf, much in little at the Playhouse', with a brief caption underneath.

42 Thomson, 2002. All quotations in this paragraph are from pp. 144–45.

43 Watts, 1947, 49.

44 Beauvoir, 1999, 129–30. All the quotations are from these two pages. Probable date of letter: Saturday, 20 December 1947, when Piaf was at the Versailles. The slightly awkward English in places is Beauvoir's own.

45 It's difficult to tell quite where Beauvoir's explanation of Breton's view ends and her own expansion on it begins. Beauvoir does, however, end the letter by saying she thinks Breton is probably right; and her own liking for Piaf is clarified in a slightly earlier letter (probably Friday, 12 December 1947): 'Édith Piaf can be cheap sometimes, but she can be wonderful; she had [*sic*] a hoarse voice which pleases me better than many "nice" ones.' Beauvoir, 1999, 122.

46 Deniot, 2012a, 132–34.

47 See Looseley, 2013c, 47–48.

48 Atkinson, 1947, 30.

49 Quoted in Burke, 2011, 168.

50 Cited in an undated flyer for Angel Records on its release of two Piaf recordings, probably around the time of her Carnegie Hall appearances, reproduced in Mazillier, Berrot and Durieux, 2010, 158. The flyer also carried a quotation from *Art Digest*: 'It's like taking a trip to Paris'.

51 Quoted in Burke, 2011, 170.

52 'Chaque fois qu'elle nous revient d'Amérique, elle nous étonne avec les mêmes refrains et nous sommes heureux de nous laisser reprendre. [...] On l'a acclamée comme jamais encore elle ne l'avait été.' Jean Antoine, 'Édith Piaf de retour d'Amérique', *Paris Presse*, 16 March 1950. Article reproduced in Marchois, 1993, 75.

53 'Dans quelques jours, elle partira à Hollywood [...] avec le fervent désir d'y faire entendre les chansons de notre pays.' J. E., 'Édith triomphe aux États-Unis avec La Vie en rose', *Regard*, 22 February 1948. Article reproduced in Marchois, 1993, 59.

54 François de Roux, '"La môme Piaf" se métamorphose en princesse', *Le Figaro littéraire*, 20 January 1949. Article reproduced in Marchois, 1993, 61. All quotations in the following paragraph are from this article.

55 'Elle ne bouge pas. Les mains derrière le dos, le nez en l'air, la tête inclinée

vers l'épaule gauche, bien plantée sur ses petites jambes, elle regarde le public sans sourire et sans saluer.'

56 'Son art est d'une extrême sobriété. Sa voix n'est pas le seul de ses dons. Chacun de ses gestes prend une signification intense. Ils sont rares, lents et mesurés. Sa mimique, d'une expression profonde, termine heureusement son chant après que la voix s'est tue.'

57 'on a la vision d'un tableau du Douanier Rousseau. La soirée se termine comme il faut.'

58 Morin, 1972, and Morin, 2005 (translation into English).

59 'Édith Piaf a changé de visage, [...]. Notre chanteuse, devenue rousse, ressemble maintenant à une vedette d'Hollywood.' Émile Cerquant, 'De la môme Piaf à Édith Piaf', *France-Soir*, 1 August 1945. Article reproduced in Marchois, 1993, 52.

60 Chevalier's diary entry is reproduced in Marchois, 2013, 119.

61 'Édith Piaf est une femme extraordinaire. On ne peut pas ne pas subir son charme étrange. [...] C'est une des grandes personnalités de l'époque. Dans son métier, elle est la première. La seule. Elle est montée si haut que le vide s'est fait autour d'elle.' Maurice Fleury, 'Édith Gassion (dite "Piaf") est-elle la George Sand du 20e siècle?', *Photo-Journal*, 11 December 1952. Article reproduced in Marchois, 1993, 79–80 (quotation: 79).

62 'Il faut qu'Édith Piaf exerce sur l'intelligence ou la sensibilité d'un individu un pouvoir bien magique pour faire naître tant de passions violentes—elle qui n'a pas la beauté d'Elizabeth Taylor ou l'éclat de Marilyn Monroe.' Maurice Fleury, 'Édith Gassion (dite "Piaf") est-elle la George Sand du 20e siècle?', *Photo-Journal*, 11 December 1952. Article reproduced in Marchois, 1993, 79–80 (quotation: 79).

Chapter 6: Ideology, tragedy, celebrity: a new middlebrow

1 Danielle Bonel in conversation with Bonini, 2008, 365.

2 Danielle Bonel in conversation with Bonini, 2008, 365.

3 Bonels, 1993, 265.

4 Danielle Bonel in conversation with Bonini, 2008, 363–64.

5 'Respectueuse des institutions, elle était en admiration devant les fortes personnalités.' Danielle Bonel in conversation with Bonini, 2008, 365.

6 Kuisel, 1993, 6.

7 Spiraux, 1959. All quotations in this paragraph are from this article.

8 'Elle chante et dès que l'on entend sa voix, la France se dessine avec tous ses détails, même pour les yeux de ceux qui n'ont jamais traversé l'Atlantique. [...] En écoutant Édith Piaf, les Américains du Waldorf Astoria ou de Carnegie Hall entendent chanter la France.'

9 'Tout comme la France, surtout celle de l'année dernière, elle était gravement

malade. L'une et l'autre semblaient condamnées. [...] Et les mots pour la [Piaf] qualifier sont les mêmes que ceux employés par la presse étrangère pour parler de la France en péril.' In fact, she was taken ill and hospitalised again two weeks after Spiraux's article.

10 Saka, 1994, 261–62. Les Grognards were the soldiers of Bonaparte's Old Guard. The song has their ghosts marching loudly and proudly down the Champs-Élysées.

11 'Il faut la voir [...] pour comprendre le pouvoir de cette créature, la magie de cette sorcière. Elle pourrait si elle voulait soulever le peuple, faire surgir des barricades: il n'est pas une "Pasionaria" qui lui damerait le pion. C'est un phénomène.' 'T.', 1958.

12 Compare for example the fulsome declarations of love in her published letters to Cerdan (Piaf and Cerdan, 2012) and to Louis (nicknamed 'Toto') Girardin, the professional cyclist (Piaf, 2011).

13 'D'une autre on a le temps de penser qu'elle chante bien ou mal. Piaf, on la subit. Son public souffre physiquement.' Jean Antoine, 'Édith Piaf de retour d'Amérique', *Paris Presse*, 16 March 1950. Article reproduced in Marchois, 1993, 75.

14 'Elle fait lever la petite fleur bleue au fond des cœurs les plus endurcis et les plus blasés, ceux à qui on ne la fait pas, sentent tout à coup un picotement inusité, un serrement des entrailles.' *Le Canard enchaîné*, 1956.

15 'Les jours de première, tous les grands noms du spectacle venaient s'effondrer en larmes dans sa loge. Elle était un peu médium, hypersensible, très psychologue. Elle subjuguait une salle après trois ou quatre chansons, même ceux qui étaient contre elle.' Bonel quoted in Bonini, 2008, 388.

16 Dax in conversation with Bonini, 2008, 388–89.

17 'Elle entre, elle a le visage sévère. Ovation. Personne n'a jamais eu les ovations qu'elle a eues. Ça dure pratiquement dix minutes. Des hurlements de bonheur, avant même qu'elle n'ait ouvert la bouche. Les gens disent merci. Merci d'être là. Merci d'être revenue.' Dax in conversation with Bonini, 2008, 404.

18 'Dès qu'elle paraît sur la scène, elle hypnotise son public'. Roland Côté, 'Épatante, cette Piaf!', *Le Petit Journal*, 18 December 1955. Article reproduced in Marchois, 1993, 104.

19 Monteaux, 1963. The quotations that follow in this paragraph are from this article.

20 'l'esprit n'était pas touché mais la sensibilité dans ce qu'elle a de plus naturel, de plus primitif, de plus humain. A l'écoute d'Édith Piaf, tout s'efface: l'intelligence comme l'esprit critique, le raffinement intellectuel comme le snobisme [...]. L'esprit analytique du spectateur est neutralisé.'

21 Barthes, 1977.

22 'Les feux de la scène s'éteignent. Un spot blanc tombe sur la droite. Une, deux, trois... Une frêle silhouette sombre s'avance. Seuls son visage et ses

deux mains plaquées sur ses hanches sont visibles. [...] la voix d'Édith s'élance dans le micro, remplit tout l'espace, jusqu'aux notes les plus hautes, qui me galvanisent, semblant sortir de ses entrailles et non plus de sa bouche, comme si leur puissance n'avait aucune limite. Je suis figé sur mon siège. [...] A la septième ou huitième [chanson], j'ai l'impression que je rentre en transe. Je vois de moins en moins la scène, alors que j'ai le sentiment que la chanteuse entre en moi, guidée par les accents de sa voix, qui me font l'effet d'un viol délicieux dont je ne peux me défendre, au point de rentrer spontanément en érection. [...] Je me retrouve comme un animal totalement possédé et alors que la voix atteint des hauteurs inouïes, qui brûlent toutes mes entrailles, une jouissance inimaginable embrase mes tempes, mon cœur bat à tout rompre. J'explose littéralement dans un orgasme jusqu'alors inconnu, qui me laisse terrassé sur mon siège.' Biro in conversation with Bonini, 2008, 387–88.

23 'les hommes sont fous de Piaf, et cela se comprend. Pourtant ce sont les seuls qu'elle dupe'. Lange, 1958.

24 'Bonne copine, camarade qui connaît la vie, on lui confierait, à coup sûr, ses embêtements, car c'est du solide et on voit bien que ça ne flanche pas. [...] La petite marchande de fleurs du coin de la rue devient brusquement, grandie à vous faire pâlir, la voix de la misère humaine.' *Le Canard enchaîné*, 1956. All quotations in this paragraph are from this article.

25 Saka, 1994, 213–14.

26 'tout un chacun se voit comme il est, un peu pauvre clown, hélas, et ravale ses larmes.'

27 'Il n'y a plus de pudeur qui tienne. Le populo et les esthètes, tous tapis au fond de leur fauteuil dans la salle obscure, se sentent tous ensemble un cœur de midinette'.

28 Hirschi, 2008, 164. Morin, 1972, 105–06.

29 'Si à ce passage ils ne chialent pas tous, c'est qu'ils ont des cœurs de pierre.' Noli, 1973, 40.

30 'Elle connaît son métier comme personne. Son tour de chant est de plus en plus beau parce qu'elle progresse toujours. On sent qu'elle travaille.' Lange, 1958.

31 Deniot, 2012a, 37.

32 Deniot, 2012a, 262–69.

33 On the notion of a new middlebrow, see Holmes and Looseley, 2013, particularly the introduction and conclusion. A central argument in that book is that the idea of a middlebrow has been and is being redefined as not necessarily a negative term.

34 See Hirschi, 2008, 163–64, for a brief but illuminating analysis of how life and chanson became imbricated in this song and the impact of that imbrication on those listening only to the record.

35 Burke, 2011, 143.

36 They did initially attempt to conceal the fact of their being lovers, as Cerdan was married with children, but unsuccessfully.

37 Deniot, 2012a, 135.

38 'quand sa voix se tait, la tête penchée, immobile, on la croit crucifiée à l'image du Christ'. Quoted in Belleret, 2013, 224.

39 Versions of this story emanating from Piaf vary, particularly concerning the period of time in which she was supposedly blind. On the TV show *La Joie de vivre* in 1954, for example, she claimed to have gone blind aged three and remained so for four years (Belleret, 2013, 562). But the more probing biographers like Belleret reduce her illness to a form of conjunctivitis and her blindness, if it existed, to at most a few weeks.

40 Piaf, 1964, 55–56, 88–89. For the English translation, see Piaf, 1992, 39, 57–58. The two accounts of the meeting with Cerdan's wife Marinette that feature in the volume are not entirely consistent with each other.

41 Saka, 1994, 315–16.

42 Henri Lemaire, 'Terrassée par une crise de nerfs', *Le Soir illustré*, 6 February 1958. Article reproduced in Marchois, 1993, 107.

43 'entraîner avec elle ses amis et son public dans une quête d'absolu qui menait finalement à Dieu'. Vassal, 2002, 107.

44 'Édith Piaf, c'est la chute de l'ange dans tout ce qu'elle a de plus vil et de plus grand. [...] Son histoire est simple: elle part de l'amour, elle arrive à la mort.' Jean-François Noël, 'Édith Piaf lance face à Dieu le cri même de la terre...', *Combat*, 15 March 1950. Article reproduced in Marchois, 1993, 76.

45 Vassal, 2002, 12.

46 Vassal, 2002, 42–43.

47 *Justice Magazine*, 1960, 6–7.

48 'Elle appela ça "la vie en rose", la dame! Une bonne douche lui ferait du bien...'. 'A la douche "la Môme"!', *L'Aurore*, 17 December 1948. Article reproduced in Marchois, 1993, 60.

49 'Édith Piaf et Jacques Pills s'envolent vers le septième ciel... via New York', *Le Parisien*, 5 September 1952. Article reproduced in Marchois, 1993, 79.

50 Saka, 1994, 178–79.

51 Rivoyre, 1953.

52 Piaf, 1964, 105. English translation: Piaf, 1992, 68.

53 Bonels, 1993, 247–48.

54 Saka, 1994, 229–30.

55 *Cinq colonnes à la une*, 1960a, 1960b and 1962.

56 Bonini, 2008, 506–07.

57 Holmes, 2007, 63. Holmes's internal quotation here is from Ginette Vincendeau. Holmes herself departs to an extent from Vincendeau by insisting that, despite Bardot's ambivalent meanings in terms of sexual politics, 'BB's stardom had a predominantly empowering effect' on her young female fans.

58 Holmes, 2007, 50.

59 Deniot, 2012a, 364. This is a quotation from an ARTE programme: see 364 n673.

60 Georges Devaise, 'Les Disques du mois'. Article reproduced with no source given in Marchois, 1993, 14.

61 'du rêve, encore du rêve [...]. Tout cela est du romantisme pur, à peine camouflé.' Émile Vuillermoz, 'Édith Piaf et Jacques Pills à Marigny', *Paris-Presse*, 24 April 1953. Article reproduced in Marchois, 1993, 80.

62 René Dunan, 'Édith Piaf au Canada', *France-Soir*, 27 August 1948. Article reproduced in Marchois, 1993, 60.

63 'Édith Piaf, grande dame de la chanson française, est incontestablement notre première chanteuse réaliste.' 'Édith Piaf, allez la voir!', *France-Soir*, 31 January 1955. Article reproduced in Marchois, 1993, 103.

64 'le public préférait son répertoire réaliste qui collait mieux, il est vrai, à sa voix et à sa petite silhouette malingre.' Canetti quoted in Marchois, 2013, 106.

65 'Trois notes et elle redevient ce à quoi elle a toujours voulu échapper: le petit oiseau triste qui est né dans la rue.' Henri Lemaire, 'Terrassée par une crise de nerfs', *Le Soir illustré*, 6 February 1958. Article reproduced in Marchois, 1993, 107.

66 'Son intelligence, c'est d'avoir su rester ce qu'elle était à ses débuts: une pauvre petite gosse. A ces réflexes, à ces cris de vaines espérances, à ces révoltes des bafoués, des malchanceux, elle a su à force de travail et de talent, donner un accent, une résonance qui provoque l'émotion.' 'Édith Piaf à l'ABC', no source cited, 14 June 1950. Article reproduced in Marchois, 1993, 76.

67 Saka, 1994, 249–50.

68 It's not clear whether it's the mother or the lyricist, J. Larue, who believes that Sydney is 'in the Americas'.

69 Deniot, 2012a, 235.

70 'Elle a transformé la chanson, et de nombreux artistes lui doivent le meilleur d'eux-mêmes.' Programme reprinted in Marchois, 1993, 103.

71 'Mais je garde toujours une sorte de tradition. Je veux rester moi-même et évoluer avec le personnage que j'ai créé. Je ne veux pas en changer.' Quoted in Bonini, 2008, 356, with no source or date. Context suggests the early to mid-1950s.

72 Burke, 2011, 175.

73 Burke, 2011, 176.

74 'ce romantisme des rues, des ports et des gares dont Carco et Mac Orlan ont célébré les misères et les joies'. *Arts*, 1957.

Chapter 7: Losing Piaf

1   'Elle partira un beau soir et la chanson française aura perdu sa raison d'être.' Maurice Fleury, 'Édith Gassion (dite "Piaf") est-elle la George Sand du 20ᵉ siècle?', *Photo-Journal*, 11 December 1952. Article reproduced in Marchois, 1993, 79–80.
2   Hiégel quoted in Marchois, 2013, 257.
3   *Cinq colonnes à la une*, 1960a.
4   Bonels, 1993, 41.
5   'Aimez les personnages que nous jouons ou les chansons que l'on vous chante, mais ne vous occupez pas des êtres qui jouent ou des êtres qui chantent.' Brasseur's letter reproduced without date in Bonels, 1993, 42–45 (quotation: 43).
6   Letter quoted in Bonini, 2008, 496–97.
7   Saka, 1994, 244–45.
8   Noli, 1973, 46.
9   Saka, 1994, 287–88.
10 'My Way', famously, turned out not to be Sinatra's swansong by a long chalk, as his career continued until a year before his death in 1998. But the song (adapted from a French original, 'Comme d'habitude' by Claude François) was received as such because of the valedictory tone of the lyric.
11 'Édith, on t'aime, on te retrouve'. 'Bravo, Édith'. 'Salut, ma belle'. Manceaux, 1961.
12 Noli, 1973, 51.
13 'De chanson en chanson, ou plutôt de litanie en litanie, car il y a vraiment quelque chose de religieux dans ce perpétuel "Hymne à l'amour", la ferveur du public s'intensifie. [...] Piaf a goûté ce soir-là les délices de la béatification. Ressuscitée, miraculée, Édith, que les fidèles supplient et glorifient. Édith-Marie-Madeleine.' Manceaux, 1961.
14 'Je n'ai rien contre les filles de joie, mais entendre hurler leur détresse pendant une demi-heure a quelque chose de récriminatoire et d'un peu lassant, surtout quand elles s'égarent dans des cathédrales pour réclamer au Bon Dieu la restitution immédiate de leur petit ami.' Charbon, 1962, 55–56.
15 Saka, 1994, 339–40.
16 Saka, 1994, 345–46.
17 Nougaro, 1963.
18 Saka, 1994, 342–43.
19 Saka, 1994, 344–45
20 This said, gay listeners have sometimes invested the song with meanings which deepen its intensity and widen its impact beyond Piaf's biography at the time.
21 Bonels, 1993, 39.
22 Saka, 1994, 365–66.

23 Bonini, 2008, 501.

24 'Le Mariage le plus insolite du siècle a mobilisé cinq cars d'agents de police', *Paris Jour*, 10 October 1962. Article reproduced in Marchois, 1993, 131.

25 'Comment une petite vieille femme maigre et pitoyable, au visage ravagé, aux épaules voûtées, peut-elle se faire un beau gars de 26 ans, plein de vie?' Unnamed source quoted by Danielle Bonel in Bonels, 1993, 39. The use of 'se faire' here is ambiguous, possibly implying, more crudely still, 'get laid by' rather than just 'get'. Given this crudeness, it's conceivable that this isn't a verbatim quotation but Bonel's own summary of the kinds of thing said when, once the shock of the marriage had passed, as she put it, 'the press coverage became dreadful' ('la presse devient terrible').

26 'on a envie de lui conseiller la discrétion des alcôves et l'opacité des rideaux tirés'. Charbon, 1962.

27 'ait cru utile de l'inviter dans sa chambre à coucher'. François Brigneau, 'Mme Édith Piaf ... avec nos regrets', *L'Aurore*, 10 October 1962. Article reproduced in Marchois, 1993, 131.

28 D'Ormesson, 1962, 36–37. All quotations in this paragraph are from this article.

29 'Notre Villon à nous, je crois bien que c'est elle.' Both quotations from d'Ormesson, 1962, 36.

30 'il est bien naturel qu'elle leur demande aussi beaucoup en échange pour l'édification de sa mythologie personnelle'.

31 'Ce qu'il y a d'immoral, ce qu'il y a d'affreux, ce qu'il y a d'obscène en vous, ce sont les autres. Une presse, un public, une société, un peuple ont les vedettes qu'ils méritent. Et je ne suis même pas sûr que les nôtres aient mérité Édith Piaf.' D'Ormesson, 1962, 37.

32 Some have maintained that Sarapo was gay but this has been the subject of some debate.

33 Bonels, 1993, 40. Simone Margantin claims that in her last days Piaf spoke to her of her plan to separate from Théo and of having even considered divorce but rejected it. Margantin's memoir of Piaf's last days is in Noli, 1973, 197–211 (reference to separation: 198–99).

34 'celui pour lequel j'ai chanté, même à l'extrême limite de mes forces, celui pour lequel je voudrais mourir en scène, à la fin d'une dernière chanson. [...] Toute cette foule qui me suivra, j'espère, le dernier jour, parce que je n'aime pas être seule.' Piaf, 1964, 8. English translation: Piaf, 1992, 10.

35 'malgré mon âge, je suis restée une sorte de pauvre gamine trop crédule et qui poursuit inlassablement le même rêve: être heureuse, être aimée! Le merveilleux, la vie s'est toujours arrangée pour me le salir.' Piaf, 1964, 96. English translation: Piaf, 1992, 63. I have replaced the translation of the last sentence here with my own, as I am doubtful of the accuracy of the translator's version.

36 'Ce légionnaire, je l'ai perdu, sans doute parce que je n'étais pas désignée pour le bonheur?' Piaf, 1964, 16. English translation: Piaf, 1992, 13. The all-important question mark is omitted in the English version; I have restored it here.

37 Piaf, 1964, 103 and 123 respectively. English translation: Piaf, 1992, 66 and 79.

38 Chiropractic was considered an alternative and dubious form of health care in France at that time. There were very few chiropractors, and Vaimber maintains that his successful treatment of Piaf did much to improve its image. Piaf, however, was reluctant to stay off drugs and medication for long, and their relationship ended shortly before her death when she called for him but refused to detoxify; he therefore declined to treat her. See Marchois, 2013, 457–75, for Vaimber's detailed account of treating her.

39 'Quand elle parut en scène, j'ai sangloté, tant je souffrais de la voir dans cet état de délabrement. Elle était vacillante, décharnée. Puis, elle a chanté et le miracle s'est produit. Ce fut du délire. Les gens, debout, trépignaient, pleuraient. Un spectacle inoubliable!' Bizet quoted in Marchois, 2013, 62.

40 'Vous finissez par nous importuner avec toutes vos affaires de cœur et de c[ul]! Quand on "gueule" comme vous—car vous ne chantez pas—, on a au moins la sagesse de ne pas nous en faire entendre davantage.' Letter quoted in Bonini, 2008, 529.

41 'Quelle est donc la fripouille qui vous a fait sortir de prison pour faire de vous une vedette, vous qui chantiez sur les trottoirs avec une voix !!! à faire fuir les chiens?' Letter quoted in Bonini, 2008, 529.

42 Saka, 1994, 362–63.

43 Berteaut claimed that it was she who spent the last hours holding Piaf's hand, having been summoned to her side by Piaf herself. Undated and unidentified press article (possibly *France-Dimanche*) in a collection of cuttings assembled by a fan: at the BNF-Richelieu, box 27, 'Coupures de presse après mort', chemise 299, 'Recueil de coupures de presse constitué par un fan (France) après sa mort'.

44 Burke, 2011, 226.

45 *Le Parisien libéré*, 1963a.

46 Respectively, 'Piaf est morte, Paris pleure', *Paris Jour*, 1963; and 'Le cœur d'Édith Piaf a cessé de battre: une authentique fleur du pavé', *Tribune de Genève*, 1963.

47 Hope-Wallace, 1963, 7.

48 Quoted in Crosland, 2002, 205.

49 *New York Times*, 1963, 1, 19 (quotation: 19).

50 *Paris Match*, 1963a and 1963b.

51 'une petite morte en robe d'orpheline avec, au bout de sa chaîne, sa croix de communiante. Son regard, d'un bleu intense, ébloui par les projecteurs,

implorait. Elle nous demandait pardon d'être si petite, si faible, si malade.' *Paris Match*, 1963a, 72.
52 *Paris Match*, 1963a, 72 and 50 respectively.
53 In the absence of verification, there seems little point discussing the letter. It is reproduced in Burke, 2011, 229.
54 Burke, 2011, 230.
55 Blistène, 1963.
56 'Ils sont tous venus. Tous ses amis inconnus. Ceux qui l'avaient applaudie sur la scène, ceux qui l'avaient entendue à la radio, ceux qui faisaient tourner ses disques. Hommes et femmes de toutes les conditions, jeunes et vieux, communiant dans une même ferveur avec cette petite bonne femme dans laquelle chacun d'eux reconnaissait la meilleure part de lui-même, la part du cœur.' *Le Parisien libéré*, 1963b.
57 'C'était une fille du peuple, comme moi, comme nous. Elle chantait avec son cœur'. *Le Parisien libéré*, 1963b.
58 *Le Parisien libéré*, 1963b; and Bonels, 1993, 327–28.
59 Bonini, 2008, 10.
60 Crosland, 2002, 200. Bonini (2008, 9–13) begins with a detailed account of the funeral.
61 Bonels, 1993, 327.
62 Burke, 2011, 228.
63 Blistène, 1963, 51.
64 'Aucun auteur populaire n'eût osé imaginer pareil début pour son héroïne. Mais dans le cas d'Édith il ne s'agissait pas d'un roman.' *Le Parisien libéré*, 1963a, 6.
65 'comme s'il fallait qu'elle ne vît plus ce monde terrible où l'on peut abandonner des enfants'. *Paris Match*, 1963a, 61, 63.
66 'Elle est la seule qui n'ait pas galvaude le mot "populaire". Elle était la chanteuse populaire par excellence, la seule qui parvenait à déplacer les foules, même en plein air, partout où elle chantait.' *Paris-Presse-L'Intransigeant*, 1963, 7.
67 '[the street in Piaf] est "peuple" avec tout ce que le mot comporte de noblesse. [...] cette noblesse du peuple qui est la noblesse humaine. Car le peuple, c'est elle, c'est vous, c'est la foule, c'est moi. [...] Le peuple n'est pas plus de Belleville que de Passy, de France que d'Allemagne: il est universel. Édith Piaf l'est.' Monteaux, 1963.
68 'Édith Piaf était une chanteuse "populaire", elle plaisait au plus grand nombre, voilà pourquoi on refuserait de prononcer le mot de génie à son sujet. [...] C'était cela le génie de Piaf.' Giannoli, 1963, 24.
69 'cette grande voix de velours noir, magnifiant ce qu'elle chante'. Cocteau quoted in Marchois, 2013, 128.

70 'rauque, immense, déchirant à pleines dents des textes d'une navrante banalité qu'un simple geste du doigt savait rendre poignant'. Sarraute, 1963.

71 'On plongeait vraiment dans un monde populaire, celui qui demeure sensible aux sentiments éternels, qui se réunit autour des chanteurs de rue, d'un accordéon, d'un accident, d'un malheur ou d'une gloire.' Guermantes, 1963. 'Guermantes' was the pen name of the writer and critic Gérard Bauër.

72 'La pauvre Môme du Boulevard du Crime prenait le masque et les gestes d'une tragédienne grecque. Une chanteuse populaire qui fait revivre la tragédie antique, c'est assez exceptionnel dans le music-hall moderne. Peu importe alors qu'elle ait interprété des airs faciles, bon marché.' 'G. B.', 1963.

73 Blistène, 1963, 150.

74 L'Amateur, 1963.

75 'Elle restera, dans notre souvenir, unique, irremplaçable, tragique petite figure de proue de la chanson française.' Sarraute, 1963.

76 Bécaud, 1963.

77 'c'est toute une part d'histoire dans la tradition de la chanson qui bascule et disparaît'. Nougaro, 1963.

78 Chevalier, 1963.

79 'Dans son style, c'était sûrement une très grande chanteuse. Sauf "Milord", je n'aimais pas ses chansons, je suis d'une autre époque.' Quoted in Bonini, 2008, 539.

80 'Oh là là! C'est du jamais entendu. Si nous voulons tenir le coup, il faudra nous bagarrer.' Quoted in Bonels, 1993, 335.

81 See for example 'Piaf chanterait du rock', recorded by Céline Dion, among others.

82 See Looseley, 2003, 29–30.

83 Perez, 1963.

84 Rebierre, 1963.

85 As a compromise, the chaplain for artists was finally permitted to officiate at her burial.

86 'une autre idole du bonheur préfabriqué: Marilyn Monroe dont la gloire s'est achevée dans un tube de barbituriques'. Quoted in Bonini, 2008, 543.

87 'Ceux qui ont été tenus en haleine deux heures durant par ce petit bout de femme au visage ingrat à jamais ne peuvent oublier la sincérité des cris de passion, de douleur et d'espoir qu'elle arrachait du tréfonds de ses entrailles.' I take this summary of the ecclesiastical quarrel from the account by Bonini, 2008, 544–45.

88 Monteaux, 1963.

89 'Parce que cette frénésie, cette fureur étaient vraies, parce que cette petite femme laide et infirme était vraiment possédée, cent mille personnes ont défilé religieusement devant sa dépouille et la voilà sainte Édith. Je ne crois pas que

cela arrivera à Sylvie Vartan.' Quoted in Bonini, 2008, 518. At the time, Sylvie Vartan was a teenage pop singer.

90 The story of Monseigneur Martin is drawn from a number of sources, notably Bonels, 1993, 326. Danielle describes him as a bishop in Rome.

Chapter 8: Remembering Piaf

1 'Piaf ne peut pas mourir... Elle ne mourra jamais... Elle est partie, c'est tout.' Blistène quoted in Marchois, 2013, 68.

2 Sciarretto, 2012.

3 'Elle reste un monstre sacré dans le cœur des Français. [...] En un demi-siècle on aurait pu l'oublier, il n'en est rien'. France 2, 2013b.

4 Nora, 1996, 6.

5 'Elle comprenait tout, elle pigeait, et ce que sa vie de pauvre môme ne lui avait pas appris, toute seule elle en avait eu l'intuition [...]. Elle n'aimait que la beauté, sous toutes ses formes, dans l'art, dans les êtres qui l'entouraient, dans la nature.' Blistène, 1963, 12.

6 Burke, 2011, 230.

7 'Il y a un an déjà ... il y a un an seulement et la distance nous paraît grande. [...] La mode a balayé cette façon-là de clamer haut à grande voix, la secrète association du cœur et du ventre [...]. Que sera-t-elle dans dix, vingt, cinquante ans, [...] quand les projecteurs du souvenir, après ceux du théâtre, se seront éteints?' Érismann, 1964, 45–46.

8 This collection has now been deposited at the BNF's Département des Arts du Spectacle.

9 Berteaut, 1969.

10 'je l'ai vue sourire; d'un sourire, ou se lisaient la joie, l'innocence, la jeunesse, et plus que tout, la volonté farouche de ne pas se laisser vaincre. Quelle belle leçon de courage, j'ai reçu ce jour-là!' Franco, 1973.

11 'cet oiseau qui aimait trop la vie et dont la seule faute est de nous avoir quittés bien trop tôt.' Letter by P. Arinthe (no first name given), 1973.

12 Burke, 2011, 233.

13 Bonini, 2008, 573.

14 For an account of this episode, see Belleret, 1996, 426–28.

15 In the French lyric, Nougaro plays with the fact that 'piaf' (slang for 'sparrow') is actually a masculine noun anyway. By making it feminine in his title, he makes an explicit allusion to Piaf from the start but also puns on his desire to be a grammatically 'masculine' Piaf.

16 During a visit I made to the museum in October 2013, Bernard Marchois spoke to me of a complete lack of interest from the Ministry of Culture. In subsequent correspondence (December 2014; February 2015), he indicated that

the subsidies available for such ventures by application are 'derisory' and come with too many conditions to be worth applying for.

17 Béhar, 1993, 29.
18 Both quotations are from Lebrun, 2009, 45.
19 Lelouch, 1983.
20 Crosland, 2002, 219.
21 Mogui, 1983.
22 Duclos and Martin, 1993, 523.
23 *Le Monde*, 1993, 27–29 (quotation: 27).
24 Marti, 1988.
25 Marti, 1988.
26 See table in Donnat and Cogneau, 1990, 229.
27 'Without love, we are nothing'. Lamour, 2003.
28 'elle n'a cessé de grandir et d'envahir notre univers ... l'adjectif qui lui va le mieux: "vivante"'.
29 Richer, 2007.
30 *Le Point*, 2013.
31 TF1, 2013.
32 For details, see Vassal's official website: www.hugues-vassal.com/#!home/ c11fx.
33 Kaas, 2012b. Part of my analysis of the show draws on my own observations as an audience member at the Albert Hall show.
34 Kaas, 2012a.
35 Saka, 1994, 251–53.
36 Saka, 1994, 292–94.
37 France 2, 2013a.
38 TF1, 2013.
39 BBC Radio 4, 2013.
40 Danielle Bonel in conversation with Bonini, 2008, 364.
41 Bret, 1988, 103.
42 Mayle's best-known title is *A Year in Provence* (Penguin, 2000).
43 I was myself phoned up by a media company for a view about how the French felt about what the questioner assumed would be a blasphemous use of the song in the advert. Its popularity in the UK can be measured by its inclusion in the *Songlines* programme (BBC Radio Scotland, 2004), which examined the popularity of a number of famous songs.
44 See Deniot, 2012a, 212, on Calvi and Piaf.
45 'Mythe de la chanson française, dépassant les frontières et transcendant les époques, elle saura apporter à la Fête de la Musique une brillante énergie auprès du public tant en France qu'à l'étranger.' Ministry of Culture, 2013. The Fête, though founded in France, has subsequently become an international event.
46 Delaunay, 2013.

Chapter 9: Performing Piaf

1   Runcie, 2013.
2   See for example BBC4, 2006. This programme's most recent UK showing was on BBC4, 21 February 2015.
3   Marchois, correspondence with author, December 2014.
4   'Son message n'est pas affaibli par le temps; il le transcende.' *Reflet*, 1988, 9.
5   'Édith Piaf est une des rares artistes à connaître un tel succès posthume et tant qu'il y aura des cœurs aimants, le monde se souviendra.' Arinthe, 1973.
6   Demay, 1988, 16–17.
7   'Ses chansons reflètent la vie de tous les jours, on ne se lasse pas de sa voix.' Demay, 1988, 16–17.
8   See table in Donnat and Cogneau, 1990, 67. Respondents were allowed to make two choices from the categories offered—hence the figures exceeding 100%.
9   Demay, 1988, 16–17.
10 'Son art nous est devenu aussi lointain, aussi étranger que celui du pétomane et du tourlourou de grand papa [*sic*]'. Macabiès, 1981.
11 *Le Quotidien de Paris*, 1983. *La nouvelle chanson française*, or new French chanson, was a classification applied to this new generation from the mid-1970s onwards.
12 Donnat and Cogneau, 1990.
13 Demay, 1988, 17.
14 'Elle ne délivrait pas de messages. Elle faisait pas "intellectuel". Elle criait, pleurait, riait, vivait sur scène les petits instants, les petites amours, les petits malheurs, les grands Bonheurs. Inimitable, inégalée parce que jamais truquée. [...] Écoutez-là être elle-même. Et laissez-vous aller à être comme elle, à conjuguer le verbe aimer sans ricaner au mélodrame. Elle savait le prix de la sincérité.' Lefebvre, 1977, 11.
15 '50 ans après sa disparition, elle reste *la* voix française.' TV5 Monde, 2013.
16 Runcie, 2013.
17 'Paris rendait hommage à sa plus authentique représentante. En elle, ces femmes et ces hommes se reconnaissaient et enterraient une des leurs.' Noli quoted in Marchois, 2013, 340.
18 'cette grande artiste qui a incarné, avec tant de passion et de vérité, l'âme du peuple de Paris'. Chirac quoted in Marchois, 2013, 511.
19 '[Piaf] est Paris, elle est la France joyeuse, gouailleuse, malheureuse, éternelle. L'Amérique, c'est-à-dire le monde entier, chante "La Vie en rose".' Leclère and Lorrain, 2007, 79.
20 'c'est encore Ménilmontant d'autrefois. Paris-Village malgré le béton envahissant. Pas loin des immeubles trop neufs, des maisons à trois étages,

avec du linge aux fenêtres, des chaises paillées sur le bord des trottoirs. [...]
Vrai décor pour la Môme.' *Le Journal illustré*, 1983.

21 'les choses graves de la vie et de l'amour paraissent ne sortir que du cœur
des femmes'. Buffier, 1990, 37–39 (quotation: 39).

22 Vincendeau, 1987, 120.

23 Vassal quoted in Leclère and Lorrain, 2007, 80.

24 Riva's claim appeared in her biography of her mother, but she repeated it in
the media, for example in a CNN interview with Larry King on 30 December
2003, where she unequivocally confirms they were lovers. See transcript of
the interview: http://transcripts.cnn.com/TRANSCRIPTS/0312/30/lkl.00.html
(consulted 1 March 2015). For Danielle's flat denial, see Bonels, 1993, 82–86.

25 'tu es tout cela et plus encore. Piaf tu resteras dans nos cœurs. Édith, je
t'aime.' 'Pablo', 1983, 28.

26 Pons, 1993, 29.

27 'pour moi, elle a été plus qu'une chanteuse, elle a été l'âme, le miroir, le
reflet vivant de la misère humaine, le cri poignant de la souffrance, l'image de
notre solitude et de notre détresse.' Carzou, 1964, 52.

28 Morin, 1972, or (for English translation) Morin, 2005.

29 'Cette vague chaude nous submerge, nous traverse, pénètre en nous. Le
tour est joué. Édith Piaf comme le rossignol invisible, installé sur sa branche,
va devenir elle-même invisible.' Reproduced in Marchois, 2013, 126.

30 'Car il y a de la magie là-dedans, dans ce charme où se mêlent nostalgie,
brume de souvenirs inventés, bribes de littérature (Zola), mauvais feuilleton
et tragédie pure, le tout sublimé par le chant. Le miracle, c'est que le charme
opère toujours. Question d'imaginaire collectif, probablement.' Leclère and
Lorrain, 2007, 76.

31 'Édith Piaf fait partie de la culture française, à proprement parler, ou
plutôt elle appartient à l'inconscient collectif populaire. C'est un monstre, un
monument, une image qui colle à la France. [...] Un peu comme un vieux
fantasme.' Guidoni, 1983.

32 'On bafouillait, on en tremblait. C'etait comme un traumatisme énorme.'
Jonasz, 1983.

33 Dyer, 1998, 18.

34 Assmann, 1995, 130.

35 'Aujourd'hui, les légendes, il faut les détruire. Toutes. Faire table rase.'
Bonels, 1993, 32–33.

36 For example Petit and Illand, 2001.

37 Aston, 2000, 162.

38 *Le Point*, 2013, 77–78.

39 'la mise en scène ne lésine pas sur les effets, la bande-son exploite à fond
le timbre d'une voix déchirante: c'est le choix d'Olivier Dahan, celui du film
populaire, sentimental, dramatique.' Drouin, 2007.

40 'une image négative, déformée et caricaturale d'une des plus grandes interprètes de la Chanson Française. Elle eut un destin exceptionnel, avec la présence permanente de l'inexplicable, de l'étrangeté, de l'irrationnel, marquée du sceau secret de la tragédie. Il y a quelque chose d'ésotérique dans la vie d'Édith. La fatalité l'a retrouvée à tous les carrefours de sa vie, pour la guider de l'amour à la gloire, une gloire qui se perpétue.' Darcy, 1996.

41 'retracer cette vie sous la forme d'un spectacle mettant en évidence le destin d'un petit être né de la rue, magnifié par la rue, et qui, telle une prêtresse vouée au culte permanent de l'amour, rend son chant incantatoire'. Darcy, 1996.

Conclusion

1 Vincendeau, 1987, 125.

2 Some of this concluding analysis was first developed in various papers delivered in the UK and France and written up in several publications, most notably Looseley, 2010, 2013b and 2013c.

3 See for example Vassal, 2002, 77–78, for a description of how she rehearsed.

4 Becker, 2008 [1982].

5 Lebrun and Lovecy, 2010, 129, 135. For a more detailed analysis of this change, see Looseley, 2013c.

6 Hawkins, 2000, 140.

7 Deniot, 2012a; see in particular 57, 67 and the following: 'How can we recognise a myth? Among other things, by the identificatory impulses to which it gives rise, by the tributes, the covers, the imitations it inspires over time' ('A quoi reconnaître un mythe? Entre autres, par ce qu'il suscite d'élans identificateurs, par ce qu'il inspire d'hommages, de reprises, de répliques au fil du temps') (239).

8 Deniot, 2012a, 243 n414.

9 Anderson, 2006.

10 Nora, 1996, 3–4.

11 Nora, 1996, 6–7.

12 Nora, 1996, 19–20.

13 Nora, 1996, 7.

14 See for example Dutheil Pessin (2004, 298) on the 'myth of the voice in Piaf'.

15 See Bennett, 2012, 79–80, which discusses 'celebrity saints' and the connections between religion and popular culture.

16 Kelly, 2014.

17 France 2, 2013a.

References

NB. Press articles are listed below by name of author. If the articles are unattributed, I have listed them by name of publication. Their page numbers are supplied where these have been visible in copies available in archives.

L'Amateur, 1963, 'La Voix d'Édith Piaf s'est éteinte'. *Journal de Genève*.

Anderson, 2006, *Imagined Communities: Reflections on the Origin and Spread of Nationalism*, new revised edition. London: Verso.

Anouilh, Jean, 2008 [1942], *La Sauvage*, in Anouilh, *Pièces noires*. Paris: La Table Ronde.

Arinthe, P., 1973, 'Édith Piaf que je n'ai pas connue...' *Le Courrier de Mantes*, 13 October.

Arts, 1957, 'Nouvelles chansons d'Édith Piaf'. 12 November.

Assmann, Jan, 1995, 'Collective memory and cultural identity'. *New German Critique*, no. 65, spring–summer, 125–33.

Aston, Elaine, 2000, 'Pam Gems: body politic and biography', in E. Aston and Janelle Reneilt (eds), *The Cambridge Companion to Modern British Women Playwrights*. Cambridge: Cambridge University Press, 156–73.

Atkinson, Brooks, 1947, 'At the theatre'. *New York Times*, 31 October.

Barthes, Roland, 1977, 'The grain of the voice', in Barthes, *Image, Music, Text*, transl. Stephen Heath. London: Fontana, 179–89.

BBC4, 2006, *Queens of Heartache*. First broadcast 10 March.

BBC Radio 4, 2013, *Desert Island Discs: Ed Miliband*. First broadcast 24 November.

BBC Radio Scotland, 2004, *Songlines: Non, je ne regrette rien*. First broadcast 3 February.

Beauvoir, Simone de, 1999, *Beloved Chicago Man: Letters to Nelson Algren 1947–64*. London: Phoenix.

Bécaud, Gilbert, 1963, 'Sur cette scène où elle a si souvent chanté'. *Les Lettres Françaises*, 17–23 October.

Becker, H. S., 2008 [1982], *Art Worlds*, updated and expanded 25th anniversary edition. Berkeley: University of California Press.

Béhar, Henri, 1993, 'Une Voix au long cours'. *Le Monde*, 7 October, 27–29.

Belleret, Robert, 1996, *Léo Ferré: une vie d'artiste*. Arles: Actes Sud.

Belleret, Robert, 2013, *Piaf: un mythe français*. Paris: Fayard.

Bennett, Oliver, 2012, 'Strategic canonisation: sanctity, popular culture and the Catholic Church', in D. Looseley (ed.), 2012, *Policy and the Popular*. Abingdon: Routledge.

Bensoussan, Albert, 2013, *Édith Piaf*. Paris: Gallimard.

Berteaut, Simone, 1969, *Piaf*. Paris: Laffont.

Berteaut, Simone, 1973 [1969], *Piaf*, transl. Ghislaine Boulanger. Harmondsworth: Penguin.

Bleustein-Blanchet, Marcel, 1964, 'Hommage à Édith Piaf: Bleustein-Blanchet, Président de Publicis'. *Musica Disques*, no. 128, November, 51–52.

Blistène, Marcel, 1963, *Au revoir Édith*. Paris: Éditions du Gerfaut.

Bonel, Marc and Bonel, Danielle, 1993, *Édith Piaf: le temps d'une vie*. Paris: Fallois.

Bonini, Emmanuel, 2008, *Piaf: la vérité*. Paris: Pygmalion.

Bonnat, Yves, 1944, 'Les 118 évadés d'Édith Piaf'. *Ce Soir*, 21 October, 1.

Bret, David, 1988, *The Piaf Legend*. London: Robson Books.

Bret, David, 1998, *Piaf: A Passionate Life*. London: Robson Books.

Brierre, Jean-Dominique, 2003, *Édith Piaf: sans amour on n'est rien du tout*. Paris: Hors Collection.

Burke, Carolyn, 2011, *No Regrets: The Life of Édith Piaf*. London: Bloomsbury. Paperback edition 2012.

Le Canard enchaîné, 1956, 'Dites-le avec des fleurs: tant qu'il y aura de l'Édith Piaf, il y aura de l'espoir…' 6 June.

Canetti, Jacques, 2008, *Mes 50 ans de chansons françaises*, Paris: Flammarion.

Carzou, 1964, 'Hommage à Édith Piaf: Carzou peintre'. *Musica disques*, no. 128, November, 52.

Cavanna, François, 1988, 'Sacrée môme!' *Télérama*, 27 January, 43.

Cavendish, Dominic, 2008, 'Piaf at Vaudeville Theatre: review'. *Daily Telegraph*, 23 October. Available at www.telegraph.co.uk/culture/theatre/drama/3562483/Piaf-at-Vaudeville-Theatre-review.html.

Chapman, John, 1947, 'Piaf, French singer, has debut; her Compagnons steal the show'. *Daily News*, 1 November.

Charbon, Catherine, 1962, 'Exercice de dissection: Édith Piaf, un phénomène d'accord, mais…' *Tribune de Genève*, 12 October, 55–56.

Chevalier, Maurice, 1963, 'Maurice Chevalier'. *Le Figaro*, 12–13 October.

Cinq colonnes à la une, 1960a, interview with Piaf by Pierre Desgraupes broadcast 15 January. Available at www.ina.fr/video/I00012771/edith-piaf-sur-le-besoin-de-chanter-a-tout-prix-video.html (consulted 15 April 2015).

Cinq colonnes à la une, 1960b, interview with Piaf by Pierre Desgraupes broadcast 2 December. Available at www.ina.fr/video/I00000109/edith-piaf-avant-sa-nouvelle-tournee-video.html (consulted 15 April 2015).

Cinq colonnes à la une, 1962, interview with Piaf by Pierre Desgraupes broadcast 1 June. Available at www.ina.fr/video/I00012860 (consulted 15 April 2015).

Cohen, Évelyne et al., *Dix ans d'histoire culturelle*. Villeurbanne: Éditions de l'ENSIBB.

Cooper, Nicola J., 2006, 'The French Foreign Legion: forging transnational identities and meanings'. *French Cultural Studies*, vol. 17, no. 3, October, 269–84.

Crosland, Margaret, 2002, *A Cry from the Heart: The Biography of Edith Piaf*. London: Arcadia. Revised edition of *Piaf*, 1985, London: Hodder and Stoughton.

Daily Telegraph, 2011, 'Pam Gems' (obituary). 16 May. Available at www.telegraph.co.uk/news/obituaries/culture-obituaries/theatre-obituaries/8517453/Pam-Gems.html (consulted 1 March 2015).

Darcy, Jacques, 1996, 'Avant-propos'. Programme for production of *Piaf je t'aime*.

Dauncey, Hugh and Le Guern, Philippe (eds), 2011, *Stereo: Comparative Perspectives on the Sociological Study of Popular Music in France and Britain*. Farnham: Ashgate, 23–42.

Delaunay, Michèle, 2013, Twitter post, @micheledelaunay, 28 August, 14:23.

Demay, Marie-Noëlle, 1988, *Voici: le nouveau magazine des femmes*. 29 February–6 March, 16–17.

Deniot, Joëlle-Andrée, 2012a, *Édith Piaf la voix, le geste, l'icône: esquisse anthropologique*. Paris: Lelivredart.

Deniot, Joëlle-Andrée, 2012b, 'Corpographies d'une voix: Piaf, la pasionara de la chanson française', in Barbara Lebrun (ed.), *Chanson et performance: mise en scène du corps dans la chanson française et francophone*. Paris: L'Harmattan.

Dillaz, Serge, 1991, *La Chanson sous la Troisième Republique: 1870–1940*. Tallandier.

Donnat, Olivier and Cogneau, Denis, 1990, *Les Pratiques culturelles des Français, 1973–1989*. Paris: La Découverte/La Documentation Française.

D'Ormesson, Jean, 1962, 'Piaf une obscénité'. *Arts*, 3 October, 36–37.

Drott, Eric, 2011, *Music and the Elusive Revolution*. Berkeley: University of California Press.

Drouin, Jean-Louis, 2007, 'Pathos et performance d'actrice pour Piaf'. *Le Monde*, 15 February.

Duclos, Pierre and Martin, Georges, 1993, *Piaf: biographie*. Paris: Seuil.

Dutheil Pessin, Catherine, 2004, *La Chanson réaliste: sociologie d'un genre*. Paris: L'Harmattan.

Dyer, Richard, 1998, *Stars*, new supplemented edition. Houndmills: Palgrave Macmillan.

Érismann, Guy, 1964, 'Édith Piaf'. *Musica Disques*, October, 45–46.

Exposito, Valérie, 2013, *Piaf intime*. TF1 Production. DVD, EDV 1035.

Fargue, Léon-Paul, 1938, 'L'Air du mois: la Môme Piaff [*sic*]'. *Nouvelle Revue Française*, no. 50, 1 March, 512–14.

Feschotte, Jacques, 1965, *Histoire du music-hall*. Que Sais-Je, Paris: Presses Universitaires de France.

Fondazione Sapegno, 2013, 'Poésie et chanson de la France à l'Europe: Colloque international'. 11–13 July, Morgex, Italy.

France 2, 2013a, *Piaf: hymnes à la Mome*. 5 October, 20:45.

France 2, 2013b, *Le Journal de 13 heures*. 10 October.

France Actualités, 1943, 'Édition du 20 août 1943'. Available at www.ina.fr/video/AFE86004341/france-actualites-edition-du-20-aout-1943-video.html (consulted 2 March 2015).

France-Soir, 1969, 'Raymond Asso'. 30 September, 8.

Franco, Victor, 1973, 'Il y a dix ans disparaissait Édith Piaf'. *Jours de France*, October.

Fréjaville, Gustave, 1943a, 'Variétés et chansons'. *Comœdia*, 13 February, 6.

Fréjaville, Gustave, 1943b, 'Variétés et chansons'. *Comœdia*, 29 May, 4.

Freyeisen, Astrid, 2006, *Chansons pour Piaf: Norbert Glanzberg, toute une vie 1910–2001*, translated from the German by Françoise Saint-Onge. Geneva: Éditions MJR.

Frith, Simon, 1998, *Performing Rites: Evaluating Popular Music*. Oxford and New York: Oxford University Press.

Frith, Simon, 2011, 'Writing the History of Popular Music', in H. Dauncey and P. Le Guern (eds), *Stereo: Comparative Perspectives on the Sociological Study of Popular Music in France and Britain*. Farnham: Ashgate, 11–21.

'G. B.', 1963, untitled. *Le Figaro*, 12–13 October.

Giannoli, Paul, 1963, 'Et pourtant...' *Candide*, 17 October, 24.

Giroud, Françoise, 1952, *Françoise Giroud vous présente le Tout-Paris*. Paris: Gallimard.

Guermantes, 1963, 'La Voix du faubourg'. *Le Figaro*, 12–13 October.

Guibert, Gérôme and Le Guern, Philippe, 2011, 'Charting the history of amplified musics in France', in H. Dauncey and P. Le Guern (eds), *Stereo: Comparative Perspectives on the Sociological Study of Popular Music in France and Britain*. Farnham: Ashgate, 23–42.

Guidoni, Jean, 1983, 'Un monstre', in 'Qu'en pense la nouvelle génération des chanteurs français?' *Le Quotidien de Paris*, 11 October.

Harvey, Ralph, 2002, 'Appendix 2: the chanteuses réalistes', in M. Crosland, *A Cry from the Heart: The Biography of Edith Piaf.* London: Arcadia, 247–66.

Hawkins, P., 2000, *Chanson: The French Singer-Songwriter from Aristide Bruant to the Present Day.* Aldershot: Ashgate.

Hirschi, Stéphane, 2008, *Chanson: l'art de fixer l'air du temps. De Béranger à Mano Solo.* Paris: Les Belles Lettres; Presses Universitaires de Valenciennes.

Holmes, Diana, 2007, '"A girl of today": Brigitte Bardot', in D. Holmes, and J. Gaffney (eds), *Stardom in Postwar France.* New York and Oxford: Berghahn, 40–66.

Holmes, Diana and Gaffney, John (eds), 2007, *Stardom in Postwar France.* New York and Oxford: Berghahn.

Holmes, Diana and Looseley, David (eds), 2013, *Imagining the Popular in Contemporary French Culture.* Manchester: Manchester University Press.

Hope-Wallace, Philip, 1963, 'Edith Piaf'. *Guardian*, 12 October, 7.

Jackson, Julian, 2003, *France: The Dark Years, 1940–1944.* Oxford: Oxford University Press.

Jonasz, Michel, 1983, 'Le Sixième Sens', in 'Qu'en pense la nouvelle génération des chanteurs français?' *Le Quotidien de Paris*, 11 October.

Le Journal illustré, 1983, 'Grand-messe pour Édith'. March.

Justice Magazine, 1960, 'Alerte aux "excitants" et "tranquillisants"'. No. 62, February, 6–7.

Kaas, Patricia, 2012a, 'Interview with Patricia Kaas'. *CompleteFrance.com*, 12 November. Available at www.completefrance.com/language-culture/interview_with_patricia_kaas_1_1690694 (consulted 15 March 2015).

Kaas, Patricia, 2012b, *Kaas chante Piaf.* CD, Richard Walter Entertainment.

Kelly, Michael, 2014, 'Le Regard de l'étranger: what French cultural studies brings to French cultural history'. *French Cultural Studies*, vol. 25, nos. 3–4, 253–61.

Kuisel, R. F., 1993, *Seducing the French: The Dilemma of Americanization.* Berkeley; Los Angeles; London: University of California Press.

Lamour, Marianne, 2003, *Sans amour on n'est rien du tout.* Zylo, Ile Productions, France 5, ARTE France.

Lange, Monique, 1958, 'Piaf la rouge'. *France-Observateur*, 10 April.

Lange, Monique, 1979, *Histoire de Piaf.* Paris: J'ai lu/Ramsay.

Lebrun, Barbara, 2009, *Protest Music in France: Production, Identity and Audiences.* Farnham: Ashgate.

Lebrun, Barbara (ed.), 2012, *Chanson et performance: mise en scène du corps dans la chanson française et francophone.* Paris: L'Harmattan.

Lebrun, Barbara and Lovecy, Jill (eds), 2010, *Une et indivisible? Plural Identities in Modern France.* Bern: Peter Lang.

Leclère, Marie-Françoise and Lorrain, François-Guillaume, 2007, 'Le Mythe Piaf'. *Le Point*, 11 February, 74–86.

Lefebvre, Monique, 1977, 'Piaf, le cri des petits bonheurs'. *Le Point*, December, 11.

Lelouch, Claude, 1983, *Édith et Marcel*. Les Films 13.

Lévy, François, 2003, *Passion Édith Piaf: La Môme de Paris*. Paris: Textuel. Catalogue of the 2003 exhibition at the Hôtel de Ville, Paris.

Looseley, David, 2003, *Popular Music in Contemporary France: Authenticity, Politics, Debate*. Oxford; New York: Berg.

Looseley, David, 2010, 'Making history: French popular music and the notion of the popular', in B. Lebrun and J. Lovecy (eds), *Une et indivisible? Plural Identities in Modern France*. Bern: Peter Lang, 127–40.

Looseley, David, 2013a, 'Outside looking in: European popular musics, language and intercultural dialogue'. *Journal of European Popular Culture*, vol. 4, no. 1, 19–28.

Looseley, David, 2013b, 'Finding the plot in French *chanson*: Édith Piaf and the narrative song', in D. Holmes, D. Platten, L. Artiaga and J. Migozzi (eds), *Finding the Plot: Storytelling in Popular Fictions*. Newcastle upon Tyne: Cambridge Scholars Publishing, 234–46.

Looseley, David, 2013c, 'Authenticity and appropriation: a discursive history of French popular music', in D. Holmes and D. Looseley (eds), *Imagining the Popular in Contemporary French Culture*. Manchester: Manchester University Press, 47–84.

Macabiès, Jean, 1981, 'Piaf toujours présente'. *L'Aurore*, 14 December.

Manceaux, Michèle, 1961, 'Piaf ressucitée'. *L'Express*, 4 January.

Marchois, Bernard, 1993, *Piaf: emportée par la foule*. Paris: Éditions du Collectionneur; Vade Retro.

Marchois, Bernard, 1995, *Édith Piaf: 'opinions publiques'*. Paris: TF1 Éditions.

Marchois, Bernard, 2013, *La Vraie Piaf: témoignages et portraits inédits*. Paris: Éditions Didier Carpentier.

Marti, Anik, 1988, 'Le crédo de Piaf'. *Le Figaro*, 30–31 January.

Mattelart, Armand and Neveu, Érik, 2003, *Introduction aux Cultural Studies*. Paris: La Découverte.

Mazillier, Jean-Paul, Berrot, Anthony and Durieux, Gilles, 2010, *Piaf: De la Môme à Édith, documents et inédits*. Paris: Le Cherche-Midi.

Ministry of Culture, 2013, *Culture Communication*, no. 210, June, 23.

Le Minotaure, 1946, 'Croquis à l'emporte-tête: Édith Piaf'. *L'Écran français*, 24 April.

Mogui, Jean-Pierre, 1983. *Le Figaro*, 1 April.

Le Monde, 1993, 'Piaf'. 7 October, 27–29.

Monteaux, Jean, 1963, 'Piaf: psychanalyse d'un succès'. *Arts*, 16–22 October.

Morel, Chloé, 2011, 'Bilan et pistes pour une histoire culturelle mondiale', in E. Cohen et al., *Dix ans d'histoire culturelle*. Villeurbanne: Éditions de l'ENSIBB, 236–42.

Morin, Edgar, 1972, *Les Stars*. Paris: Seuil. First published 1957; 3rd (revised) edition, 1972.

Morin, Edgar, 2005, *The Stars*, transl. R. Howard. Minneapolis; London: University of Minnesota Press.

Mortaigne, Véronique, 2007, 'Le Cas Piaf, ou l'art de tourner autour du pot'. *Le Monde*, 11–12 February.

Neveu, Érik, 2011, 'La Ligne Paris-Londres des *Cultural Studies*: une voie à sens unique?', in E. Cohen et al., *Dix ans d'histoire culturelle*. Villeurbanne: Éditions de l'ENSIBB, 159–73.

New York Herald Tribune, 1947, 'Bravo'. 4 November, 21.

New York Times, 1963, 'Song stylist, 47, cast a spell over many audiences. Tragedy marked life'. 12 October, 1, 19.

Noli, Jean, 1973, *Piaf secrète*. Paris: L'Archipel.

Nora, Pierre, 1996 (ed.), *Realms of Memory: Rethinking the French Past*. Columbia: Columbia University Press. Revised and abridged translation by Arthur Goldhammer of Nora, 1992, *Lieux de mémoire*, Paris: Gallimard.

Nougaro, Claude, 1963, 'Elle était l'amour de chanter'. *Les Lettres Françaises*, 17–23 October.

Obaldia, René de, 1946, 'De la chanson à la mélodie'. *Masques*, no. 10 (2nd year).

'Pablo', 1983, 'Édith Piaf, junkie du rideau rouge'. *Gai-Pied*, 8 October, 28.

Le Parisien libéré, 1963a, 'La Mort d'Édith Piaf a tué Jean Cocteau'. 12–13 October, 1, 6.

Le Parisien libéré, 1963b, 'Le Peuple de Paris a rendu hier un fervent hommage à la chanteuse'. 14 October.

Paris Jour, 1963, 'Piaf est morte, Paris pleure'. 12–13 October.

Paris Match, 1963a, 'Édith Piaf: cette fois le rideau est tombé'. 19 October.

Paris Match, 1963b, 'Édith Piaf: sa voix ne mourra pas'. 26 October.

Paris-Presse-L'Intransigeant, 1963, 'La Mort d'Édith Piaf'. 12 October, 1, 6–7.

Paris-Soir, 1936a, 'Quatre jeunes gens revolver au poing font irruption dans l'appartement d'un ancient artiste'. 7 April, 1, 5.

Paris-Soir, 1936b, various short items covering Leplée's murder. 8 April, 1, 2, 3, 5.

Pénet, Martin (ed.), 2004, *Mémoire de la chanson*. Paris: Omnibus.

Perez, Michel, 1963, 'Celle qu'on ne pourra jamais oublier'. *Combat*, 12–13 October.

Peterson, Richard A., 1997, *Creating Country Music: Fabricating Authenticity*. Chicago; London: University of Chicago Press.

Petit, Olivier and Illand, Cédric (eds), 2001, *Chansons d'Édith Piaf en bandes dessinées*. Darnétal: Petit à Petit.

Le Petit Parisien, 1935, 'Une chanteuse qui vit sa chanson'. 10 November, 7.

Piaf, Édith, 1964, *Ma vie*. Paris: Union générale d'éditions.

Piaf, Édith, 1992, *My Life*, transl. M. Crosland. London: Penguin.

Piaf, Édith, 2003 [1958], *Au bal de la chance*. Paris: L'Archipel. Originally published 1958, Geneva: Éditions Jeheber.

Piaf, Édith, 2004, *The Wheel of Fortune: The Autobiography of Édith Piaf*, transl. P. Trewartha and A. Masoin de Virion. London: Peter Owen.

Piaf, Édith, 2011, *Mon amour bleu*. Paris: Grasset.

Piaf, Édith and Cerdan, Marcel, 2012, *Moi pour toi: lettres d'amour*. Paris: J'ai lu.

Le Point, 2013, 'Piaf: un destin français'. Hors série, October–November.

Le Point, 2015, '"Mistral gagnant", chanson préférée de tous les temps par les Français'. Available at www.lepoint.fr/societe/mistral-gagnant-chanson-preferee-de-tous-les-temps-par-les-francais-30-05-2015-1932284_23.php (consulted 23 June 2015).

Pons, Philippe, 1993, 'La Reine de la "shanson"'. *Le Monde*, 7 October, 29.

Le Quotidien de Paris, 1983, 'Qu'en pense la nouvelle génération des chanteurs français?'. 11 October.

Reader, Keith, 2003, 'Flaubert's sparrow, or the Bovary of Belleville: Édith Piaf as cultural icon', in H. Dauncey and S. Cannon (eds), *Popular Music in France from Chanson to Techno: Culture, Identity and Society*. Aldershot: Ashgate, 205–23.

Rebierre, Jean-Roger, 1963, 'La "Bouche d'ombre" s'est tue'. *La Tribune de Genève*, 12–14 October.

Reflet (*Revue des Enseignants de Français Langue Etrangere*), 1988, 'Emblèmes: la Môme Piaf'. No. 27, September.

Reiner, Sylvain, 1999, *Piaf: le livre d'Édith*. L'Archipel.

Richard, Lionel, 1991, *Cabaret, cabarets*. Plon.

Richer, 2007, *Piaf mon amie*. Denoël. An earlier edition (2004), entitled *Mon amie Édith Piaf* (Avignon: L'Instantané, 2004), also exists.

Rifkin, Adrian, 1995, *Street Noises: Studies in Parisian Pleasure, 1900–40*. Manchester: Manchester University Press.

Rioux, Jean-Pierre and Sirinelli, Jean-Francois (eds), 2002, *La Culture de masse en France: de la Belle Époque à aujourd'hui*. Paris: Fayard.

Rivoyre, Christine de, 1953, 'Édith Piaf et Jacques Pills'. *Le Monde*, 25 April.

Runcie, Charlotte, 2013, 'Edith Piaf: still an inspiration 50 years after her death'. *Daily Telegraph*, 10 October. Available at www.telegraph.co.uk/culture/music/music-news/10367807/Edith-Piaf-still-an-inspiration-50-years-after-her-death.html (consulted 15 April 2015).

Saka, Pierre, 1994, *L'Hymne à l'amour*. Paris: Librairie Générale Française; Livre de Poche.

Sarraute, Claude, 1963, 'Édith Piaf est morte'. *Le Monde*, 12 October.

Sciarretto, Amy, 2012, 'Lady Gaga purchases French singer Édith Piaf's songs, clothes and … toenail clippings'. *PopCrush.com*, 16 October. Available at http://popcrush.com/lady-gaga-edith-piaf-songs-clothes-toenail-clippings/ (consulted 15 April 2015).

Singer, Barnett, 2013, *The Americanization of France: Searching for Happiness after the Algerian War*. Lanham; Plymouth: Rowman and Littlefield.

Sizaire, Anne, 1996, *Édith Piaf: la voix de l'émotion*. Paris: Desclée de Brouwer.

Spiraux, Alain, 1959, 'Édith Piaf, comme la France'. *Combat*, 10 March.

Spotts, Frederic, 2008, *The Shameful Peace: How French Artists and Intellectuals Survived the Nazi Occupation*. New Haven; London: Yale University Press.

'T.', 1958, 'Le Centième d'Édith Piaf'. *Le Canard enchaîné*, 15 April.

Taubman, Howard, 1947, 'Records: La Piaf'. *New York Times*, 7 December.

TF1, 2013, *Le Journal de 13 heures*. 11 October.

Thomson, Virgil, 2002, 'La Môme Piaf', in *Virgil Thomson: A Reader. Selected Writings 1924–1984*, ed. Richard Kostelanetz. New York; London: Routledge, 144–45.

Tournès, Ludovic, 2011, 'L'Histoire culturelle face au tournant transnational', in E. Cohen et al., *Dix ans d'histoire culturelle*. Villeurbanne: Éditions de l'ENSIBB, 249–52.

Tribune de Genève, 1963, 'Le cœur d'Édith Piaf a cessé de battre: une authentique fleur du pavé'. 11–12 October.

TV5 Monde, 2013, *Le Journal*. 10 October, 13:00.

Vadelorge, Loïc, 2011, 'Introduction', in E. Cohen et al., *Dix ans d'histoire culturelle*. Villeurbanne: Éditions de l'ENSIBB, 12–15.

Vassal, Hugues, 2002, *Dans les pas de … Édith Piaf*. Éditions Les Trois Orangers.

Vedettes, 1943, 'Nos vedettes chez les prisonniers'. September.

Vian, Boris, 1997, *Derrière la zizique*, revised and enlarged edition by Georges Unglik. Paris: Christian Bourgois.

Vincendeau, Ginette, 1987, 'The mise-en-scène of suffering: French *chanteuses réalistes*'. *New Formations*, no. 3, winter, 107–28.

Vinneuil, François, 1941, 'Faux pas'. *Je suis partout*, 29 November, 11.

Wainwright, Martha, 2009, *Sans fusils, ni souliers, à Paris*. CD, Republic of Music.

Watts Junior, Richard, 1947, 'France's Edith Piaf has local triumph'. *New York Post*, 31 October, 49.

Index

Piaf's songs are listed individually by title. Given the very large number of proper names listed below, the lyricists and composers of Piaf songs are only indexed if they appear in the main text. Songs not performed by Piaf are also listed by title unless the songwriter or performer is referred to in the body of the book, in which case they are cross-referenced. Films, plays and musicals are generally listed by director or playwright; but by title in cases where director or playwright is not mentioned in the book or is little known today. I have also excluded names that appear only in passing, unless they are of some biographical or cultural-historical significance. Similarly, I have not indexed the names of biographers, journalists, historians or critics, unless they have a significant place in my argument, as in the cases of Deniot, Frith and Nora.

Anglophone and global perceptions
of 115–16, 167–69, 175, 185–86,
188
as middlebrow *see* middlebrow art
la nouvelle chanson française 173,
229n11
chanson réaliste (realist song)
as interpreted by Piaf 47–50,
54–61, 70–73, 147, 149–50
as tragic myth 19, 48–49
her attempts to reinvent and move
away from realism 3, 36–37,
72, 83–84, 89–92, 99, 101, 103,
127–30, 135, 138, 142, 186
nature of 34–38, 41, 176–77,
193n2
'neo-realist chanson' 160, 174
Charlie Hebdo 15, 52, 193n3
Chauvigny, Monique 95
Chauvigny, Robert 4, 11, 84–85, 93,
95, 103, 131
'Chevalier de Paris, Le' 6, 126
Chevalier, Maurice 11, 28, 36, 68,
74, 103, 111, 146–47, 149, 176,
187
'Prosper (Yop la boum!)' 38
'Quand un vicomte' 38
Chirac, Jacques 12, 161, 175
Christ *see* religion and spirituality
Christianity *see* religion and
spirituality
cinema 28–29, 35–36, 41, 55, 77, 111,
187
New Wave 121
Cinq colonnes à la une see
Desgraupes, Pierre
Clerc, Julien 167, 193n3
Cocteau, Jean 3, 10, 35–36, 49, 61,
64, 77, 83–85, 99, 127, 143, 147,
162, 177–78, 210n66
Le Bel Indifférent 3, 7, 34, 126,
130

Cohen, David
Édith Piaf: A Remembrance 12,
158
collaboration *see* Occupation, the
colonialism 22, 42, 53–54, 191,
204n44
see also Algerian war of
independence; decolonisation
Columbia (label) *see* Pathé Marconi
Combelle, Alix 60
Commaret, Noël 94, 136
commemoration and commemorative
consciousness 15, 21–22, 153–70,
171, 180, 184, 189–90
'Comme une Piaf' *see* Nougaro,
Claude
'Comme un moineau' 34
Communist Party (French) 4, 53,
113
Compagnons de la chanson 4–5,
58, 94–95, 131, 145, 149
in the USA with Piaf 103–04,
107–08, 216n41
'Les Trois Cloches' 75–77, 123
Constantine, Eddie 5–6, 85, 94, 125,
130–31, 162, 189
Contet, Henri 3, 27, 33, 42–43, 50,
65, 68–69, 143
as lyricist 84, 86–87, 90–91,
93–94, 119–20, 130, 148, 212n31
'Contrebandier, Le' 41, 46, 53
Copeau, Jacques 107
Coquatrix, Bruno 117, 145, 155,
199–200n73
cultural history
definitions and uses of 20–22,
168–69, 185–86, 188–90,
195n26
cultural memory 21, 73, 129, 157–58,
175, 179–80, 182–83, 189–90
cultural theory (French) 21–22,
195n26